The Latest Type 2 Diabetes

Cookbook

Simple & Quick Diabetic Friendly Recipes for Beginners and Advanced Users

Lisa Sadler

Table of Contents

Chapter 6: Appetizers, Soups and Snacks 97

"Health is wealth" indicates the importance of being healthy but what if you're silently caught in a chronic situation that shakes you. Yes, Diabetes is a silent chronic disease. Diabetes is a situation when your pancreas makes no or insufficient insulin in the body.

There are two types of diabetes, one named Type-1 and the other is Type-2 diabetes. Type 1 diabetes is incurable but type-2 diabetes can be put in remission with a healthy lifestyle.

Type 2 diabetes mellitus is a condition in which the body controls and uses sugar (glucose) for fat. These long-term infections cause too much sugar in the arteries. Finally, high blood sugar can damage blood vessels, the nervous system, and the immune system. There is no cure for type 2 diabetes mellitus, but weight loss, eating a healthy diet, and exercising can help control the disease. If diet and exercise are not enough to control your blood sugar, you may need diabetes medication or insulin therapy.

Differences between Type-1 and Type-2 Diabetes

We know that some people develop type 1 diabetes mellitus with type 2 diabetes. And we often ask questions about the differences between them.

Type 1 diabetes and type 2 diabetes have many similarities, but there are many differences. What is the reason, who affects it and how is it managed? There are other types of diabetes, such as pregnancy and MODY.

First of all, type 1 affects 8% of all diabetics. When type 2 diabetes affects up to 90%, many people have mistaken type-2 diabetes for type 1 diabetes. It could mean that what works for one type doesn't work for another and has to explain with another reason.

The important thing to remember is that both weigh the same as each other. High blood sugar can lead to health problems, even if you have type 1 or type 2 diabetes. So, if you have both of these situations, then you need to take the necessary steps to deal with them.

The below table shows some basic knowledge about the type-1 and type-2 Diabetes.

	Type 1 Diabetes	Type 2 Diabetes
What is happening	Your Pancreas is not making insulin to dissolve glucose in cells.	The pancreas is making insulin but the amount is not sufficient for cells to work properly.
Risk Factor	No current reason is known about the type-1 occurrence.	Obesity and ethnicity put you towards the type-2 diabetes.
Symptoms	The quick appearance of symptoms	Symptoms appearance mildly and slowly
How to Manage	Taking insulin to control blood sugar	Healthy lifestyle, walking, and exercise, healthy eating, and mild medication
Prevention and cure	Not curable	Not curable but can be put into remission with a healthy lifestyle

Type 1 diabetes means you have an autoimmune disease. This means that the body attacks and destroys the cells that make insulin. It can therefore no longer produce insulin. We need insulin because it helps absorb sugar from the blood into the cells of our body. This sugar is then used for energy. Without insulin, blood sugar is too high. Type 2 diabetes is different. In type 2, the body either does not make enough insulin or does not function properly. This is called insulin resistance. According to type 1, this means the blood sugar is too high.

About Type-2 Diabetes

Type 2 diabetes mellitus, the most common type of diabetes mellitus, is a type of disease that occurs in diabetes mellitus, also called diabetes mellitus. Diabetes is your life energy and comes from the foods you eat. Insulin, a substance produced by the pancreas, helps sugar enter cells and use it for energy. In type 2 diabetes, the body either does not make enough insulin or uses insulin poorly. Too much sugar is in the blood and cannot reach the cells.

- Some of the symptoms of diabetes include;
- increased thirst and urination
- increased hunger
- feeling tired
- blurred vision
- numbness or tingling in the feet or hands
- sores that do not heal
- unexplained weight loss

Symptoms of type 2 diabetes usually appear slowly over many years and can be so minor that you may not notice it. Many people have no symptoms. Some people don't know they have the disease until they have a health problem, such as blindness or heart disease.

This cookbook and diet plan in it is here to help you manage your health well by managing your blood sugar and your health.

Formation of Type-2 Diabetes

The risk of developing type 2 diabetes is determined by some factors that can be modified and others that cannot.

1. Obesity

It is not known why some people make insulin, but obesity and lack of physical function are known to cause insulin resistance. Improving insulin resistance is important for improving type 2 diabetes. A link can also be seen in the fact that losing weight can improve the management or treatment of type 2 diabetes. In addition to obesity, the location of excess body fat is also important in determining the risk of type 2 diabetes. Levels of insulin resistance and the incidence of type 2 diabetes mellitus are highest in individuals of the "apple" type. These people carry most of their heaviest weight on their stomachs. In contrast, people with "pear" appear to have most of their weight on their hips and thighs, which is less likely to be associated with insulin resistance.

2. Gestation Period

Researchers believe gestational diabetes, type 2 diabetes that occurs during pregnancy, is caused by hormonal changes during pregnancy, including genetics and lifestyle. Hormones produced by the NIH placental network externally activate insulin resistance, which occurs in all women after pregnancy. Most women can produce enough insulin during pregnancy to beat insulin resistance, but some do not. Gestational diabetes mellitus occurs when the pancreas does not produce enough insulin. As with type 2 diabetes mellitus, obesity is also associated with gestational diabetes. Overweight women can avoid insulin during pregnancy. Excessive weight gain during pregnancy can also cause diabetes. Hormonal changes, weight gain, and family history all contribute towards gestational diabetes but sometimes it is just temporary and ended after delivery.

3. Hypertension

High blood pressure, or hypertension, can also cause type 2 diabetes. Hypertension can cause or worsen many types of diabetes, including diabetes mellitus and kidney infections. Most people with diabetes eventually develop high blood pressure as well as other heart and circulatory problems. Diabetes damages the arteries and makes them targeted for a hardening called arteriosclerosis. This can lead to high blood pressure which, if left untreated, can lead to problems such as blood vessel damage, heart attack, and kidney failure.

The combination of high blood pressure and type 2 diabetes is particularly deadly and can increase the risk of heart disease or stroke. Diabetic retinopathy can lead to blindness. Some people can improve their type 2 diabetes and high blood pressure with lifestyle changes, but most need medication. Depending on their general health, some people may need more than one medicine to control their blood pressure.

4. Other Causes

Genetic mutations, NIH external link, other, damage to the pancreas, and certain medicines may also cause diabetes.

Genes And Family History

Family history puts women at risk for gestational diabetes. This indicates that the seeds are playing a role. Genetic studies explain why this problem is more prevalent among African Americans, American Indians, Asians, and Hispanics. Diabetes alone is caused by a mutation or a change in a gene. These mutations are usually passed down through the family, but sometimes genetic mutations do occur. Most of these mutations cause insulin levels to drop, leading to diabetes.

Type 1 diabetes is more common in children and mature-onset diabetes mellitus (MODY). Neonatal diabetes develops at 6 months. NIH cystic fibrosis externally causes thick mucus in the scar tissue which can prevent the pancreas from making enough insulin. Hemochromatosis issue causes too much iron in the body. If left untreated, iron can build up and cause cuts and other infections.

Hormonal Diseases

Diabetes is caused by a hormonal imbalance. The pancreas produces the hormone insulin, which is absorbed into the blood by fat, muscle, and liver cells and used for energy. Insulin also helps other metabolic processes in the body.

If you have type 2 diabetes, your body will fight off insulin. In response, the cutter works harder to produce more insulin to lower blood sugar, but it doesn't store it. The result is uncontrolled diabetes.

For example;

Hormonal changes during menopause affect blood sugar levels, and postmenopausal women may experience faster changes in blood sugar levels if they have diabetes. The weight gain associated with pregnancy may require changes in blood sugar levels, and low hormones can interfere with sleep, making it more difficult to control blood sugar. Women with diabetes are also more likely to have sex than usual. The reason is that the disease is associated with damage to the cells of the vagina.

Men experience similar issues when their bodies produce low testosterone, including muscle loss and decreased sex drive. However, many people are unaware that low testosterone can also lead to insulin resistance.

Some other hormonal problems cause the body to make too many hormones, sometimes leading to insulin resistance and diabetes.

Cushing's syndrome occurs when the body makes too much cortisol, often referred to as a "stress hormone". Acromegaly occurs when the body makes too many hormones. Hyperthyroidism occurs when the thyroid gland overproduces thyroid hormone.

Damage to or Removal of the Pancreas

Pancreatitis, leukemia, and injury can damage any beta cells or reduce their ability to produce insulin, leading to diabetes. When pancreatic cancer is eliminated, beta cells disappear, leading to diabetes.

How to Prevent and Control Diabetes

If you are at risk for diabetes, you can prevent or delay diabetes. Most of all you need to do are stay healthy. Therefore, this change has other health benefits as well. You can lower your risk of getting other illnesses and make you feel better and stronger. Here are the changes:

Develop Good Habits

Type-2 diabetes can be put to remission by developing good habits like a healthy lifestyle, healthy eating, and proper medication. You should have quit smoking and drinking which lead you towards managing active metabolic activities that can help you to reduce your diabetes and allow you to live a healthy lifestyle with this chronic disease.

Some of the following activities help you to manage type-2 diabetes. Following are;

Cut of Refined Carbs and Sugar from the Diet

Avoiding these foods can help lower your risk, as eating a diet high in good carbohydrates and sugar can increase blood sugar and insulin levels, which can lead to hypoglycemia. Your body very quickly breaks down sugars and carbohydrate-rich foods into small pieces that your brain absorbs. The result is high blood sugar. Replacing sugary foods or foods low in carbohydrates can help control diabetes. People who eat a lot of carbohydrates quickly are more likely to have type 2 diabetes than those who take less.

Drink a Lot of Water

Water is the best drink for you. Helps reduce the risk of diabetes, which can increase blood sugar. Studies show that drinking helps the body make the best insulin and control blood sugar. Water reduces cravings for sweet and salty drinks which can help control blood sugar.

Quit Smoking

Smoking is associated with an increased risk of diabetes, especially in heavy smokers. Smoking has been shown to cause or worsen serious illnesses, including heart disease, emphysema, lung cancer, breast cancer, prostate cancer, and indigestion. You may have a risk for type 2 diabetes. Quitting smoking has been shown to reduce these risks over time.

Take Coffee and Tea

While water should be your first drink, research shows that including coffee or tea in your diet can help prevent diabetes. Studies indicate that daily coffee intake reduces the risk of type 2 diabetes. Coffee and tea contain antioxidants called polyphenols, which can help prevent diabetes. Green tea also contains a special antioxidant called epigallocatechin gallate (EGCG), which has been shown to reduce the release of blood sugar from the liver and increase insulin secretion.

Minimized Processed Food Intake

Cutting back on your diet and focusing on healthy whole foods can help lower your risk for diabetes. One easy step that you can take to improve your health is to cut back on your processed foods. It caused all kinds of health problems, including heart disease, obesity, and diabetes. Cutting back on fatty foods, whole grains, and supplements can help lower your risk for diabetes. It is part of fruits, vegetables, berries, and other food crops.

Eat High Fiber Diet

Eating good fiber with every meal can help lower your risk of diabetes by preventing high blood sugar and insulin levels. Eating fiber helps with stomach health and weight management. Fiber can be divided into two groups: soluble and insoluble. Soluble fiber can absorb water, while insoluble fiber does not.

Intake of Vitamin D

Eating a diet rich in vitamin D or taking supplements can help lower your risk of diabetes by improving your vitamin D levels. Vitamin D is important for managing diabetes. Studies have shown that not getting enough vitamin D or having low blood pressure increases the risk of developing all types of diabetes. When people become malnourished by taking vitamin D, it improves the function of insulin-producing cells, normalizes blood sugar levels, and reduces the risk of diabetes. Oily fish and cod liver oil are good sources of vitamin D. Sun exposure can increase the amount of vitamin D in the blood. However, for many people, it is necessary to supplement 2,000 to 4,000 IU of vitamin D per day to achieve and maintain high levels.

Regular Exercises

Daily physical activities, such as exercising and walking, help your brain break down the sugars and fats in your body by digesting food and releasing insulin from your pancreas. Exercise increases insulin sensitivity in the brain. So when you exercise, you need less insulin to control your blood sugar. Aerobic exercise, high-intensity exercise, and strength training can help obese people lower blood sugar and control type 2 diabetes. Regular physical activity increases insulin secretion and sensitivity, which helps prevent type 2 diabetes and lower blood sugar.

Dietary Requirements for Type-2 Diabetes

People with type-2 diabetes find it difficult to get enough sugar to the brain. When the sugar does not reach the desired level, the sugar in the blood rises. which can lead to problems such as kidneys, brain, eye damage, and heart disease.

The best diet for type 2 diabetes includes simple carbohydrates such as brown rice, whole grains, quinoa, oatmeal, fruits, vegetables, beans, and lentils. Foods to avoid include simple carbohydrates such as sugar, pasta, white bread, flour, cookies, and pastries.

Foods that do not have a glycemic load (index) raise blood sugar levels only slightly and are a better choice for diabetics. Effective blood sugar control can help prevent the long-term problems of type 2 diabetes. Fat does not have a direct effect on blood sugar, but it can help slow the absorption of carbohydrates.

Protein provides constant energy with little cause on blood sugar. It can help to even blood sugar levels and ease sugar cravings. Foods high in protein include beans, legumes, eggs, seafood, dairy products, soybeans, soybeans, lean meats, and chicken. Diabetic "superfoods" contain chia seeds, wild salmon, cinnamon white balsamic vinegar, and lentils. They help you to maintain diabetes and fulfill you as well.

A healthy diet includes lots of vegetables, a limited amount of sugar, and red meat. Dietary recommendations for people with type 2 diabetes include a vegetarian or vegan diet with the importance of exercise. The diet of people with type 2 diabetes includes a diet that is low in glycemic load, high in vegetables, and high in vegetable fats and proteins.

In type-2 diabetes, Which foods are not allowed to eat: soft drinks (regularly and on a diet), refined sugars, processed carbohydrates, saturated fat, fatty junk food, foods high in fat, fruit juices high in fructose, sweets, and all processed foods.

What to Eat

You can follow a variety of diets and diets to meet your health needs. For type 2 diabetes, you need to choose foods that contain nutritious foods that can help provide your body with the fiber, vitamins, and minerals it needs. You should eat a diversity of heart oils, including monounsaturated and polyunsaturated fatty acids. These fatty acids can help you to maintain a healthy heart by lowering cholesterol.

Likewise, eating a diet high in fiber can improve blood sugar control and allow you to eat longer, preventing you from overating when you're not hungry. The diet should be safe and easy to follow as well as tasty at the same time. A diet that is restricted or does not suit your lifestyle can be difficult to manage in the long term.

Here are some examples of foods you should include in your diet.

- **Fruits:** apples, oranges, strawberries, melons, pears, and peaches.
- **Vegetables:** cauliflower, cabbage, cucumber, pumpkin, etc.
- **Whole grains:** quinoa, couscous, oats, brown rice, Faro

- **Beans:** beans, lentils, and chickpeas
- **Nuts:** almonds, walnuts, pistachios, macadamia nuts, cashews
- **Seeds:** chia seeds, pumpkin seeds, flax seeds, hemp seeds
- **Foods rich in protein:** lean chicken, seafood, lean meats, beans, tempeh
- **Heart-healthy fats:** olive oil, avocado, canola oil, sesame oil
- **Drinks:** water, black coffee, unsweetened tea, soup

What to Avoid

There aren't many foods that you should avoid completely when you have type 2 diabetes. However, some foods have more choices than others in terms of healthy nutrients. This means that it is rich in vitamins and minerals and low in fat.

Limiting your intake of foods high in fat, and sugar can help improve blood sugar control and prevent the health effects associated with diabetes.

Here are some of the foods you should limit or avoid in your diet with type-2 diabetes:

- **Fatty meats:** beef, lamb, chicken, black chicken
- **Fatty foods:** whole milk, butter, cheese, sour cream
- **Sweets:** candies, cookies, toast, ice cream, candies
- **Non-alcoholic drinks:** non-alcoholic drinks, tea sweeteners, processed juices
- **Sweeteners:** sugar, brown sugar, honey, maple syrup, molasses
- **Processed foods:** chips, microwave popcorn, processed meats, ready meals
- **Fatty foods:** short vegetables, fried foods, dairy-free coffee, semi-hydrogenated fats

Breakfast Bark with Berries

Prep Time: 10minutes| Cook Time: 0 minutes| Servings: 8
Ingredients:
3-4 strawberries, sliced
1 ½ cup plain Greek yogurt
½ cup blueberries
What you'll need from the store cupboard:
½ cup low-fat granola
3 tbsp. sugar-free maple syrup
Directions:
Using parchment paper, line a baking sheet.
Combine yoghurt and syrup in a medium mixing basin. Spread in a thin even layer on the prepared pan.
Add the remaining Ingredients on top. Wrap in foil and place in the freezer for two hours or overnight.
To serve, cut the cake into squares and serve right away. When bark thaws out too much, it loses its shape. Any leftover bark should be frozen in an airtight container.
Nutritional Information: Calories 69; Total Carbs 18g; Net Carbs 16g; Protein 7g; Fat 6g; Sugar 7g; Fiber 2g

French Toast with Blueberries

Prep Time: 15 minutes| Cook Time: 20 minutes| Servings:8
Ingredients:
4 eggs
1 ½ cup blueberries
½ cup orange juice
1 tsp. orange zest
What you'll need from store cupboard:
16 slices bread, (chapter 14)
3 tbsp. Splenda, divided
⅛ tsp. salt
Blueberry Orange Dessert Sauce, (chapter 16)
Nonstick cooking spray
Directions:
Preheat the oven to 400 degrees Fahrenheit.
Coat a large baking sheet in cooking spray., coat a large baking sheet.
Combine the berries and 2 tablespoons of Splenda in a small bowl.
On a work surface, arrange 8 slices of bread.
Place the second slice of bread on top and top with about 3 tablespoons of berries. Slightly flatten.
In a small mixing dish, combine the remaining Ingredients. Dip both sides of the bread into the egg mixture and place on the preheated pan.
Cook for 7-12 minutes per side in the oven, or until gently browned
Warm the dessert sauce until it is warm. Top the French toast with 1-2 teaspoons of the sauce.
Serve.
Nutritional Information: Calories 208; Total Carbs 20g ;Net Carbs 18g; Protein 7g; Fat 10g; Sugar 14g; Fiber 2g

Coconut Porridge

Prep Time: 02 minutes| Cook Time:10 minutes| Servings:4
Ingredients:
4 cup vanilla almond milk, unsweetened
What you'll need from store cupboard
1 cup unsweetened coconut, grated
8 tsp. coconut flour
Directions:
In a saucepan, roast the coconut over medium-high heat until it is lightly toasted. Make sure it doesn't burn.
Bring the milk to a boil. Slowly add the flour, stirring constantly, and simmer and stir until the mixture thickens, about 5 minutes.
Remove the pan from the heat; the mixture will thicken as it cools. Pour into bowls, top with blueberries.
Serve and enjoy.
Nutritional Information: Calories 231; Total Carbs 21g; Net Carbs 8g; Protein 6g; Fat 14g ;Sugar 4g; Fiber 13g

Swedish Pancake with Apple Filling

Prep Time: 25 minutes| Cook Time: 20 minutes| Servings:6
Ingredients:
2 apples, cored and sliced thin
¾ cup egg substitute
½ cup fat-free milk
½ cup sugar-free caramel sauce
1 tbsp. reduced calorie butter
What you'll need from the store cupboard
½ cup flour
1½ tbsp. brown sugar substitute
2 tsp. water
¼ tsp. cinnamon
⅛ tsp. cloves
⅛ tsp. salt
Nonstick cooking spray
Directions:
Preheat the oven to 400 degrees Fahrenheit.
Place the low-fat butter in a cast iron skillet or an ovenproof skillet and bake until melted.
Whisk together flour, milk, egg substitute, cinnamon, cloves, and salt in a medium mixing bowl until smooth.
Pour batter into a heated skillet and bake for 20–25 minutes, or until golden brown and puffy.
Using cooking spray, coat a medium saucepan. Heat over a medium heat setting.
Combine the apples, brown sugar, and water in a mixing bowl. Cook, stirring periodically, for 4–6 minutes, or until apples are soft and golden brown.
In a microwave-safe measuring glass, pour the caramel sauce and heat for 30–45 seconds, or until warmed through.
To serve, put apples into the pancakes and top with caramel sauce. Cut the wedges in half.
Nutritional Information: Calories 193 Total Carbs 25g Net Carbs 23g Protein 6g Fat 2g Sugar 12g Fiber 2g

Avocado Pesto Zucchini Noodles

Prep Time: 10 minutes| Cook Time: 05 minutes| Servings:2

Ingredients:
6 cups of spiralized zucchini
1 tablespoon olive oil
6 oz. of avocado
1 basil leaf
3 garlic cloves
⅓ oz. pine nuts
2 tablespoons lemon juice
½ teaspoon salt
¼ teaspoon black pepper

Directions:
Spiralize the zucchini and place them on paper towels to absorb any excess liquid.
Put avocados, basil leaves, garlic, pine nuts, and sea salt in a food processor and pulse until finely chopped. Then slowly drizzle in the vegetable oil until it is emulsified and creamy.
In a skillet over medium-high heat, drizzle vegetable oil and add zucchini noodles, cooking for about 2 minutes or until cooked.
Toss zucchini noodles with avocado pesto in a large mixing bowl. Serve with cracked pepper.
Nutritional Information: Calories 110; Total Carbs 7.1g Net Carbs 12.6g Protein 2.3g Fat 9.2g Sugar 2.3g Fiber 3.3g

Salad with Avocado and Chicken Dice

Prep Time: 05 minutes| Cook Time: 10 minutes| Servings:2

Ingredients:
10 oz. diced cooked chicken
½ cup 2% Plain Greek yogurt
3 oz. chopped avocado
12 teaspoon garlic powder
¼ teaspoon salt
⅛ teaspoon pepper
1 tablespoon lime juice
¼ cup fresh cilantro, chopped

Directions:
Combine all of the Ingredients in a medium mixing basin. Keep refrigerated until ready to eat.
Cut the salad in half and combine it with your favourite greens to serve.
Nutritional Information: Calories 403; Total Carbs 13.1g Net Carbs 20.6g Protein 50.6g Fat 13.2g Sugar 6.3g Fiber 4.3g

Pancakes with Coconut

Prep Time: 05 minutes| Cook Time:15 minutes| Servings:4

Ingredients:
1 cup coconut flour
2 tablespoons of arrowroot powder
1 teaspoon. baking powder
1 cup of coconut milk
3 tablespoons coconut oil

Directions:
Combine all of the dry Ingredients in a medium container.
Mix in the coconut milk and a couple of tablespoons of copra oil until thoroughly combined.
1 teaspoon copra oil, melted in a skillet

Pour a ladle of batter onto the skillet and swirl it around to properly distribute the batter into a smooth pancake.
Cook for about 3 minutes over medium heat, or until firm.
Turn the pancake over and cook for another 2 minutes, or until golden brown on the other side.
Cook the remaining pancakes in the same manner as before.
Serve.
Nutritional Information: Calories 258; Total Carbs 9.3g Net Carbs 4.3g Protein 1.9g Fat 25g Sugar 2.3g Fiber 2.3g

Quinoa Porridge with Blueberries

Prep Time: 05 minutes| Cook Time:25 minutes| Servings:2

Ingredients:
2 cups of coconut milk
1 cup rinsed quinoa
⅛ teaspoon ground cinnamon
1 cup fresh blueberries

Directions:
Boil the coconut milk in a pot over high heat.
Allow the quinoa to soak in the milk before bringing it to a boil.
Then, on medium heat, let it simmer for a quarter-hour until the milk is reduced.
The cinnamon should be added last, and the mixture should be thoroughly mixed in the saucepan.
Cook, covered, for at least 8 minutes, or until the milk has been absorbed.
Cook for another 30 seconds after adding the blueberries.
Serve.
Nutritional Information: Calories 480; Total Carbs 68g Net Carbs 53g Protein 14g Fat 17.4g Sugar 7.2g Fiber 7.9g

Low-Fat Cheddar Apple Muffins

Prep Time: 10 minutes| Cook Time: 20 minutes| Servings:12

Ingredients:
1 egg
¾ cup tart apple, peel & chop
⅔ cup reduced fat cheddar cheese, grated
⅔ cup skim milk
What you'll need from store cupboard:
2 cup low carb baking mix
2 tbsp. vegetable oil
1 tsp. cinnamon.

Directions:
Preheat the oven to 400 degrees Fahrenheit.
A 12-cup muffin pan should be lined with paper liners.
Lightly beat the egg in a medium basin. Stir in the remaining Ingredients until they are barely moistened. Divide evenly between the muffin cups.
Bake for 17-20 minutes, or until golden brown.
Serve warm.
Nutritional Information: Calories 162 ;Total Carbs 17g; Net Carbs 13g; Protein 10g; Fat 5g; Sugar 8g ;Fiber 4g

Berry Parfaits

Prep Time: 7 minutes| Cook Time: 23 minutes|
Servings: 4
Ingredients:
For The Nut Granola
2 cups mixed nuts
1 tablespoon flax seed
1 tablespoon sesame seeds
1 tablespoon chia seeds
2 tablespoons pumpkin seeds
2 tablespoons coconut oil, melted
Pinch of salt
For The Blueberry Sauce
2 cups frozen blueberries
3 tablespoons Xylitol or (sugar alternative)
1 tablespoon water
For The Parfait
Plain Greek yoghurt
Fresh raspberries or other fruit of your choice
Directions:
Preheat the oven to about 175°C and line a
baking tray with parchment paper.
In a bowl, mix all the granola Ingredients and
place them in a baking tray evenly.
Place the granola in the oven and bake.
Bake the granla until golden brown for 5-10
minutes.
For blueberry sauce, mix all Ingredients in a
saucepan and cook for 5 to 10 minutes to bring
a boil on low flame until the juice is released.
Cool the sauce.
For serving, place the yoghurt with the granola,
fresh fruit and blueberry sauce in a bowl to
make the parfaits. Cool the parfait for at least
30 minutes or overnight in refrigerator.
Nutritional Information: Calories 217; Total
Carbs 12g; Net Carbs 8g; Protein 65g; Fat 16g;
Sugar 3g; Fiber 1g

Baked Sweet Potatoes with egg

Prep Time: 30 minutes| Cook Time: 60
minutes| Servings: 4
Ingredients:
For The Potatoes:
4 medium Sweet Potatoes
2 heads of garlic
2 teaspoons Extra Virgin Olive Oil
½ tablespoon Taco Seasoning
¼ cup fresh cilantro, plus additional for garnish
salt and pepper
4 eggs
For The Sauce:
½ cup avocado, about 1 medium avocado
1 tablespoon fresh lime juice
1 teaspoon lime zest
salt and pepper
2 tablespoons water
Directions:
Preheat the oven to 395°F.
Line the baking pan with foil.
Place the potatoes in the baking pan.
Make garlic pocket by placing garlic in the olive
oil and little salt and roll in the foil. Then fold to
make pocket.
Place garlic pocket on the baking pan with
potatoes.
Bake the garlic and potatoes for about 40
minutes, until it is tender.

Remove the garlic pocket from the pan and
proceed to cook the potatoes for additional 25-
35 minutes, until fork tender and soft.
When the potatoes are tender, set them aside
for about 10 minutes until they're cool.
Lower the temperature of the oven to 375°.
Break the potatoes into half and peel the skin
back, leaving the skin intact on the sides.
Carefully scoop out the pulp, leaving a little
amount on the sides of the potato to help
maintain its form.
Mash the flesh of the sweet potato and then cut
½ of it from the bowl.
Add in the taco seasoning, cilantro, salt, and
pepper to taste into the mashed flesh. Squeeze
all the fluffy garlic in the mash and blend well.
Divide the flesh between the 4 sweet potatoes,
spreading it softly to fill the mash, leaving a
large hole in the middle of each potato.
Place the potatoes boats on the baking sheet
and crack an egg into each hole and season it
with pepper and salt.
Bake until the egg is well fried for about 10-15
minutes and blend until smooth.
For the avocado sauce,add all Ingredients in a
food blender along with little water and blend
until well mixed.
Sprinkle the sauce with salt and pepper to
taste.
Spread the avocado sauce between the
potatoes until cooked, spreading it out on top.
Garnish the potatoes with sliced tomatoes and
cilantro in addition. And enjoy!
Nutritional Information: Calories 399; Total
Carbs 21g; Net Carbs 14g; Protein 18g; Fat
32g; Sugar 8g; Fiber 5g

Black Beans and Egg Tacos

Prep Time: 9 minutes| Cook Time: 13 minutes|
Servings: 4
Ingredients:
½ cup red onion, diced
86-inch white soft corn tortillas, warmed
1 clove of garlic, minced
1 teaspoon avocado oil
¼ cup chopped fresh cilantro
4 eggs
1 15-ounce can black beans, rinsed and drained
1 small avocado, diced
¼ teaspoon ground chipotle powder
½ cup fresh or your favorite jarred salsa
Directions:
Make scrambled egg as you always do.
Take a pan and heat the avocado oil in it. Add
onions and sauté for 3 minutes until tender.
Add garlic and beans and cook for 2-5 minutes
until heated through and shinny.
Toast the tortillas until little tender .
Put aside, wrapped to keep them warm, in a
cloth napkin.
Take a tortilla and layer the beans, ¼ cup per
taco, then add the eggs.
Top up the taco with salsa, avocado and
cilantro.
Nutritional Information: Calories 349; Total
Carbs 12g; Net Carbs 9g; Protein 11g; Fat 15g;
Sugar 5g; Fiber 6g

Simple Amaranth Porridge

Prep Time: 05 minutes| Cook Time:30 minutes| Servings:2

Ingredients:
2 cups of coconut milk
2 cups alkaline water
1 cup amaranth
2 tablespoons coconut oil
1 tablespoon ground cinnamon

Directions:
In a pot, combine the milk and water and bring to a boil.Reduce the heat to medium after stirring in the amaranth.
Cook, stirring occasionally, over medium heat for at least half an hour.
Turn down the heat.
Stir in the cinnamon and copra oil.
Serve.

Nutritional Information: Calories 520; Total Carbs 40.3g Net Carbs 27.3g Protein 9.9g Fat 38.2g Sugar 4.9g Fiber 8.1g

Salad with Pickled Cucumbers and Onions

Prep Time: 10minutes| Cook Time:00 minutes| Servings:2

Ingredients:
½ cucumber, peeled and sliced
¼ cup red onion, sliced thin
What you'll need from store cupboard:
1 tbsp. olive oil
1 tbsp. white vinegar
1 tsp. dill

Directions:
Mix all of the Ingredients together in a medium mixing basin.
Serve.

Nutritional Information: Calories 79 Total Carbs 4g Net Carbs 3g Protein 1g Fat 7g Sugar 2g Fiber 1g

Salad with Pomegranate and Brussels Sprouts

Prep Time: 10minutes| Cook Time:00 minutes| Servings:6

Ingredients:
3 cup Brussels sprouts, shredded
3 cup kale, shredded
1 ½ cup pomegranate seeds
What you'll need from store cupboard:
½ cup almonds, toasted & chopped
¼ cup reduced fat parmesan cheese, grated
Citrus Vinaigrette, (chapter 16)

Directions:
In a large mixing basin, add all of the Ingredients.
Mix the salad in the vinaigrette to thoroughly coat it.
Serve.

Nutritional Information: Calories 256 Total Carbs 15g Net Carbs 10g Protein 9g Fat 18g Sugar 5g Fiber 5g

Berry Avocado Smoothie

Prep Time: 7 minutes| Cook Time: 0 minutes| Servings: 2

Ingredients::
½ avocado
1 cup strawberries
¼ cup blueberries
½ cup low-fat milk
½ cup 2% Greek yogurt

Directions:
Place the avocado, strawberries, blueberries and milk in a blender.
Blend the fruits until perfectly smooth.
Serve or put in a refrigerator for up to 2 days.

Nutritional Information: Calories 350; Total Carbs 25g; Net Carbs 15g; Protein 24g; Fat 17g; Sugar 9g; Fiber 5g

Hummus Toast

Prep Time: 30 minutes| Cook Time: 4 hours| Servings: 2

Ingredients:
1 soft boiled egg, halved
6 tablespoons plain hummus
2 pieces gluten-free bread, toasted
1 pinch of paprika
2 teaspoons everything bagel Spice
drizzle of olive oil

Directions:
Spread hummus on each bread slice approximately 3 tablespoons each.
Place the halved egg on it top with 1 teaspoon 'Bagel' spice each.
Sprinkle small amount of paprika, muzzle with olive oil and make sandwich and serve at once.

Nutritional Information: Calories 213; Total Carbs 15g; Net Carbs 8g; Protein 6.5g; Fat 11g; Sugar 4g; Fiber 9g

Strawberry Coconut Breakfast Cake

Prep Time: 11 minutes| Cook Time: 23 minutes| Servings: 2

Ingredients:
½ cup chopped walnuts
2 cups unsweetened coconut flakes
1 teaspoon cinnamon
¼ cup chia seeds
2 cups diced strawberries
1 ripe banana, mashed
1 teaspoon baking soda
4 large eggs
¼ teaspoon of salt
1 cup unsweetened nut milk
2 tablespoons coconut oil, melted

Directions:
Preheat the oven to 375 °F for 10 minutes.
Grease a square 8-inch baking pan and set aside.
In a bowl, combine the dried Ingredients walnuts, chia seeds, cinnamon, salt and baking soda.
In another bowl, whisk the eggs and milk together. Add mashed banana and coconut oil to the egg mixture.
Add the wet Ingredients to the dry Ingredients and mix properly.
Fold the strawberries in.
Pour the batter in the greased baking pan and bake for about 40 minutes, or until the top is golden and solid.
Serve hot!

Nutritional Information: Calories 395; Total Carbs 12g; Net Carbs 10g; Protein 7g; Fat 40g; Sugar 2g; Fiber 3g

Paleo Hash

Prep Time: 7 minutes| Cook Time: 33 minutes|
Servings: 5
Ingredients:
8 ounces white mushroom, quartered
1 pound brussels sprout, quartered
Everything bagel seasoning
1 tablespoon olive oil or avocado oil
3 cloves of garlic, minced
1 small onion, diced
Crushed red pepper, optional
8 slices of nitrate free bacon sugar free, for
Whole30, cut into pieces
Sea salt and pepper to taste
6 large eggs
Directions:
Preheat the oven to 425 ° F for 5 minutes.
On a baking tray, arrange the mushrooms and
Brussels sprouts in a single layer.
Drizzle with the olive oil and seasoned salt and
pepper.
Sprinkle the onions on top and place the strips
of bacon equally over all the vegetables.
Roast the veggies for 15 mins in the preheated
oven, then sprinkle with the garlic and stir
gently.
Roast the veggies with garlic for another 10
minutes or until the bacon and vegetables are
crisp and fluffy, then extract from the oven.
Make tiny gaps in the veggies and place the egg
gently on it, careful not to 'split' the yolk.
Sprinkle the bagel seasoning and crushed red
pepper over the top of hash.
Bake the hash with eggs for another 5-10
minutes or until the eggs are fried.
Remove from the oven and quickly serve.
Enjoy!
Nutritional Information: Calories 250; Total
Carbs 14g; Net Carbs 10g; Protein 14g; Fat
18g; Sugar 4g; Fiber 5g

Avocado Toast

Prep Time: 5 minutes| Cook Time: 13 minutes|
Servings: 4
Ingredients:
1 avocado peeled and seeded
2 tablespoons chopped cilantro
Juice of ½ lime
½ tablespoon red pepper flakes optional
Salt & pepper to taste
2 slices of whole grain bread or bread of your
choice
2 eggs fried, scrambled, optional
Directions:
Toast 2 whole grain slices until they are crispy
and golden.
In a bowl, add the avocado, lime, cilantro and
salt and pepper and crushed them until well
incorporated.
Spread the avocado sauce on all the toasted
slices with ½ of the combination.
Top with fried poached or scrambled egg, as
desired and serve.
Nutritional Information: Calories 501; Total
Carbs 11g; Net Carbs 6g; Protein 16g; Fat 28g;
Sugar 2g; Fiber g

Chickpea Flour Omelet

Prep Time: 10 minutes| Cook Time: 20
minutes| Servings: 1
Ingredients:
1 cup chickpea flour
⅓ cup nutritional yeast
3 finely chopped green onions
4 ounces sautéed mushrooms
½ teaspoon onion powder
¼ teaspoon black pepper
½ teaspoon garlic powder
½ teaspoon baking soda
¼ teaspoon white pepper
Directions:
In a bowl, combine the onion powder, white
pepper, chickpea flour, garlic powder, black and
white pepper, baking soda, and yeast.
Add 1 cup water and mix well until smooth
batter formd.
Heat the frying pan over medium heat and add
the batter like pancakes.
Sprinkle some green onion and mushrooms on
top of batter.
Flip the omelet and cook evenly on both sides.
Serve the omelet with spinach, tomatoes, hot
sauce, and salsa.
Nutritional Information: Calories 150; Total
Carbs 2.4g; Net Carbs 1.5g; Protein 10.2g; Fat
1.9g; Sugar 0g; Fiber 2.2g

Hite Sandwich

Prep Time: 10 minutes| Cook Time: 20
minutes| Servings: 1
Ingredients:
1 cup warm water
1 cup warm unsweetened almond milk
2 tablespoons active dry yeast
4 tablespoons oil
2 ½ teaspoons salt
2 tablespoons splenda
6 cups all-purpose flour
Directions:
In a bowl, add warm water, yeast, and sugar
and stir. Set aside for 5 minutes or until lots of
tiny bubbles are formed, sort of frothy.
Add flour and salt into a mixing bowl and stir.
Pour the oil, yeast mix and milk and mix into
dough. Knead the dough until soft and supple.
Use hands or hook attachment of the stand
mixer.
Keep the bowl covered with a towel. Let it rest
until it doubles in size. Remove the dough from
the bowl and place on your countertop. Punch
the dough.
Line a loaf pan with parchment paper. You can
also grease with some oil if you prefer.
Place the dough in the loaf pan.
Keep the loaf pan covered rest until the dough
doubles in size.
Bake in a preheated oven at 370 ° F for about
40 to 50 minutes.
Let it cool to room temperature.
Cut into 16 equal slices and use as required.
Store in a breadbox at room temperature.
Nutritional Information: Calories 209; Total
Carbs 11g; Net Carbs 6g; Protein 1g; Fat 4g;
Sugar 0.6g; Fiber 0.2g

Sprouted Toast with Avocado

Prep Time: 10 minutes| Cook Time: 15 minutes| Servings: 3
Ingredients:
2 small sized bread sprouts
1 cup finely cut tomatoes
2 moderate size avocados
1 small cup alfalfa
Pure sea salt and bell pepper
Directions:
In a bowl, add the avocado, alfalfa, and tomatoes and mix.
Place the sauce to the bread and season to taste with pure sea salt and pepper.
Have a delicious breakfast with any freshly extracted juice of your choice.
Nutritional Information: Calories 82; Total Carbs 25g; Net Carbs 23g; Protein 30g; Fat 15g; Sugar 8g; Fiber 15g

Scrambled Tofu with Spinach

Prep Time: 5 minutes| Cook Time: 15 minutes| Servings: 4
Ingredients:
1 crumbled serve of tofu
1 small cup finely chopped onions
1 teaspoon the fresh parsley
1 teaspoon coconut oil
1 cup soft spinach
1 small teaspoon Turmeric
2 avocado serves
75g of tomatoes
1 small spoon of roasted paprika
Directions:
In a bowl, make tofu crumbs with your hands and keep it aside.
In a pan, sauté diced onions in oil till it softens.
Put your tofu, tomatoes, and other seasonings in a pan and mix well until combine till tofu is well prepared.
Add veggies in it and stir.
Serve in a bowl alongside some avocado and fresh salad.
Nutritional Information: Calories 91; Total Carbs 5g; Net Carbs 3g; Protein 30g; Fat 3g; Sugar 4g; Fiber 8g

Goddess Bowl with Spiced Avocado Dressing

Prep Time: 10 minutes| Cook Time: 20 minutes| Servings: 4
Ingredients:
3 heaping cups finely sliced kale
1 small cup diced broccoli florets
½ cup zucchini spiralized noodles
½ cup soaked Kelp noodles
3 cups tomatoes
2 tablespoons hemp seeds
Tahini dressing
1 small cup sesame butter
1 cup alkaline water
1 cup freshly extracted lemon
1 garlic, finely chopped clove
¾ tablespoon pure sea salt
1 spoon of olive oil
bell pepper
Avocado dressing
1 big avocado
2 freshly extracted lime
1 cup alkaline water
1 tablespoon olive oil
bell pepper
1 tablespoon powdered cumin
Directions:
In a pan, simmer veggies, kale, and broccoli for about 4 minutes until tender.
In a bowl, add all dressing Ingredients and noodles and mix well.
Add cooked noodles and add prepared avocado cumin dressing in the veggies and toss well.
Add tomatoes in it and combine well.
In a blender add all tahini Ingredients and pulse until smooth.
Put the cooked kale and broccoli in a plate, add Tahini dressing, add noodles and tomatoes.
Add hemp seeds to the whole dish and enjoy it.
Nutritional Information: Calories 109; Total Carbs 14g; Net Carbs 10g; Protein 25g; Fat 6g; Sugar 2g; Fiber 6g

Breakfast Salad

Prep Time: 5 minutes| Cook Time: 15 minutes| Servings: 3
Ingredients:
1 cup finely diced kale
1 cup cabbage, red and Chinese
2 tablespoons coconut oil
1 cup spinach
2 moderate avocados
1.2kg of chickpeas sprout
2 tablespoons sunflower seed sprouts
pure sea salt (seasoning)
bell pepper (seasoning)
lemon juice (seasoning)
Directions:
In a bowl, add spinach, Chinese and red cabbage, kale, coconut oil, and mix well.
Add seasoning to taste and mix adequately.
Add other Ingredients in salad and mix.
Serve and enjoy.
Nutritional Information: Calories 112; Total Carbs 14g; Net Carbs 10g; Protein 28g; Fat 8g; Sugar 4g; Fiber 6g

Quinoa Burrito

Prep Time: 15 minutes| Cook Time: 10 minutes| Servings: 1
Ingredients:
1 cup quinoa
2 cups black beans
4 finely chopped onions, green
4 finely chopped garlic
2 freshly cut limes
1 big tablespoon cumin
2 beautifully diced avocado
1 small cup beautifully diced cilantro
Directions:
Boil quinoa as per instructions.
Heat up beans over low heat.
Add other Ingredients to the beans pot and let it mix well for about 15 minutes.
Serve quinoa and add the prepared beans on top.
Nutritional Information: Calories 117; Total Carbs 22g; Net Carbs 18g; Protein 27g; Fat 8g; Sugar 2g; Fiber 10g

Veggie Wrap

Prep Time: 12 minutes| Cook Time: 13 minutes| Servings: 2
Ingredients:
2 teaspoons olive oil or other
1 cup sliced mushrooms
2 eggs
½ cup egg white or egg replacement
1 cup firmly packed spinach or other greens
2 tablespoons of sliced scallions.
nonstick cooking spray
2 whole wheat and low-carb flour tortillas
2 tablespoons salsa
Directions:
Add the oil to the pan over a medium flame.
Add the mushrooms and sauté until the edges turn golden (about 33 minutes).
Beat the eggs with the whites or egg substitute in a medium sized bowl using a blender or by hand until they are emulsified. Mix sliced spinach and green onion.
Add fresh or dried vegetables such as basil or parsley to taste like Moe.
Start heating the medium/large pan to a medium-low temperature. Put on the pan with a change of spray. Go to the egg mixture and stir the mixture while cooking with a spatula.
Once the eggs in the area unit are grilled as you feel, turn off the heat and stir in the mushrooms. Spread ½ egg mixture into 36 halves of each dough.
High each with a spoonful of fresh herbs or alternate sauce in your alternative.
Garnish with extra toppings such as avocado, bell, or tomato slices if desired, and then roll them up and create a wrapper.
Nutritional Information: Calories 220; Total Carbs 14g; Net Carbs 10g; Protein 19g; Fat 11g; Sugar 2g; Fiber 2g

Egg and Avocado Toasts

Prep Time: 17 minutes| Cook Time: 0 minutes| Servings: 4
Ingredients:
4 eggs
4 slices of hearty whole grain bread
1 avocado, mashed
½ teaspoon salt, optional
¼ teaspoon black pepper
¼ cup Greek yogurt, non-fat
Directions:
To pour each egg, fill ½ cup water into 1 cup bowl suitable for microwave.
Slowly break the eggs into water and make sure they are completely submerged.
Cover at high temperature for about 1 minute with a container and microwave, or before the egg whites solidify and the yolk begins to solidify, but still soft (not running).
Toast the bread and use ¼ of the mashed avocado to sprinkle on each toast.
Sprinkle salt (optional) and pepper.
Place a piece of porched egg on top.
Pour a tablespoon of Greek yogurt and serve.
Nutritional Information: Calories 230; Total Carbs 26g; Net Carbs 18g; Protein 17g; Fat 13g; Sugar 2g; Fiber 5g

Turkey and Egg Casserole

Prep Time: 13 minutes| Cook Time: 13 minutes| Servings: 5
Ingredients:
½ cup green chopped onions
2 cups nonfat milk
nonstick cooking spray
½ teaspoon mustard powder
¼ teaspoon salt
¼ teaspoon black pepper
egg substitute
4 slices of whole wheat bread, cut into ½ –inch cubes
3 precooked diced turkey breakfast sausage patties
¼ cup cheddar cheese, reduced-fat, shredded
Directions:
Preheat oven to 350 degrees F. Grease a 9x13 baking tin with cooking spray.
In a medium pot, mix skim milk, green onions, dried mustard, salt (optional), pepper, and egg substitute.
Place the bread cubes and sausage under the pan and pour the egg mixture over the bread and sausage.
Put cheddar cheese on top.
Cover the baking pan with foil and bake for 20 minutes.
Remove the foil and cook for another 40 minutes.
Serve hot and enjoy.
Nutritional Information: Calories 120; Total Carbs 9g; Net Carbs 5g; Protein 10g; Fat 3g; Sugar 0.5g; Fiber 1g

Scrambled Eggs and Onion for Lox

Prep Time: 12 minutes| Cook Time: 15 minutes| Servings: 4
Ingredients:
6 eggs
4 egg whites
1 teaspoon canola oil
⅓ cup sliced green onions
4 ounces smoked salmon, cut into ½ -inch pieces
¼ cup reduced-fat cream
nonfat cheese, cut into 12 pieces
¼ teaspoon freshly ground black pepper
4 slices pumpernickel bread, toasted
Directions:
Place the eggs and egg whites in a bowl. Stir with a whisk until combined.
Preheat a medium nonstick skillet to medium.
Use oil in the shower. Swirl to coat
Put the green onions in the pan. Fry for 2 minutes or until tender. Connect a bowl of the egg mixture. Cook without stirring until the mixture is on the edges.
Draw a spatula to create a curd at the bottom of the pan. Add sour cream and salmon.
Continue to draw a spatula on the bottom of the pan until the egg mixture is slightly thick but still moist. Do not stir. Removed directly from the pan.
Sprinkle Pepper on egg mixture and serve.
Nutritional Information: Calories 297; Total Carbs 11g; Net Carbs 6g; Protein 22g; Fat 14g; Sugar 2g; Fiber 7g

Huevos Rancheros

Prep Time: 12 minutes| Cook Time: 33 minutes| Servings: 2
Ingredients:
4 corn tortillas
1 can tomato(es) (14.5-ounce, no-salt-added, diced, drained)
1 teaspoon ground cumin
⅛ teaspoon cayenne pepper (optional)
½ teaspoon salt
4 large eggs
1 ounce part-skim mozzarella cheese or reduced-fat feta (shredded)
¼ cup cilantro (chopped)
Directions:
Preheat oven to 425 degrees F.
Put the tortillas in a pan and fry them on each side for 3 minutes.
Meanwhile, place tomatoes, cumin, cayenne pepper, and salt in a medium non-stick pan and cook over medium-high heat.
Reduce heat to medium-low and cook covered until soft or 3 minutes.
Divide one egg into a beaker for the calculation. Carefully move the eggs over the tomato mixture.
Repeat with the remaining eggs. Slowly simmer, covered, over medium, 2½ to 3 minutes or until the whites completely solidify and the yolks begin to thicken slightly.
Place a tortilla to eat on each of the four plates. Cover with eggs and tomato mixture. Use cheese and coriander to spread and enjoy!
Nutritional Information: Calories 162; Total Carbs 14.6g; Net Carbs 9g; Protein 10g; Fat 8g; Sugar 2g; Fiber 5g

Chicken and Egg Salad

Prep Time: 5 minutes| Cook Time: 25 minutes| Servings: 2
Ingredients:
2 cooked chicken breasts
3 hard-boiled eggs
2 tablespoons fat-free mayo
1 tablespoon curry powder
Chives or basil (optional)
Salt (optional)
Directions:
Bake the chicken for 15 minutes in the oven around 360° F. Cook the eggs for 8 minutes.
Cut the eggs and chicken into a small-bite size piece.
Combine the cream cheese with curry powder.
In a large bowl, combine everything and mix.
Allow a minimum of 10 minutes to chill in the refrigerator.
Serve with chives on toast or muffins.
Nutritional Information: Calories 139; Total Carbs 23g; Net Carbs 20g; Protein 18g; Fat 9g; Sugar 1g; Fiber 3g

Curried Apple Chicken Salad

Prep Time: 12 minutes| Cook Time: 13 minutes| Servings: 3
Ingredients:
1 pound of cooked, diced chicken breast.
1 Granny Smith diced apple.
2 celery stalks, (diced)
2 green onions, (diced)
½ cup sliced cashew.
1 cup plain Greek yogurt
1 tablespoon tahini
4 teaspoons curry powder
1 teaspoon ground cinnamon
Directions:
In a big mixing bowl, add the milk, tahini, curry powder, and cinnamon.
Add the chicken, apple, celery, cashews and green onions. Stir to mix well.
Serve with papya chunks if desire.
Nutritional Information: Calories 139; Total Carbs 19g; Net Carbs 11g; Protein 14g; Fat 8g; Sugar 1g; Fiber 5g

Chicken Nuggets

Prep Time: 15 minutes| Cook Time: 23 minutes| Servings: 2
Ingredients:
½ cup almond flour
1 tablespoon Italian seasoning
2 tablespoons extra virgin olive oil
½ teaspoon salt
½ teaspoon pepper
Directions:
Preheat the oven to 400° F.
Using parchment paper to arrange a large baking dish.
In a bowl, combine the Italian seasoning, almond flour, pepper, and salt together.
Start cutting, remove the fat from the chicken breast, then cut it into 1 inch thick slices.
Drizzle the chicken with extra virgin olive oil.
Place each piece of chicken in a bowl of flour and toss until well covered in the mix, then transfer the chicken to a lined baking sheet.
Bake chicken chunks for 20 minutes.
To make the outside crispy, turn on the oven and place the chicken nuggets under the oven for 3-4 minutes.
Nutritional Information: Calories 149; Total Carbs 29g; Net Carbs 22g; Protein 23g; Fat 9g; Sugar 3g; Fiber 8g

Keto Salad

Prep Time: 11 minutes| Cook Time: 0 minutes| Servings: 2
Ingredients:
4 cherry tomatoes
½ avocado
1 hardboiled egg
2 cups mixed green salad
2 ounce of chicken breast, shredded
1 ounce of low-fat feta cheese, crumbled
¼ cup cooked nitrate-free bacon, sugar-free, crumbled
Directions:
Cut the avocado and tomatoes.
Cut the hard-boiled eggs.
Place the mixed vegetables on a large plate.
Add the chicken breast, mashed bacon, and feta cheese.
Arrange tomatoes, eggs, chicken, avocado, feta, and bacon in a horizontal line over the vegetables.
Serve and enjoy.
Nutritional Information: Calories 152; Total Carbs 24g; Net Carbs 19g; Protein 17g; Fat 9g; Sugar 1.1g; Fiber 6.2g

Niçoise Salad Tuna

Prep Time: 12 minutes| Cook Time: 5 minutes| Servings: 1
Ingredients:
4 ounces ahi tuna steak
1 whole egg
2 cups baby spinach (3 ounces)
2 ounces green beans
1 and ½ ounces broccoli
½ red bell peppers
3 and ½ ounces cucumber
1 radish
3 large black olives
Handful of parsley
1 teaspoon olive oil
1 teaspoon balsamic vinegar
½ teaspoon Dijon mustard
½ teaspoon pepper
Directions:
Cook the eggs and let them cool.
Steam the beans and broccoli and drain 2-3 minutes in the microwave or 3 minutes in boiling water.
Heat oil at a high temperature in a pan.
Pepper the seafood on each side and put them on the heat, stirring both sides for about 2 minutes.
Place the spinach in a bowl.
Cut the red peppers, oranges, and eggs into small pieces. Put the spinach on it.
Cut the radish and toss the broccoli, beans, and olives together. Add the spinach salad on top.
Cut the tuna into pieces and add to the salad.
In a bowl, add olive oil, balsamic vinegar, mustard, salt, and pepper.
Finely chop the parsley and add it to the vinaigrette.
Use a spoon to spread the dressing over the salad.
Nutritional Information: Calories 149; Total Carbs 21g; Net Carbs 15g; Protein 19g; Fat 6g; Sugar 1.5g; Fiber 2.5g

Spinach Rolls

Prep Time: 15 minutes| Cook Time: 40 minutes| Servings: 4
Ingredients:
16 ounces frozen spinach leaves
3 eggs
2 and ½ ounce of onion
2 ounces carrot
1 ounce of low-fat mozzarella cheese
4 ounce of fat-free cottage cheese
½ cup parsley
1 clove of garlic
1 teaspoon curry powder
¼ teaspoon chili flakes
1 teaspoon salt
1 teaspoon pepper
Cooking spray
Directions:
Preheat the oven to 400 ° F.
Thaw the spinach and squeeze out the water. You can cook the spinach in the microwave for a few minutes to speed up the defrosting process.
In an ovenproof dish, combine the spinach, 2 eggs, mozzarella, ginger, ½ salt, and pepper together.

Place parchment paper on a baking sheet and coat with cooking spray. Turn the spinach mixture about ½ inch thick and about 10 to 12 inches high into a leaf and press it down. Bake for 15 minutes, then place on a wire rack to cool.
Finely chop the onion and parsley. Grate the carrots.
Brown the onion in a pan with a little oil for 1 minute. Add the carrots and parsley to the pan and simmer for 2 minutes.
Add cottage cheese, curry, chili, salt, and pepper to the other half.
Put the pan on fire, add the eggs and mix everything together.
Spread the filling over the cooled spinach.
Gently roll the spinach mat to the filling and bake for 25 minutes.
When the time is up, remove the roll and let cool for 5-10 minutes, then cut into pieces and serve.
Nutritional Information: Calories 149; Total Carbs 26g; Net Carbs 15g; Protein 17g; Fat 11g; Sugar 0.5g; Fiber 2g

Cajun-Style Shrimp and Grits

Prep Time: 12 minutes| Cook Time: 20 minutes| Servings: 6
Ingredients:
1 tablespoon olive oil
½ cup (2 ounces) of non-nitrite ham, minced
1 cup chopped onion
1 garlic clove, minced
36 medium shrimp, peeled (about 1 ¼ pounds)
1 teaspoon Cajun seasoning
2 and ½ cups water, divided
1 tablespoon unsalted butter
1 cup fat-free milk
1 quarter teaspoon salt
1 cup uncooked quick-cooking grits
1 cup (4 ounces) of sharp cheddar cheese, shredded
½ cup sliced green onions
Directions:
Heat olive oil in a large skillet over medium heat. Add Tasso; Fry for 2 minutes or until edges are golden. Add onions. Fry for 2 minutes.
Stir in the garlic. Fry for 1 minute.
Sprinkle with Cajun seasoning, add the shrimp on the grill and cook in the oven for 3 minutes in turn.
Use ¼ glass of water to loosen the brown flakes and scrape the pan. Remove from fire. Stir and mix with the butter until melted. Wrap up and stay warm. Add milk, salt, and 2 cups of water to a boil over medium heat. remove heat.
Continue to add the oatmeal and cook until thick and crisp, stirring constantly with a whisk. Place the grain at room temperature. Add the cheese and stir with a whisk until the cheese is melted.
Place an equal spoon on the plate.
Mix together the eafood, mixed ham, and green onions for serving.
Nutritional Information: Calories 346; Total Carbs 14g; Net Carbs 9g; Protein 24g; Fat 14g; Sugar 3g; Fiber 4g

Creamy Smoked Salmon Wraps

Prep Time: 12 minutes| Cook Time: 15 minutes| Servings: 2
Ingredients:
1 8-inch low carb flour tortilla
2 ounces smoked salmon
2 teaspoons low-fat cream cheese
One and ½ ounce of red onion
Handful of arugulas
½ teaspoon fresh or dried basil
A pinch of pepper
Directions:
In the oven or microwave, warm the tortillas.
In a bowl, mix the cream cheese, basil, and pepper and then scattered over the tortilla.
Place the salmon, arugula, and finely sliced onion on top of cream mix.
Roll the tortilla up and enjoy the wrap!
Nutritional Information: Calories 138; Total Carbs 19g; Net Carbs 15g; Protein 14g; Fat 6g; Sugar 1.5g; Fiber 3.2g

Balanced Turkey Meatballs

Prep Time: 12 minutes| Cook Time: 26 minutes| Servings: 2
Ingredients:
20 ounces ground of turkey
3 and ½ ounce of fresh or frozen spinach
¼ cup oats
2 egg whites
Celery sticks
3 cloves' garlic
½ green bell peppers
½ red onion
½ cup parsley
½ teaspoon cumin
1 teaspoon mustard powder
1 teaspoon thyme
½ teaspoon turmeric
½ teaspoon chipotle pepper
1 teaspoon salt
A pinch of pepper
Directions:
Preheat the oven to 350 °F .
Finely chop the onion, garlic, and celery (or use a food processor) and place them in a large mixing bowl.
In a bowl, put the ham, egg whites, oatmeal, and spices and mix well. Make sure the mixture does not contain spices or oats.
Finely chop the spinach, pepper, and parsley. Add the vegetables to the mix and mix until well combined.
Place the parchment paper on the baking sheet. Roll the turkey mixture into 15 balls and place them on a baking sheet.Bake for 25 minutes, until fully baked and serve with salad.
Nutritional Information: Calories 129; Total Carbs 22g; Net Carbs 17g; Protein 25g; Fat 9g; Sugar 2g; Fiber 3g

Beef Fajitas

Prep Time: 6 minutes| Cook Time: 19 minutes| Servings: 4
Ingredients:
1 lbs. beef stir-fry strips
1 medium red onion
1 red bell pepper
1 yellow bell pepper
½ teaspoon cumin
½ teaspoon chili powder
Splash of oil
Salt
Pepper
½ juice of lime
Freshly chopped cilantro (also called coriander)
1 avocado
Directions:
Steam a cast-iron saucepan over medium heat.
Wash and clean the peppers, cut them into slices 0.5 cm thick, and leave them separately.
Wash the red onions and cut them into strips. Separate.
When the pan is heated, add a little oil.
Add 2-3 packets of stir-fry strips while the oil is hot.
In a skillet, lightly brown a loaf of beef with salt and pepper. Bake for 1 minute on each side and place on a plate to warm.
When the beef is cooked, add the chopped onion and red pepper to the rest of the broth and set aside.
Spice with chili powder and cumin, then simmer until desired consistency.
Transfer the roasted vegetables and beef to a plate and serve with chopped avocado, a drop of lemon juice, and a drop of fresh cilantro.
Nutritional Information: Calories 151; Total Carbs 27g; Net Carbs 20g; Protein 37g; Fat 6g; Sugar 0.4g; Fiber 11g

Traditional Omelet with Turmeric

Prep Time: 8 minutes| Cook Time: 15 minutes| Servings: 2
Ingredients:
4 large eggs
Kosher salt
1 tablespoon olive oil
¼ teaspoon brown mustard seeds Turmeric powder
2 green onions, finely chopped
¼ cup diced plum tomato
Dash of black pepper
Directions:
Whisk the eggs and salt together.
Heat oil in a large cast-iron skillet over medium heat.
Use mustard and turmeric seeds. Stir constantly for 30 seconds or until the seeds crackled.
Add the onions and cook for 30 seconds or until tender, stirring constantly. Add the tomatoes.
Cook for 1 minute, stirring constantly, or until very tender.
Pour the bowl with the egg mixture. Spread evenly. Cook until edges are set (about 2 minutes).
Slide the edges of the spatula between the edges of the omelet and the plate. Carefully lift the edges of the omelet by tilting the pan so that it comes in contact with the egg mixture. Duplicate procedure from the opposite edge. Continue cooking until the setting is ready.
Loosen the omelet and fold it in half with a spatula. Carefully slide the omelet onto the plate. Cut the omelet in half and sprinkle with pepper.
Nutritional Information: Calories 216; Total Carbs 14g; Net Carbs 9g; Protein 13.3g; Fat 16.9g; Sugar 0.6g; Fiber 4g

Instant Pot Chicken Chili

Prep Time: 6 minutes| Cook Time: 21 minutes| Servings: 2

Ingredients:
1 tablespoon vegetable oil
1 yellow diced onion
4 minced garlic cloves
1 teaspoon ground cumin
1 teaspoon oregano
2 and halls' chicken breasts, boneless & skinless
16 ounce of salsa Verde
For Toppings
2 packages of queso fresco(crumbled) or sour cream
2 diced avocados
Finely chopped radishes
8 springs cilantro (optional)

Directions:
Set the Instant Pot to a medium sauté setting.
Add oil and vegetables to the pot.
Add the onion and simmer for 3 minutes, stirring constantly, until the onion begins to melt.
Add the garlic and stir for 1 minute.
Add oregano and cumin and simmer for 1 minute.
Add ½ of the salsa verde to the pan.
Top with the chicken breast and pour the chicken with most of the leftover salsa verde.
Place the cover on the instant pot, change the nozzle to "Seal" and select "Manual". Set the timer for 10 minutes.
Then let the pressure release naturally after done.
Remove the lid and transfer the chicken to a small bowl and chop it with a fork.
Transfer the meat to a pot and stir to combine most of the remaining Ingredients.
Serve hot and enjoy.

Nutritional Information: Calories 144; Total Carbs 20g; Net Carbs 18g; Protein 15g; Fat 7g; Sugar 3g; Fiber 8g

Summer Fruits Smoothie

Prep Time: 12 minutes| Cook Time: 0 minutes| Servings: 4

Ingredients:
1 cup fresh blueberries
1 cup fresh strawberries (chopped)
2 peaches (peeled, seeded and chopped)
Peach flavored Greek style yogurt (non-fat)
1 cup unsweetened almond milk
2 tablespoons ground flax seed
½ cup ice

Directions:
Put all Ingredients in a blender and puree until creamy.
Serve chilled.

Nutritional Information: Calories 130; Total Carbs 23g; Net Carbs 20g; Protein 15g; Fat 4g; Sugar 1g; Fiber 4g

Tex-mex Migas

Prep Time: 9 minutes| Cook Time: 15 minutes| Servings: 4

Ingredients:
3 large eggs - 3 egg whites
1 tablespoon canola oil
4 corn tortillas, cut into ½ -inch-wide strips
½ cup chopped onion
2 large seeded jalapeño peppers
⅔ cup lower-sodium salsa
½ cup non-fat Monterey Jack cheese, shredded
½ cup sliced green onions
Hot sauce (optional)
Lower-sodium red salsa (optional)
Lower-sodium green salsa (optional)

Directions:
Place the eggs and egg whites in a bowl. Stir with a whisk until combined.
Set to medium and heat in a medium nonstick skillet. Use oil in the shower. Swirl on the shirt.
Spread tortilla strips on the pan and cook for 3 minutes or until golden brown, stirring constantly.
Add the onions and jalapeño peppers to the sauce. Fry for 2 minutes or until tender. Add ⅔ cup of salsa and simmer for 1 minute, stirring constantly.
Add the egg mixture. Cook for 2 minutes or until eggs is tender, stirring frequently. Sprinkle the cheese with the egg mixture.
Bake 3 minutes or until cheese is melted. Cover with green onions and serve immediately.
Serve with hot sauce, red salsa, or green salsa of your choice.

Nutritional Information: Calories 193; Total Carbs 12g; Net Carbs 9g; Protein 10.2g; Fat 10.4g; Sugar 1.4g; Fiber 6.2g

Turkey Meatballs

Prep Time: 16 minutes| Cook Time: 25 minutes| Servings: 5

Ingredients:
20 ounces ground turkey
4 ounces fresh or frozen spinach
¼ cup oats
2 egg whites
2 celery sticks
3 cloves' garlic
½ green bell peppers
½ red onion
½ cup parsley
½ teaspoon cumin
1 teaspoon mustard powder
1 teaspoon thyme
½ tablespoon turmeric
½ teaspoon chipotle pepper
1 teaspoon salt
Pinch of pepper

Directions:
Preheat the oven to 350° F.
Chop very finely the onion, garlic, and celery, and add to a large mixing bowl.
In the dish, add the ham, egg whites, oats, and spices and combine well.
Make sure the blend has no pockets of spices or oats. Spinach, green peppers and parsley are chopped.
To the bowl, add the vegetables and mix it until well-combined.
Line the parchment paper with a baking sheet.
Roll the turkey mixture into 15 balls and put them on the baking sheet.
Bake for 25 minutes, until fully baked.

Nutritional Information: Calories 349; Total Carbs 7g; Net Carbs 4g; Protein 19g; Fat 7g; Sugar 0g; Fiber 1.2g

Savory Egg Muffins

Prep Time: 12 minutes| Cook Time: 33 minutes| Servings: 6
Ingredients:
1 and ½ cups water
2 tablespoons unsalted butter
1 (6-ounce) package Stove, top lower-sodium stuffing mix for chicken
3 ounces bulk pork sausage
Cooking spray
6 eggs, beaten
½ cup nonfat (1.5 ounces) Monterey Jack cheese, shredded -
½ cup finely chopped red bell pepper –
¼ cup sliced green onions
Directions:
Preheat oven to 400°F.
Boil 1½ cups of water and butter. Mix the Ingredients. Cover, remove from heat, and let stand 5 minutes.
Use a pork to fluff the filling. Leave it for 10 minutes.
Cook the sausages in a small skillet over medium heat until they are brown while the stuffing is cooling. Stir to break.
Press about ¼ cup into the bottom and sides of 12 oil-coated muffin cups.
Pour in eggs equal to cups of filling. If desired, top the eggs evenly with cheese, ham, bell peppers, and green onions.
Bake at 400°F for 18-20 minutes.
Let stand 5 minutes before eating. Loosen the glass muffin with a thin, sharp knife along the edge.
Remove from the casserole dish.
Serve immediately.
Nutritional Information: Calories 292; Total Carbs 18g; Net Carbs 12g; Protein 14.6g; Fat 16.7g; Sugar 3g; Fiber 9g

Pancakes with Blueberry and Peaches

Prep Time: 12 minutes| Cook Time: 16 minutes| Servings: 6
Ingredients:
One and ½ cups all-purpose flour
2 tablespoons splenda
2 tablespoons flaxseed (optional) One tablespoon baking powder
½ teaspoon kosher salt
1 and ½ cups nonfat buttermilk
1 teaspoon grated lemon rind
2 eggs
1 cup fresh or frozen blueberries, thawed
1 cup chopped fresh or frozen peaches, thawed
2 tablespoons unsalted butter
Fresh blueberries (optional)
Directions:
Whisk or gently pour the flour into a measuring cup. Level with a knife.
In a large bowl, combine flour, splenda, flax seeds, baking powder, and salt as needed and stir with a fork.
In a small cup, put the buttermilk, lemon zest, and eggs and stir with a fork.
Use the buttermilk mixture to mix and stir until it is just moist. Thinly fold the blueberries and peaches.
Heat a nonstick skillet or nonstick skillet over medium heat. Pour ⅓ cup of flour into a pancake in the pan.
Cook over medium heat for 2-3 minutes or until the foam covers the top and fry the edges.
Slowly turn the pancake over.
Cook 2-3 minutes or until the underside is golden brown.
Nutritional Information: Calories 238; Total Carbs 14g; Net Carbs 10g; Protein 8.1g; Fat 2.8g; Sugar 3g; Fiber 2.5g

Bulgur Porridge

Prep Time: 5 minutes| Cook Time: 15 minutes| Servings: 4
Ingredients:
4 cups 1% low-fat milk
1 cup bulgur
⅓ cup dried cherries
¼ tablespoon salt
⅓ cup dried apricots, coarsely chopped
½ cup sliced almonds
Directions:
In a large saucepan, put the milk, bulgur, dried cherries, and salt. Bring to a boil.
Reduce heat to low and simmer, stirring constantly, until tender and oatmeal are tender for 10-15 minutes.
Divide among 4 bowls.
Garnish with apricots and almonds and serve.
Nutritional Information: Calories 340; Total Carbs 21g; Net Carbs 18g; Protein 15g; Fat 6.7g; Sugar 2g; Fiber 5g

Yummy Bean and Veggie Cups

Prep Time: 10minutes| Cook Time:05 minutes| Servings:4

Ingredients:
1 cup fat-free grated Parmesan cheese, divided
1 (15-ounce / 425-g) can low-sodium white beans, drained and rinsed
1 cucumber, peeled and finely diced
½ cup finely diced red onion
¼ cup thinly sliced fresh basil
1 garlic clove, minced
½ jalapeño pepper, diced
1 tablespoon extra-virgin olive oil
1 tablespoon balsamic vinegar
¼ teaspoon salt
Freshly ground black pepper, to taste

Direction:
Over medium heat, heat a medium nonstick skillet.
Spatula 2 tablespoons of cheese in the centre of the pan and spread out in a thin circle.
When the cheese has melted, flip it over and lightly brown the other side with a spatula.
Remove the cheese "pancake" from the pan and set it in the cup of a muffin tin, gently bending it to fit into the cup.
Continue with the remaining cheese until you have a total of 8 cups.
Toss together the beans, cucumber, onion, basil, garlic, jalapeo, olive oil, and vinegar in a mixing bowl, seasoning with salt and pepper.
Just before serving, spoon the bean mixture into each cup.

Nutritional Information: calories: 260 | fat: 12.1g | protein: 14.9 | carbs: 23.9g | fiber: 8.0g | sugar: 3.9g | sodium: 552mg

Summer Vegetables with Green Lentils

Prep Time: 15 minutes| Cook Time:00 minutes| Servings:4

Ingredients:
3 tablespoons extra-virgin olive oil
2 tablespoons balsamic vinegar
2 teaspoons chopped fresh basil
1 teaspoon minced garlic
Sea salt , according to taste
freshly ground black pepper, according to taste
2 (15-ounce / 425-g) cans sodium-free green lentils, rinsed and drained
½ English cucumber, diced
2 tomatoes, diced
½ cup halved Kalamata olives
¼ cup chopped fresh chives
2 tablespoons pine nuts

Direction:
In a medium mixing bowl, combine the olive oil, vinegar, basil, and garlic. Salt & pepper to taste.
Combine the lentils, cucumber, tomatoes, olives, and chives in a large mixing bowl.
Serve with pine nuts as a garnish.

Nutritional Information: calories: 400 | fat: 15.1g | protein: 19.8g | carbs: 48.8g | fiber: 18.8g | sugar: 7.1g | sodium: 439mg

Herbed Brown Rice with Beans

Prep Time: 15 minutes| Cook Time:15minutes| Servings:8

Ingredients:
2 teaspoons extra-virgin olive oil
½ sweet onion, chopped
1 teaspoon minced jalapeño pepper
1 teaspoon minced garlic
1 (15-ounce / 425-g) can sodium-free red kidney beans, rinsed and drained
1 large tomato, chopped
1 teaspoon chopped fresh thyme
Sea salt according to taste
freshly ground black pepper, to taste
2 cups cooked brown rice

Direction:
In a large skillet, heat the olive oil over medium-high heat.
Sauté the onion, jalapeo, and garlic for 3 minutes, or until softened.
Combine the beans, tomato, and thyme in a mixing bowl.
Cook, stirring occasionally, for about 10 minutes, or until completely cooked.
Season with salt and pepper to taste.
Serve with a side of warm brown rice.

Nutritional Information: calories: 200 | fat: 2.1g | protein: 9.1g | carbs: 37.1g | fiber: 6.1g | sugar: 2.0g | sodium: 40mg

Baked Tomatoes and Navy Beans

Prep Time: 10 minutes| Cook Time:25 minutes| Servings:8

Ingredients:
1 teaspoon extra-virgin olive oil
½ sweet onion, chopped
2 teaspoons minced garlic
2 sweet potatoes, peeled and diced
1 (28-ounce / 794-g) can low-sodium diced tomatoes
¼ cup sodium-free tomato paste
2 tablespoons granulated sweetener
2 tablespoons hot sauce
1 tablespoon Dijon mustard
3 (15-ounce / 425-g) cans sodium-free navy or white beans, drained
1 tablespoon chopped fresh oregano

Direction:
In a large saucepan, heat the oil over medium-high heat.Sauté the onion and garlic for 3 minutes, or until transparent.
Bring to a boil with the sweet potatoes, diced tomatoes, tomato paste, sweetener, spicy sauce, and mustard.
Reduce the heat to low and allow the tomato sauce to simmer for 10 minutes.
Stir in the beans and continue to cook for another 10 minutes.
Serve with oregano on top.

Nutritional Information: calories: 256 | fat: 2.1g | protein: 15.1g | carbs: 48.1g | fiber: 11.9g | sugar: 8.1g | sodium: 150mg

Wild Rice with Blueberries

Prep Time: 15 minutes| Cook Time:45minutes| Servings:4

Ingredients:
1 tablespoon extra-virgin olive oil
½ sweet onion, chopped
2½ cups sodium-free chicken broth
1 cup wild rice, rinsed and drained
Pinch sea salt
½ cup toasted pumpkin seeds
½ cup blueberries
1 teaspoon chopped fresh basil

Direction:
Add the oil to a medium saucepan over medium-high heat. 3 minutes later, the onion should be softened and transparent.
Bring the broth to a boil, gradually stirring.
Reduce the heat to low and stir in the rice and salt. Cook for 40 minutes, or until the rice is cooked, covered. If necessary, drain any surplus broth.
Combine the pumpkin seeds, blueberries, and basil in a mixing bowl.
Warm the dish before serving.

Nutritional Information: calories: 259 | fat: 9.1g | protein: 10.8g | carbs: 37.1g | fiber: 3.9g | sugar: 4.1g | sodium: 543mg

Beans Chili

Prep Time: 20 minutes| Cook Time:60 minutes| Servings:8

Ingredients:
1 teaspoon extra-virgin olive oil
1 sweet onion, chopped
1 red bell pepper, seeded and diced
1 green bell pepper, seeded and diced
2 teaspoons minced garlic
1 (28-ounce / 794-g) can low-sodium diced tomatoes
1 (15-ounce / 425-g) can sodium-free black beans, rinsed and drained
1 (15-ounce / 425-g) can sodium-free red kidney beans, rinsed and drained
1 (15-ounce / 425-g) can sodium-free navy beans, rinsed and drained
2 tablespoons chili powder
2 teaspoons ground cumin
1 teaspoon ground coriander
¼ teaspoon red pepper flakes

Direction:
In a large saucepan, heat the oil over medium-high heat.
Sauté the onion, red and green bell peppers, and garlic for about 5 minutes, or until the veggies have softened.
Toss in the tomatoes, black beans, red kidney beans, navy beans, chilli powder, cumin, coriander, and red pepper flakes, as well as chilli powder, cumin, coriander, and red pepper flakes.
Bring the chilli to a boil, then turn it down to a low heat.
Cook, stirring occasionally, for at least one hour.
Serve immediately.

Nutritional Information: calories: 480 | fat: 28.1g | protein: 15.1g | carbs: 45.1g | fiber: 16.9g | sugar: 4.0g | sodium: 16mg

Savory Linguine with Pesto

Prep Time: 10 minutes| Cook Time:20minutes| Servings:6

Ingredients:
½ cup shredded kale
½ cup fresh basil
½ cup sun-dried tomatoes
¼ cup chopped almonds
2 tablespoons extra-virgin olive oil
8 ounces (227 g) dry whole-wheat linguine
½ cup grated fat-free Parmesan cheese

Direction:
In a food processor or blender, pulse the kale, basil, sun-dried tomatoes, almonds, and olive oil until a thick paste forms, about 2 minutes.
Place the pesto in a mixing dish and set aside.
Bring a big pot filled with water to a boil over high heat.
Cook the pasta until it is al dente, as directed on the package.
Drain the pasta and combine it with the pesto and Parmesan cheese in a large mixing bowl.
Serve right away.

Nutritional Information: calories: 218 | fat: 10.1g | protein: 9.1g | carbs: 25.1g | fiber: 1.1g | sugar: 2.9g | sodium: 195mg

Quinoa with Fresh Vegetables

Prep Time: 15 minutes| Cook Time: 30 minutes| Servings:12

Ingredients:
4 cups low-sodium vegetable broth
2 cups quinoa, well rinsed and drained
2 teaspoon extra-virgin olive oil
1 sweet onion, chopped
4 teaspoons minced garlic
1 large green zucchini, halved lengthwise and cut into half disks
2 red bell pepper, chopped into small strips after being sown
2 cup fresh or frozen corn kernels
2 teaspoon chopped fresh basil
Sea salt, to taste
Freshly ground black pepper, to taste

Direction:
Place the veggie broth in a medium saucepan over medium heat. Bring the stock to a boil before stirring in the quinoa. Cover and reduce to a low heat setting.
Cook for 20 minutes, or until the quinoa has absorbed all of the broth. It should be removed from the heat and left aside to cool. Heat the oil in a big skillet over medium-high heat while the quinoa is cooking.
Sauté the onion and garlic for 3 minutes, or until softened and transparent.
Sauté the zucchini, bell pepper, and corn for about 7 minutes, or until the vegetables are tender-crisp.
Turn off the heat in the skillet. Stir in the cooked quinoa and basil until everything is well combined.
Season with a touch of salt and pepper before serving.

Nutritional Information: calories: 159 | fat: 3.0g | protein: 7.1g | carbs: 26.1g | fiber: 2.9g | sugar: 3.0g | sodium: 300mg

Lime Yogurt Black Bean Soup with Tomatoes

Prep Time: 8 hours 10 minutes | Cook Time: 1 hour 33 minutes | Servings:8
Ingredients:
2 tablespoons avocado oil
1 medium onion, chopped
1 (10-ounce / 284-g) can diced tomatoes and green chilies
1 pound (454 g) dried black beans, soaked in water for at least 8 hours, rinsed
1 teaspoon ground cumin
3 garlic cloves, minced
6 cups vegetable broth, or water
Kosher salt, to taste
1 tablespoon freshly squeezed lime juice
¼ cup plain Greek yogurt
Direction:
In a nonstick skillet, heat the avocado oil over medium heat until it shimmers.
Sauté for 3 minutes, or until the onion is transparent.
In a large pot, combine the onion, tomatoes, green chilies, and their juices, black beans, cumin, garlic, broth, and salt. Stir everything together thoroughly.
Bring to a boil over medium-high heat, then lower to a low setting. Cook for an hour and a half, or until the beans are tender.
Meanwhile, in a small bowl, combine the lime juice and Greek yoghurt. Stir everything together thoroughly.
Before serving, pour the soup into a large serving bowl and drizzle with lime yoghurt.
Nutritional Information: Calories 285; Total Carbs 42g; Net Carbs 31g; Protein 19g; Fat 6g; Sugar 3g; Fiber 10g

Eggplant and Bulgur Pilaf with Basil

Prep Time: 10 minutes| Cook Time:60 minutes| Servings:4
Ingredients:
1 tablespoon extra-virgin olive oil
½ sweet onion, chopped
2 teaspoons minced garlic
1 cup chopped eggplant
1½ cups bulgur
4 cups low-sodium chicken broth
1 cup diced tomato
Sea salt , to taste
freshly ground black pepper, to taste
2 tablespoons chopped fresh basil
Direction:
Warm the oil in a big pan over medium heat.Sauté the onion and garlic for 3 minutes or until softened and transparent.
Add the eggplant and cook for 4 minutes to soften it.
Combine the bulgur, broth, and tomatoes in a mixing bowl. Bring the water to a boil in a kettle. Reduce the heat to low, cover, and cook for about 50 minutes, or until the water has been absorbed.
Add salt and pepper to taste to the pilaf.
Garnish with basil leaves and serve.
Nutritional Information: calories: 300 | fat: 4.0g | protein: 14.0g | carbs: 54.0g | fiber: 12.0g | sugar: 7.0g | sodium: 358mg

Mushroom and Rice Bowl with Hazelnuts

Prep Time: 20 minutes| Cook Time:35minutes| Servings:8
Ingredients:
1 tablespoon extra-virgin olive oil
1 cup chopped button mushrooms
½ sweet onion, chopped
1 celery stalk, chopped
2 teaspoons minced garlic
2 cups brown basmati rice
4 cups low-sodium chicken broth
1 teaspoon chopped fresh thyme
Sea salt , to taste
freshly ground black pepper, to taste
½ cup chopped hazelnuts
Direction:
Warm the oil in a big pan over medium heat.
Sauté the mushrooms, onion, celery, and garlic for about 10 minutes, or until gently browned.
Cook for another minute after adding the rice.
Increase the heat to high and bring the chicken broth to a boil.
Lower the heat to a low setting and cover the pot. Cook for about 20 minutes, or until the liquid has been absorbed and the rice is soft.
Season with salt and pepper after adding the thyme.
Sprinkle the hazelnuts over top and serve.
Nutritional Information: calories: 240 | fat: 6.1g | protein: 7.1g | carbs: 38.9g | fiber: 0.9g | sugar: 1.1g | sodium: 388mg

Curried Black-Eyed Peas

Prep Time: 15minutes| Cook Time:40 minutes| Servings:12
Ingredients:
1 pound (454 g) dried black-eyed peas, rinsed and drained
4 cups vegetable broth
1 cup coconut water
1 cup chopped onion
4 large carrots, coarsely chopped
1½ tablespoons curry powder
1 tablespoon minced garlic
1 teaspoon peeled and minced fresh ginger
1 tablespoon extra-virgin olive oil
Kosher salt (optional)
Lime wedges, for serving
Direction:
Combine the black-eyed peas, broth, coconut water, onion, carrots, curry powder, garlic, and ginger in an electric pressure cooker. Over the top, drizzle the extra virgin olive oil.
Close and lock the pressure cooker's lid. To close the valve, turn it to the closed position. Cook for 25 minutes on high pressure.
When the cooking is finished, press Cancel and let the pressure naturally release for 10 minutes before quick-releasing any leftover pressure. Unlock and remove the cover once the pin has dropped.
If desired, season with salt and squeeze fresh lime juice over each serving.
Nutritional Information: calories: 113 | fat: 3.1g | protein: 10.1g | carbs: 30.9g | fiber: 6.1g | sugar: 6.0g | sodium: 672mg

Kale, Suqash, and Barley Risotto with Pistachio

Prep Time: 10 minutes| Cook Time:15minutes| Servings:6

Ingredients:
1 teaspoon extra-virgin olive oil
½ sweet onion, finely chopped
1 teaspoon minced garlic
2 cups cooked barley
2 cups chopped kale
2 cups cooked butternut squash, cut into ½-inch cubes
2 tablespoons chopped pistachios
1 tablespoon chopped fresh thyme
Sea salt, to taste

Direction:
Warm the oil in a big pan over medium heat.
Sauté the onion and garlic for 3 minutes, or until softened and transparent.
Stir in the barley and kale for about 7 minutes, or until the grains are heated through and the greens are wilted.
Combine the squash, pistachios, and thyme in a mixing bowl.
Season with salt and cook until the dish is heated, about 4 minutes.
Nutritional Information: calories: 160 | fat: 1.9g | protein: 5.1g | carbs: 32.1g | fiber: 7.0g | sugar: 2.0g | sodium: 63mg

Flavorful Wax Beans

Prep Time: 05 minutes| Cook Time:15 minutes| Servings:4

Ingredients:
2 pounds (907 g) wax beans
2 tablespoons extra-virgin olive oil
Sea salt, to taste
Freshly ground black pepper, to taste
Juice of ½ lemon

Direction:
Preheat the oven to 400 degrees Fahrenheit (205 degrees Celsius).
A baking pan should be lined with aluminium foil. Toss the beans with the olive oil in a large mixing dish. According to taste, season with salt and pepper.
Place the beans on the baking pan and evenly distribute them.
Roast the beans for 10 to 12 minutes, or until they are caramelised and soft.
Serve the beans on a serving plate with a squeeze of lemon juice.
Nutritional Information: calories: 99 | fat: 7.1g | protein: 2.1g | carbs: 8.1g | fiber: 4.2g | sugar: 3.9g | sodium: 814mg

Navy Beans with Pico de Gallo

Prep Time: 20 minutes| Cook Time:00 minutes| Servings:4

Ingredients:
2½ cups cooked navy beans
1 tomato, diced
½ red bell pepper, seeded and chopped
¼ jalapeño pepper, chopped
1 scallion, white and green parts, chopped
1 teaspoon minced garlic
1 teaspoon ground cumin
½ teaspoon ground coriander
½ cup low-sodium feta cheese
Direction:
In a medium mixing bowl, combine the beans, tomato, bell pepper, jalapeo, scallion, garlic, cumin, and coriander.
Serve with feta cheese on top.
Nutritional Information: calories: 225 | fat: 4.1g | protein: 14.1g | carbs: 34.1g | fiber: 13.1g | sugar: 3.9g | sodium: 165mg

Avocado and Farro

Prep Time: 05minutes| Cook Time:25 minutes| Servings:4

Ingredients:
3 cups water
1 cup uncooked farro
1 tablespoon extra-virgin olive oil
1 teaspoon ground cumin
½ teaspoon salt
½ teaspoon freshly ground black pepper
4 hardboiled eggs, sliced
1 avocado, sliced
⅓ cup plain low-fat Greek yogurt
4 lemon wedges

Direction:
In a medium saucepan over high heat, bring the water to a boil.Pour the boiling water over the farro and whisk to fully submerge the grains. Cook for another 20 minutes after lowering the heat to medium-low.
Drain and set aside the water.
Over medium-low heat, heat a medium skillet. Pour in the oil when the pan is heated, then add the farro, cumin, salt, and pepper. Cook, stirring periodically, for 3 to 5 minutes.
Top each portion of farro with one-quarter of the eggs, avocado, and yoghurt. Serve with a squeeze of lemon on top of each serving.
Nutritional Information: calories: 333 | fat: 16.1g | protein: 15.1g | carbs: 31.9g | fiber: 7.9g | sugar: 2.0g | sodium: 360mg

Traditional Texas Caviar

Prep Time: 10 minutes | Cook Time:00 minutes | Servings:6

Ingredients:
For the Salad:
1 ear fresh corn, kernels removed
1 cup cooked lima beans
1 cup cooked black-eyed peas
1 red bell pepper, chopped
2 celery stalks, chopped
½ red onion, chopped
For the Dressing:
3 tablespoons apple cider vinegar
1 teaspoon paprika
2 tablespoons extra-virgin olive oil

Direction:
In a large mixing basin, combine the corn, beans, peas, bell pepper, celery, and onion. Stir everything together thoroughly.
In a small bowl, combine the vinegar, paprika, and olive oil. Stir everything together thoroughly.
Toss the salad in the dressing to evenly distribute it. Allow it infuse for 20 minutes before serving.
Nutritional Information: Calories 170; Total Carbs 29g; Net Carbs 15g; Protein 10g; Fat 6g; Sugar 4g; Fiber 10g

Black Beans with Dandelion and Beet Greens

Prep Time: 9 minutes | Cook Time:14 minutes | Servings:4

Ingredients:
1 tablespoon olive oil
½ Vidalia onion, thinly sliced
1 bunch dandelion greens, cut into ribbons
1 bunch beet greens, cut into ribbons
½ cup low-sodium vegetable broth
1 (15-ounce) can no-salt-added black beans
Salt , to taste
Freshly ground black pepper, to taste

Direction:
In a nonstick skillet, heat the olive oil over low heat until it shimmers.
Cook for 3 minutes, or until the onion is clear.
In a skillet, combine the dandelion and beet greens with the broth. Cook, covered, for 8 minutes, or until the spinach has wilted.
Cook for 4 minutes, or until the black beans are tender. Season to taste with salt and pepper.
Stir everything together thoroughly.
Serve right away.

Nutritional Information: Calories 161; Total Carbs 26g; Net Carbs 17g; Protein 9g; Fat 4g; Sugar 1g; Fiber 10g

Chickpea Spaghetti Bolognese

Prep Time: 05 minutes | Cook Time:25 minutes | Servings:4

Ingredients:
1 (3- to 4-pound / 1.4- to 1.8-kg) spaghetti squash
½ teaspoon ground cumin
1 cup no-sugar-added spaghetti sauce
1 (15-ounce) can low-sodium chickpeas, drained and rinsed
6 ounces (170 g) extra-firm tofu

Directions:
Preheat the oven to 400 degrees Fahrenheit (205 degrees Celsius).
Squash should be cut in half lengthwise. Scoop out the seeds and toss them away.
Season both sides of the squash with cumin and set cut-side down on a baking pan. Cook for 25 minutes at 350°F.
Meanwhile, simmer the spaghetti sauce and chickpeas in a medium skillet over low heat.
Squeeze off any excess water by pressing the tofu between two layers of paper towels.
Cook for 15 minutes after crumbling the tofu into the sauce.
Remove the squash from the oven and comb thin strands of flesh through each half with a fork.
Divide the "spaghetti" into four sections and drizzle one-quarter of the sauce over each.

Nutritional Information: Calories 276; Total Carbs 41.9g; Net Carbs 24.8g; Protein 7g; Fat 7.1g; Sugar 7g; Fiber 10.1g

Savory Sofrito Dumplings

Prep Time: 20 minutes | Cook Time:15 minutes | Servings:10

Ingredients:
4 cups water
4 cups low-sodium vegetable broth
1 cup cassava flour
1 cup gluten-free all-purpose flour
2 teaspoons baking powder
1 teaspoon salt
1 cup fat-free milk
2 tablespoons bottled chimichurri or sofrito

Directions:
Bring the water and broth to a slow boil in a large pot over medium-high heat.
Whisk together the cassava flour, all-purpose flour, baking powder, and salt in a large mixing basin.
Whisk the milk and chimichurri together in a small bowl until smooth.
Combine the wet Ingredients in a mixing bowl. Place the dry Ingredients in a large mixing bowl. A bit at a time until a firm dough is formed.
Pinch off a tiny piece of dough with clean hands. Form a disc by rolling the dough into a ball and gently flattening it in the palm of your hand. Repeat till there is no more dough.
Insert a fork into the dumpling to check for doneness; it should come out clean.
Warm the dish before serving.

Nutritional Information: Calories 133; Total Carbs 25.9g; Net Carbs 20.7g; Protein 4.1g; Fat 1.1g; Sugar 2.0g; Fiber 3.2g

Black Bean and Corn Soup

Prep Time: 10 minutes | Cook Time:25 minutes | Servings:7

Ingredients:
2 tablespoons olive oil
½ onion, diced
1 pound boneless and skinless chicken breast, cut into ½-inch cubes
½ teaspoon Adobo seasoning, divided
¼ teaspoon black pepper
1 (15-ounce) can washed and drained black beans with no salt added
1 (14.5-ounce) can fire-roasted tomatoes
½ cup frozen corn
½ teaspoon cumin
1 tablespoon chili powder
5 cups low-sodium chicken broth

Directions:
Heat the olive oil in a stockpot over medium-high heat until it shimmers.
Sauté the onion for 3 minutes, or until it is transparent.
Spread the Adobo seasoning and pepper over the chicken breasts. Cook for 6 minutes, or until gently browned, with the lid on. Halfway through the cooking period, give the pot a good shake.
Combine the remaining Ingredients in a mixing bowl. Reduce to a low heat and continue to cook for another 15 minutes, or until the black beans are tender.
Serve right away.
To make your own Adobo seasoning, combine paprika, black pepper, onion powder, dried oregano, cumin, garlic powder, chilli powder, and salt.

Nutritional Information: Calories 170; Total Carbs 15g; Net Carbs 7g; Protein 20g; Fat 3.6g; Sugar 3g; Fiber 5g

Garlic Zucchini and Chicken Soup

Prep Time: 8 minutes | Cook Time:14 minutes | Servings:4

Ingredients:
2 tablespoons extra-virgin olive oil
12 ounces (336 g) chicken breast, chopped
1 onion, chopped
2 carrots, chopped
2 celery stalks, chopped
2 garlic cloves
6 cups unsalted chicken broth
1 teaspoon dried thyme
1 teaspoon sea salt
2 medium zucchinis cut into noodles (or store-bought zucchini noodles)

Directions:
In a large pot, warm the olive oil over medium-high heat until it shimmers.
Add the chicken and simmer for 5 minutes, or until it is opaque. Remove the chicken from the saucepan with a slotted spoon and place it on a plate.
In a large pot, combine the onion, carrots, and celery. Cook, stirring periodically, for about 5 minutes, or until the vegetables are tender.
Add the garlic and simmer for 30 seconds, stirring regularly. Combine the chicken stock, thyme, and salt in a large mixing bowl. Stir to a boil, then reduce to a low heat.
Return the chicken to the pan with the zucchini and any liquids that have gathered on the dish. Cook for another 1 to 2 minutes, stirring periodically, until the zucchini noodles are tender.

Nutritional Information: Calories 236; Total Carbs 11g; Net Carbs 1.6g; Protein 27g; Fat 10g; Sugar 17.3g; Fiber 3g

Black Bean Fritters

Prep Time: 10 minutes | Cook Time:25 minutes | Servings: 20

Ingredients:
1¾ cups all-purpose flour
½ teaspoon cumin
2 teaspoons baking powder
2 teaspoons salt
½ teaspoon black pepper
4 egg whites, lightly beaten
1 cup salsa
2 (16-ounce / 454-g) cans no-salt-added black beans, rinsed and drained
1 tablespoon canola oil, plus extra if needed

Directions:
In a large mixing bowl, combine the flour, cumin, baking powder, salt, and pepper, then add the egg whites and salsa. Stir in the black beans until everything is fully combined.
In a nonstick skillet, heat the canola oil over medium-high heat.
To make a fritter, put 1 teaspoon of the mixture into the skillet. Make extra fritters to cover the skillet's bottom. Maintain a small gap between each pair of fritters. To avoid overpopulation, you may need to work in bunches.
Cook for 3 minutes, or until both sides of the fritters are golden brown. Halfway through the cooking time, flip the fritters and flatten using a spatula. Rep with the rest of the mixture. As needed, add more oil.

Serve right away.

Nutritional Information: Calories 115; Total Carbs 20g; Net Carbs 13g; Protein 6g; Fat 1g; Sugar 2g; Fiber 5g

Lime Yogurt Chili Soup with Tomatoes

Prep Time: 8 hours10 minutes | Cook Time:1 hour 33 minutes | Servings:8

Ingredients:
2 tablespoons avocado oil
1 medium onion, chopped
1 (10-ounce / 284-g) can diced tomatoes and green chilies
1 pound (454 g) dried black beans, soaked in water for at least 8 hours, rinsed
1 teaspoon ground cumin
3 garlic cloves, minced
6 cup vegetable broth, or water
Kosher salt, to taste
1 tablespoon freshly squeezed lime juice
¼ cup low-fat Greek yogurt

Directions:
In a nonstick skillet, heat the avocado oil over medium heat until it shimmers.
Cook for 3 minutes, or until the onion is clear.
In a large pot, combine the onion, tomatoes, green chilies, and their juices, black beans, cumin, garlic, broth, and salt. Stir everything together thoroughly.
Bring to a boil over medium-high heat, then lower to a low setting. Cook for 1 hour and 30 minutes, or until the beans are soft.
Meanwhile, in a small bowl, combine the lime juice and Greek yoghurt. Stir everything together thoroughly.
Before serving, pour the soup into a large serving bowl and drizzle with lime yoghurt.

Nutritional Information: Calories 285; Total Carbs 42g; Net Carbs 29g; Protein 19g; Fat 6g; Sugar 3g; Fiber 10g

Black Beans and Low-Sodium Veggie Greens

Prep Time: 10 minutes | Cook Time:15minutes | Servings:4

Ingredients:
1 tablespoon olive oil
½ Vidalia onion, thinly sliced
1 bunch dandelion greens cut into ribbons
1 bunch beet greens, cut into ribbons
½ cup low-sodium vegetable broth
1 (15-ounce / 425-g) can no-salt-added black beans
Salt and freshly ground black pepper, to taste

Directions:
In a nonstick skillet, heat the olive oil over low heat until it shimmers.
Sauté the onion for 3 minutes, or until it is transparent.
In a skillet, combine the dandelion and beet greens, as well as the broth. Cook, covered, for 8 minutes, or until the spinach has wilted.
Simmer for 4 minutes, or until the black beans are tender. Season to taste with salt and pepper. Stir everything together thoroughly.
Serve right away.

Nutritional Information: Calories 161; Total Carbs 26g; Net Carbs 15g; Protein 9g; Fat 4g; Sugar 1g; Fiber 10g

Greens and Beans

Prep Time: 9 minutes | Cook Time:14 minutes | Servings:4

Ingredients:
1 tablespoon olive oil
½ Vidalia onion, thinly sliced
1 bunch dandelion greens, cut into ribbons
1 bunch beet greens, cut into ribbons
½ cup low-sodium vegetable broth
1 (15-ounce) can no-salt-added black beans
Salt , to taste
Freshly ground black pepper, to taste

Directions:
In a nonstick skillet, heat the olive oil over low heat until it shimmers.
Sauté the onion for 3 minutes, or until it is transparent.
In a skillet, combine the dandelion and beet greens, as well as the broth. Cook, covered, for 8 minutes, or until the spinach has wilted.
Simmer for 4 minutes, or until the black beans are tender. Season to taste with salt and pepper. Stir everything together thoroughly.
Serve right away.
Tips: Replace the beet greens or dandelion greens with collard greens, spinach, arugula, or Swiss chard.

Nutritional Information: Calories 161; Total Carbs 26g; Net Carbs 5g; Protein 9g; Fat 4g; Sugar 1g; Fiber 10g

Kale and Carrots Soup

Prep Time: 8 minutes | Cook Time: 14 minutes | Servings:4

Ingredients:
4 tablespoons extra-virgin olive oil
2 onion, finely chopped
2 carrot, chopped
2 cup chopped kale (stems removed)
6 garlic cloves, minced
2 cups canned lentils, drained and rinsed
2 cups unsalted vegetable broth
4 teaspoons dried rosemary (or 1 tablespoon chopped fresh rosemary)
1 teaspoon sea salt
½ teaspoons freshly ground black pepper

Directions:
Heat the olive oil in a big pot over medium-high heat until it shimmers.
Add the onion and carrot and cook for 3 minutes, stirring periodically, or until the vegetables soften.
Cook for another 3 minutes after adding the kale.
Cook, stirring regularly, for 30 seconds after adding the garlic.
Add the lentils, vegetable broth, rosemary, salt, and pepper and stir to combine.
After heating to a low boil, reduce to a low heat. Cook for an additional 5 minutes., stirring periodically.

Nutritional Information: Calories 160; Total Carbs 19g; Net Carbs 0g; Protein 6g; Fat 7g; Sugar 15g; Fiber 6g

Stuffed Kale Wrap

Prep Time: 10 minutes | Cook Time:00 minutes | Servings: 4

Ingredients:

1 teaspoon Dijon mustard
1 tablespoon chopped fresh dill
½ teaspoon sea salt
¼ teaspoon paprika
4 hard-boiled large eggs, chopped
1 cup shelled fresh peas
2 tablespoons finely chopped red onion
4 large kale leaves

Directions:
Combine mustard, dill, salt, and paprika in a medium mixing basin.
Add the eggs, peas, and onion and stir to combine.
Serve with kale leaves wrapped around it.

Nutritional Information: Calories 295; Total Carbs 18g; Net Carbs 10.3g; Protein 17g; Fat 18g; Sugar 3.7g; Fiber 4g

Pepperoni Pita

Prep Time: 10 minutes | Cook Time:00 minutes | Servings:2

Ingredients:
½ cup tomato sauce
½ teaspoon oregano
½ teaspoon garlic powder
½ cup chopped black olives
2 canned artichoke hearts, drained and chopped
2 ounces pepperoni, chopped
½ cup shredded low-fat mozzarella cheese
1 whole-wheat pita, halved

Directions:
Combine the tomato sauce, oregano, and garlic powder in a medium mixing basin.
Combine the olives, artichoke hearts, pepperoni, and cheese in a mixing bowl. To blend, stir everything together.
Spoon the mixture into the pita halves and fold them in half.

Nutritional Information: Calories 376; Total Carbs 27g; Net Carbs 3.2g; Protein 17g; Fat 23g; Sugar 17.8g; Fiber 6g

Lettuce Wraps with Chestnuts

Prep Time: 10 minutes | Cook Time:00 minutes | Servings:2

Ingredients:
1 tablespoon freshly squeezed lemon juice
1 teaspoon curry powder
1 teaspoon reduced-sodium soy sauce
½ teaspoon sriracha (or to taste)
½ cup drained and sliced canned water chestnuts
2 (2.6-ounce/73.7 g) package tuna packed in water, drained
2 large butter lettuce leaves

Directions:
Combine the lemon juice, curry powder, soy sauce, and sriracha in a medium mixing bowl.
Combine the water chestnuts and tuna in a mixing bowl. To blend, stir everything together.
Wrap the lettuce leaves around the meat and serve.

Nutritional Information: Calories 271; Total Carbs 18g; Net Carbs 6.9g; Protein 19g; Fat 14g; Sugar 8.1g; Fiber 3g

Veggie Macaroni Pie

Prep Time: 15 minutes | Cook Time: 30 minutes | Servings:6

Ingredients:
1 (1-pound / 454-g) package whole-wheat macaroni
2 celery stalks, thinly sliced
1 small yellow onion, chopped
2 garlic cloves, minced
Salt, to taste
¼ teaspoon freshly ground black pepper
2 tablespoons chickpea flour
2 cups grated reduced-fat sharp Cheddar cheese
1 cup fat-free milk
2 large zucchinis, finely grated and squeezed dry
2 roasted red peppers, ¼-inch pieces, chopped

Directions:
Preheat the oven to 350 degrees Fahrenheit (180 degrees Celsius).
Bring a pot of water to a boil, then add the macaroni and cook until al dente, about 4 minutes.
Drain the macaroni and place it in a big mixing dish. 1 cup of the macaroni water should be set aside.
In an oven-safe skillet, heat the macaroni water over medium heat.
In a large skillet, sauté the celery, onion, garlic, salt, and black pepper for 4 minutes, or until soft.
Fold in the cheese and milk after gently mixing in the chickpea flour. Whisk the liquid until it is thick and smooth.
Combine the cooked macaroni, zucchini, and red peppers in a large mixing bowl. Stir everything together thoroughly.
Preheat the oven to 350°F and cover the skillet with aluminium foil.
Bake for 15 minutes, or until the cheese has melted, then remove the foil and bake for another 5 minutes, or until the top is lightly browned.
Get the pie out of the oven and serve right away.
Tip: To make this meal gluten-free, substitute the macaroni with organic quinoa pasta.
Nutritional Information: Calories 378; Total Carbs 67g; Net Carbs 53g; Protein 24g; Fat 4g; Sugar 6g; Fiber 8g

Kidney Beans Bowl

Prep Time: 10 minutes | Cook Time: 12minutes | Servings:8

Ingredients:
2 tablespoons olive oil
1 medium yellow onion, chopped
1 cup crushed tomatoes
2 garlic cloves, minced
2 cups low-sodium canned red kidney beans, rinsed
1 cup roughly chopped green beans
¼ cup low-sodium vegetable broth
1 teaspoon smoked paprika
Salt, to taste

Directions:
In a nonstick skillet, warm the olive oil over medium heat until it shimmers.

In a large mixing bowl, combine the onion, tomatoes, and garlic. Sauté for 3 to 5 minutes, or until the onion is transparent and fragrant.
In a skillet, combine the kidney beans, green beans, and broth. Season with paprika and salt, then sauté until everything is nicely combined.
Cook for 5 to 7 minutes, or until the vegetables are soft, covered in the skillet.
Serve right away.
Nutritional Information: Calories187; Total Carbs 34g; Net Carbs 20g; Protein 13g; Fat 1g; Sugar 4g; Fiber 10g

Baby Spinach Salad with Walnuts

Prep Time: 8 minutes | Cook Time: 00minutes | Servings:2

Ingredients:
4 cups baby spinach
½ pear, cored, peeled, and chopped
¼ cup whole walnuts, chopped
2 tablespoons apple cider vinegar
2 tablespoons extra-virgin olive oil
1 teaspoon peeled and grated fresh ginger
½ teaspoon Dijon mustard
½ teaspoon sea salt

Directions:
In the bottom of two mason jars, layer the spinach. Add the pear and walnuts on top.
Combine the vinegar, oil, ginger, mustard, and salt in a small bowl. Place in a closed container.
Before serving, give the dressing a good shake and pour it into the mason jars. To evenly distribute the dressing, close the jars and shake them.
Nutritional Information: Calories 254; Total Carbs 18g; Net Carbs 6g; Protein 4g; Fat 23g; Sugar 7g; Fiber 4g

Tomatoes and Red Kidney Beans

Prep Time: 10 minutes | Cook Time: 12 minutes | Servings:8

Ingredients:
2 tablespoons olive oil
1 medium yellow onion, chopped
1 cup crushed tomatoes
2 garlic cloves, minced
2 cups low-sodium canned red kidney beans, rinsed
1 cup roughly chopped green beans
¼ cup low-sodium vegetable broth
1 teaspoon smoked paprika
Salt, to taste

Directions:
In a nonstick skillet, heat the olive oil over medium heat until it shimmers.
In a large mixing bowl, combine the onion, tomatoes, and garlic. Sauté for 3 to 5 minutes, or until the onion is transparent and fragrant.
In a skillet, combine the kidney beans, green beans, and broth. Season with paprika and salt, then sauté until everything is nicely combined.
Cook for 5 to 7 minutes, or until the vegetables are soft, covered in the skillet. Serve right away.
Tip: You can replace the veggie broth with the same amount of water.
Nutritional Information: Calories 187; Total Carbs 34g; Net Carbs 20g; Protein 13g; Fat 1g; Sugar 4g; Fiber 10g

Green Beans with Onion

Prep Time: 8 minutes | Cook Time: 28 minutes | Servings:8

Ingredients:

½ cup vegetable broth (here) or store-bought low-sodium vegetable broth
2 celery stalks, thinly sliced
½ Vidalia onion, thinly sliced
1 garlic clove, minced
2 (15-ounce / 425-g) cans low-sodium butter beans
¼ teaspoon Not Old Bay Seasoning

Direction:

Bring the broth to a low simmer in a medium skillet over medium heat.

In the skillet, add onion, celery, and garlic and then cook for 3 to 5 minutes, or until the celery, onion, and garlic are softened.

Add the beans and seasonings, cover, and simmer for another 5 to 7 minutes, or until the flavours meld.

Serve alongside your favorite greens.

Nutritional Information: Calories 101; Total Carbs 19.02g; Net Carbs 11.2g; Protein 0.7g; Fat 0.7g; Sugar 2.3g; Fiber 5.5g

Carrots, Brown Rice, and Scrambled Egg

Prep Time: 15minutes | Cook Time: 20 minutes | Servings:4

Ingredients:

1 tablespoon extra-virgin olive oil
1 bunch collard greens, stemmed and cut into chiffonade
1 carrot, cut into 2-inch matchsticks
1 red onion, thinly sliced
½ cup low-sodium vegetable broth
2 tablespoons coconut aminos
1 garlic clove, minced
1 cup cooked brown rice
1 large egg
1 teaspoon red pepper flakes
1 teaspoon paprika
Salt, to taste

Directions:

In a Dutch oven or nonstick pan, heat the olive oil over medium heat until it shimmers.

Add the collard greens and cook until wilted, about 4 minutes.

In a Dutch oven, combine the carrots, onion, broth, coconut aminos, and garlic; cover and cook for 6 minutes, or until the carrots are soft.

Cook the brown rice in the oven for 4 minutes. Throughout the cooking process, keep stirring.

Break an egg over them, then heat and scramble it for 4 minutes, or until it's set.

Before serving, remove from the fire and season with red pepper flakes, paprika, and salt.

You may replace the coconut aminos with low-sodium soy sauce.

Nutritional Information: Calories 154; Total Carbs 22g; Net Carbs 14g; Protein 6g; Fat 6g; Sugar 2g; Fiber 6g

Black Eyed Beans and Rice Bowl

Prep Time: 14 minutes | Cook Time: 45 minutes | Servings:8

Ingredients:

1 tablespoon canola oil
2 celery stalks, thinly sliced
1 small yellow onion, chopped
1 medium green bell pepper, chopped
1 tablespoon tomato paste
2 garlic cloves, minced
2 cups brown rice, rinsed
5 cups low-sodium vegetable broth, divided
2 bay leaves
1 teaspoon smoked paprika
1 teaspoon Creole Seasoning
1¼ cups frozen black-eyed peas

Direction:

In a Dutch oven, warm the canola oil over medium heat.

Then add onion, celery, tomato paste, garlic, and bell pepper in the oven. Cook, stirring frequently, for 3 to 5 minutes, or until the celery, onion, bell pepper, tomato paste, and garlic are softened.

Combine the rice, 4 cups broth, bay leaves, paprika, and Creole seasoning in a large mixing bowl.

Reduce the heat to low, cover, and cook for 30 minutes, or until the rice is tender.

Add the remaining 1 cup of broth and the black-eyed peas. Cook for 12 minutes, or until the peas soften, stirring occasionally.

Remove the bay leaves and toss them out. Enjoy with Broccoli Stalk Slaw.

Nutritional Information: Calories 185; Total Carbs 35.6g; Net Carbs 26.8g; Protein 4.6g; Fat 3.3g; Sugar 5.8g; Fiber 3g

Spicy Brown Rice with Collard

Prep Time: 14 minutes | Cook Time: 18 minutes | Servings:4

Ingredients:

1 tablespoon extra-virgin olive oil
1 bunch collard greens, stemmed and chiffonade-style
1 carrot, cut into 2-inch matchsticks
1 red onion, thinly sliced
½ cup low-sodium vegetable broth
2 tablespoons coconut amino
1 garlic clove, minced
1 cup cooked brown rice
1 large egg
1 teaspoon red pepper flakes
1 teaspoon paprika
Salt, to taste

Directions:

In a Dutch oven or nonstick pan, heat the olive oil over medium heat until it shimmers.

Add the collard greens and cook until wilted, about 4 minutes.

In a Dutch oven, combine the carrots, onion, broth, coconut amino, and garlic; cover and cook for 6 minutes, or until the carrots are soft.

Cook for 4 minutes after adding the brown rice. Throughout the cooking process, keep stirring.

Break an egg over them, then heat and scramble it for 4 minutes, or until it is set.

Before serving, remove from the fire and season with red pepper flakes, paprika, and salt.

Nutritional Information: Calories 154; Total Carbs 22g; Net Carbs 14g; Protein 6g; Fat 6g; Sugar 2g; Fiber 6g

Carolina Green Beans

Prep Time: 08 minutes | Cook Time: 28 minutes | Servings:8

Ingredients:
1 pound (454 g) green beans, trimmed, cut into bite-size pieces
3 tablespoons extra-virgin olive oil, divided
8 ounces / 227-g brown mushrooms, diced
3 garlic cloves, minced
1½ tablespoons whole-wheat flour
1 cup low-sodium vegetable broth
1 cup unsweetened plain almond milk
¼ cup almond flour
2 tablespoons dried minced onion

Direction:
Preheat the oven to 400 degrees Fahrenheit (205 degrees Celsius).
Bring a big saucepan of water to a rolling boil. Cook the green beans for 3 to 5 minutes, or until they are just barely soft but bright green. Drain the water and set it aside.
Once the 2 tablespoons oil is heated in a medium skillet over medium-high heat, toss in the mushrooms and toss to combine. Cook for 3 to 5 minutes, or until the mushrooms are golden brown and liquid has evaporated. Stir in the garlic for approximately 30 seconds, or until it is barely aromatic.
Stir in the whole-wheat flour until everything is fully combined. Add the broth and simmer for 1 minute.
Reduce the heat to a low setting and stir in the almond milk. Return to a low heat and cook for 5–7 minutes, or until the sauce has thickened. Turn off the heat. Stir with the green beans and then turn on the heat.
Mix the almond flour, the remaining 1 tablespoon of olive oil, and the dried onion minces in a small bowl until well combined.
Thrn Sprinkle over the beans. Cook for 12 to 20 minutes until it is bubbling and browned.

Nutritional Information: Calories 241; Total Carbs 7.1g; Net Carbs 0.1g; Protein 7g; Fat 20g; Sugar 3.4g; Fiber 4.8g

One Pot Hot Corn

Prep time: 10 minutes | Cook time: 20 minutes | Serves 12
Ingredients:
6 ears corn
Direction:
Corn husks and silk should be removed. Each ear should be cut or broken in half.
Fill the bottom of the electric pressure cooker with 1 cup of water. Place a wire rack or trivet on the table.
Cut-side down, stand the corn upright on the rack. Close and lock the pressure cooker's lid.
To close the valve, turn it to the closed position.
Cook for 5 minutes on high pressure.
When the cooking is finished, press Cancel and release the pressure quickly.
Unlock and remove the cover once the pin has dropped.
To remove the corn from the pot, use tongs.
Season with salt and pepper to taste, and serve immediately away.
Nutritional Information: Calories 64; Total Carbs 13.9g; Net Carbs 8 g; Protein 2.1g; Fat 17.1g; Sugar 5g; Fiber 0.9g

Garlic Onion and Tomato

Prep time: 10 minutes | Cook time: 20 minutes | Serves 2
Ingredients:
2 tablespoons extra-virgin olive oil
1 chopped onion
1 red bell pepper, seeded and chopped
2 minced garlic cloves
1 (14-ounce / 397-g) can crushed tomatoes
2 cups green beans (fresh or frozen; halved if fresh)
3 cups low-sodium vegetable broth
1 tablespoon Italian seasoning
½ cup dried whole-wheat elbow macaroni
Pinch red pepper flakes (or to taste)
½ teaspoon sea salt
Direction:
Warm the olive oil in a large saucepan over medium heat till it shimmers.
Add onion and bell pepper in the saucepan. Cook, stirring regularly, for about 3 minutes, or until the onion and bell pepper begin to soften. Then add garlic. Cook, stirring occasionally, for 30 seconds, or until the garlic is aromatic.
Bring the mixture to a boil, stirring in the tomatoes, green beans, vegetable broth, and Italian seasoning.
Combine the elbow macaroni, red pepper flakes, and salt in a large mixing bowl. Cook for another 8 minutes, or until the macaroni is cooked through, stirring periodically.
Remove the pan from the heat and place it in a large mixing bowl to cool for 6 minutes before serving.
Nutritional Information: Calories 202; Total Carbs 29.2g; Net Carbs 19.1 g; Protein 5.2 g; Fat 7.2g; Sugar 2.9g; Fiber 7.2g

Lemony Broccoli

Prep time: 08 minutes | Cook time: 24 minutes | Serves 8
Ingredients:
2 large broccoli heads, cut into florets
2 tablespoons extra-virgin olive oil
3 garlic cloves, minced
¼ teaspoon salt
¼ teaspoon ground black pepper
2 tablespoons freshly squeezed lemon juice
Direction:
Preheat to 425 degrees Fahrenheit (220 degrees Celsius) and grease a large baking sheet.
Combine the broccoli, olive oil, garlic, salt, and pepper in a large mixing basin. Toss until the broccoli is well covered. Place the broccoli on the baking sheet that has been prepped.
Roast for about 25 minutes, or until the broccoli is browned and fork-tender, in a preheated oven, flipping halfway through.
Remove the pan from the oven and place it on a dish to cool for 5 minutes.
Serve with a squeeze of lemon juice on top.
Nutritional Information: Calories 33; Total Carbs 3.1g; Net Carbs 0.9 g; Protein 21.2g; Fat 2.1g; Sugar 1.1g; Fiber 1.1g

Butter Yams

Prep time: 7 minutes | Cook time: 45 minutes | Serves 8 (½ cup each)
Ingredients:
2 medium jewel yams cut into 2-inch dices
2 tablespoons unsalted butter
Juice of 1 large orange
1½ teaspoons ground cinnamon
¼ teaspoon ground ginger
¾ teaspoon ground nutmeg
⅛ Teaspoon ground cloves
Direction:
Preheat the oven to 350 degrees Fahrenheit (180 degrees Celsius) .
Arrange the yam dices in a single layer on a rimmed baking sheet. Remove from the equation.
In a medium saucepan over medium-low heat, combine the butter, orange juice, cinnamon, ginger, nutmeg, and garlic cloves. Cook, stirring constantly for 3 to 5 minutes, or until the sauce thickens and bubbles.
Toss the yams in the sauce to thoroughly coat them.
Preheat the oven to 400°F and bake for 40 minutes, or until the potatoes are soft.
Allow 8 minutes for the yams to cool on the baking sheet before serving.
Nutritional Information: Calories 129; Total Carbs 24.7g; Net Carbs 16.8g; Protein 2.1g; Fat 2.8g; Sugar 2.9g; Fiber 5g

Veggie Fajitas with Guacamole (Homemade)

Prep time: 08 minutes | Cook time: 14 minutes | Serves 4

Ingredients:

Guacamole:
2 small avocados, pitted and peeled
1 teaspoon freshly squeezed lime juice
¼ teaspoon salt
9 halved cherry tomatoes
Fajitas:
1 red bell pepper, cut into into ½-inch slices
1 green bell pepper, cut into into ½-inch slices
1 small white onion, cut into into ½-inch slices
1 cup black beans, drained and rinsed
¼ teaspoon garlic powder
¼ teaspoon chili powder
½ teaspoon ground cumin
4 (6-inch) yellow corn tortillas
Avocado oil cooking spray

Direction:

Combine the avocados and lime juice in a mixing basin. Mash with a fork until a consistent consistency is reached. Season with salt and pepper after adding the cherry tomatoes. Set aside after thoroughly stirring.

Until a large skillet is heated, heat it over medium heat. Coat the pan's bottom with cooking spray.

In a large skillet, combine the bell peppers, white onion, black beans, garlic powder, chilli powder, and cumin. Cook, stirring occasionally, until the beans are cooked, about 15 minutes. Place the pan on a platter and turn off the heat. Arrange the corn tortillas on a clean work area and distribute the fajita mixture evenly among them.

Serve with guacamole on top.

Nutritional Information: Calories 273; Total Carbs 30.1g; Net Carbs 13.7 g; Protein 8.1g; Fat 7.1g; Sugar 5.2g; Fiber 11.2g

Lemony Brussels Sprouts

Prep time: 09 minutes | Cook time: 18 minutes | Serves 4

Ingredients:

1 pound (454 g) Brussels sprouts
2 tablespoons avocado oil, divided
1 cup chicken bone broth
1 tablespoon minced garlic
½ teaspoon kosher salt
Freshly ground black pepper, to taste
½ medium lemons
½ tablespoon poppy seeds

Direction:

Trim the Brussels sprouts by removing any loose outer leaves and cutting off the stem ends. Each one should be cut in half lengthwise (through the stem).

Select the Sauté/More setting on an electric pressure cooker. Pour 1 tablespoon avocado oil into the saucepan once it is hot.

Half of the Brussels sprouts, cut-side down, should be added to the saucepan and left to brown for 3 to 5 minutes without being stirred. Transfer to a bowl and return to the saucepan with the remaining tablespoon of avocado oil and Brussels sprouts. Return all of the Brussels sprouts to the pot by pressing Cancel.

Combine the broth, garlic, salt, and a few grinds of pepper in a mixing bowl. To evenly distribute the seasonings, give it a good stir. Close and lock the lid of the pressure cooker. Set the valve to sealing. Sauté on high pressure for 2 minutes.

Close and lock the pressure cooker's lid. Set the valve to the closed position Sauté on high pressure for 2 minutes.

Zest the lemon and chop it into quarters while the Brussels sprouts are cooking.

When the cooking is finished, press Cancel and release the pressure quickly. Unlock and remove the cover once the pin has dropped. Transfer the Brussels sprouts to a serving bowl with a slotted spoon.

Toss with the poppy seeds, lemon zest, and a squeeze of lemon juice.

Serve right away.

Nutritional Information: Calories 126; Total Carbs 12.9g; Net Carbs 5 g; Protein 4.1g; Fat 8.1g; Sugar 3g; Fiber 4.9g

Tahini Zucchini with Bell Pepper

Prep time: 10 minutes | Cook time: 0 minutes | Serves 4

Ingredients:

2 zucchini, chopped
3 garlic cloves
2 tablespoons extra-virgin olive oil
2 tablespoons tahini
Juice of 1 lemon
½ teaspoon sea salt
1 red bell pepper, seeded and cut into sticks

Direction:

Combine the zucchini, garlic, olive oil, tahini, lemon juice, and salt in a blender or food processor. Blend until completely smooth.

Serve with the red bell pepper sticks.

Nutritional Information: Calories 120; Total Carbs 6.9g; Net Carbs 0g; Protein 2.1g; Fat 11.1g; Sugar 4g; Fiber 2.9g

Baked Asparagus with Bell Peppers

Prep time: 5 minutes | Cook time: 15 minutes | Serves 4

Ingredients:

1 pound (454 g) asparagus, woody ends trimmed, cut into 2-inch segments
2 red bell peppers, seeded, 1 inch thick slices
1 small onion, quartered
2 tablespoons Italian dressing

Direction:

Preheat the oven to 400 degrees Fahrenheit (205 degrees Celsius). and line a baking sheet with parchment paper.

In a large mixing basin, toss the asparagus with the peppers, onion, and dressing.

Arrange the vegetables on the baking sheet and roast until tender, about 15 minutes. Using a spatula, flip the vegetables once during cooking.

Serve immediately on a big dish.

Nutritional Information: Calories 92; Total Carbs 10.7g; Net Carbs 1g; Protein 2.9 g; Fat 4.8g; Sugar 5.7g; Fiber 4.0g

Squash with Black Pepper

Prep time: 08 minutes | Cook time: 18 minutes | Serves 4

Ingredients:
1 (1- to 1½-pound/454-680 g) delicate squash, halved, seeded, and cut into ½-inch-thick strips
1 tablespoon extra-virgin olive oil
½ teaspoon dried thyme
¼ teaspoon salt
¼ teaspoons freshly ground black pepper

Direction:
Preheat the oven to 400 degrees Fahrenheit (205 degrees Celsius). and line a baking sheet with parchment paper.
In a large mixing bowl, toss the squash strips with the olive oil, thyme, salt, and pepper until well covered.
Place the squash strips in a single layer on the prepared baking sheet. Roast for 20 minutes, turning the strips halfway through, until lightly browned.
Remove the dish from the oven and place it on plates to serve.

Nutritional Information: Calories 78; Total Carbs 11.8g; Net Carbs 6.8g; Protein 1.1 g; Fat 4.2g; Sugar 2.9g; Fiber 2.1g

Roasted Brussels Sprouts with Tomatoes

Prep time: 15 minutes | Cook time: 20 minutes | Serves 4

Ingredients:
1 pound (454 g) trimmed and halved Brussels sprouts
1 tablespoon extra-virgin olive oil
Sea salt , to taste
Freshly ground black pepper, to taste
½ cup sun-dried tomatoes, chopped
2 tablespoons freshly squeezed lemon juice
1 teaspoon lemon zest

Direction:
Preheat the oven to 400 degrees Fahrenheit (200 degrees Celsius) (205 degrees Celsius). A large baking sheet should be lined with aluminium foil.
In a large mixing bowl, toss the Brussels sprouts with the olive oil until completely coated. Season with salt and pepper to taste.
Place the seasoned Brussels sprouts in a single layer on the baking sheet that has been prepared. Roast for 20 minutes, stirring the pan halfway through, or until the Brussels sprouts are crispy and browned on the outside, in a preheated oven.
Remove the dish from the oven and place it in a serving bowl.
Stir in the tomatoes, lemon juice, and lemon zest to combine. Serve right away.

Nutritional Information: Calories 111; Total Carbs 13.7g; Net Carbs 6.1g; Protein 5.0g; Fat 5.8g; Sugar 2.7g; Fiber 4.9g

Portobello Mushrooms with Spinach

Prep time: 04 minutes | Cook time: 18 minutes | Serves 4

Ingredients:
8 large Portobello mushrooms
3 teaspoons extra-virgin olive oil, divided
4 cups fresh spinach
1 medium red bell pepper, diced
¼ cup low-fat feta cheese, crumbled

Direction:
Preheat the oven to 450 degrees Fahrenheit (235 degrees Celsius).
Remove the mushroom stems from your cutting board. Remove the gills with a spoon and throw them away. Use 2 teaspoons olive oil to coat the mushrooms.
Place the mushrooms cap-side down on a baking sheet. Roast for 20 minutes, or until browned on top, in a preheated oven.
Meanwhile, heat the remaining olive oil in a skillet over medium heat until it shimmers. Add the spinach and red bell pepper to the skillet and cook, turning occasionally, for 8 minutes, or until the veggies are soft. Remove the pan from the heat and place it in a basin.
Place the mushrooms on a platter after removing them from the oven. Fill the mushrooms with the vegetables and feta cheese, using a spoon to do so. Warm the dish before serving.

Nutritional Information: Calories 118; Total Carbs 12.2g; Net Carbs 13.7 g; Protein 7.2 g; Fat 6.3g; Sugar 6.1g; Fiber 4.1g

Jicama Slices with Avocado

Prep time: 5 minutes | Cook time: 0 minutes | Serves 4

Ingredients:
1 avocado, cut into cubes
Juice of ½ limes
2 tablespoons finely chopped red onion
2 tablespoons chopped fresh cilantro
1 garlic clove, minced
¼ teaspoon sea salt
1 cup sliced jicama

Direction:
Combine the avocado, lime juice, onion, cilantro, garlic, and salt in a small bowl. Lightly mash with a fork.
Dip the jicama into the sauce.

Nutritional Information: Calories 74; Total Carbs 7.9g; Net Carbs 0g; Protein 4.6g; Fat 3.3g; Sugar 3g; Fiber 4.9g

Garlic Cauliflower Bowl

Prep time: 04 minutes | Cook time: 18 minutes | Serves 4

Ingredients:
1 head cauliflower, separated into bite-sized florets
¼ teaspoon garlic powder
¼ teaspoon salt
⅛ Teaspoon black pepper
Butter-flavored cooking spray

Direction:
Preheat the oven to 400 degrees Fahrenheit (200 degrees Celsius) (205 degrees Celsius).
In a large mixing bowl, spray the cauliflower with cooking spray, making sure to coat all sides. Mix with a pinch of salt and pepper to coat.
Arrange in a single layer on a cookie sheet. Cook for 20–25 minutes, or until the cauliflower begins to colour. Warm the dish before serving.

Nutritional Information: Calories 55; Total Carbs 11.1g; Net Carbs 1.1g; Protein 4.2g; Fat 0g; Sugar 5.0g; Fiber 5.0g

Baked Eggs with Vegetables

Prep time: 5 minutes | Cook time: 25 minutes | Serves 4

Ingredients:
2 tablespoons extra-virgin olive oil
1 red onion, chopped
1 sweet potato, cut into ½-inch pieces
1 green bell pepper, seeded and chopped
½ teaspoon sea salt
1 teaspoon chili powder
4 large eggs
½ cup shredded pepper Jack cheese
1 avocado, cut into cubes

Direction:
Preheat the oven to 350 degrees Fahrenheit (180 degrees Celsius).
Warm the olive oil in a large skillet over medium-high heat until it shimmers.
Combine the onion, sweet potato, bell pepper, salt, and chilli powder in a large mixing bowl.
Cook, stirring regularly for about 10 minutes, or until the veggies are gently browned.
Turn off the heat. Make 4 wells in the vegetables with the back of a spoon, then crack an egg into each well. Over the vegetables, strew the grated cheese.
Bake for about 10 minutes, or until the cheese has melted and the eggs have set.
Remove the pan from the heat and top with the avocado before serving.
Nutritional Information: Calories 286; Total Carbs 16.2g; Net Carbs 1.9 g; Protein 12.3 g; Fat 21.3g; Sugar 9.1g; Fiber 5.2g

Garlic Spinach Quiches

Prep time: 10 minutes | Cook time: 15 minutes | Serves 6

Ingredients:
2 tablespoons olive oil, divided
1 onion, finely chopped
2 garlic cloves, minced
2 cups baby spinach
8 large eggs
¼ cup 1% skim milk
½ teaspoon sea salt
¼ teaspoons freshly ground black pepper
1 cup low-fat Swiss cheese, shredded
Special Equipment:
A 6-cup muffin tin

Direction:
Preheat the oven to 375 degrees Fahrenheit (190 degrees Celsius).Using 1 tablespoon olive oil, grease a 6-cup muffin tray.
Warm the olive oil in a nonstick skillet over medium-high heat. In the same skillet, add the onion and garlic and cook for 4 minutes, or until transparent.
Toss in the spinach and cook for 1 minute, or until soft. Place them on a plate and leave them to cool.
In a mixing dish, whisk together the eggs, milk, salt, and black pepper. Toss the cooked veggies in the egg mixture, then sprinkle with the cheese.
Fill the muffin cups halfway with the mixture.
Preheat the oven to 350°F and bake for 15 minutes, or until puffed and golden brown around the edges.

Serve the quiches hot from the oven on six small plates.
Nutritional Information: Calories 220; Total Carbs 4.2g; Net Carbs 0.7 g; Protein 14.3 g; Fat 21.3g; Sugar 2.7g; Fiber 0.8g

Baked Lemony Cauliflower

Prep time: 5 minutes | Cook time: 25 minutes | Serves 4

Ingredients:
1 cauliflower head, broken into small florets
2 tablespoons extra-virgin olive oil
½ teaspoon salt, or more to taste
½ teaspoon ground chipotle chili powder
Juice of 1 lime

Direction:
Preheat to 425 degrees Fahrenheit (220 degrees Celsius) and grease a large baking sheet.Remove from the equation.
Toss the cauliflower florets with the olive oil in a large mixing dish. Salt and chipotle chile powder to taste.
Arrange the cauliflower florets in an equal layer on the baking sheet. Roast for 15 minutes in the preheated oven until lightly browned.
Continue to roast until the cauliflower is crisp and soft, about 10 minutes.
Remove from the oven and season with salt as needed.
Allow it cool for 6 minutes. Then drizzle over the cauliflower with lime juice and serving.
Nutritional Information: Calories 100; Total Carbs 8.1g; Net Carbs 1.7 g; Protein 3.2g; Fat 7.1g; Sugar 3.2g; Fiber 3.2g

Cheese Coated Egg Muffins

Prep time: 08 minutes | Cook time: 18 minutes | Serves 4

Ingredients:
4 egg whites
½ teaspoon fresh parsley, diced fine
3 tablespoons reduced fat Parmesan cheese, divided
2 teaspoons water
½ teaspoon salt
truffle oil to taste
nonstick cooking spray

Direction:
Preheat at 400 degrees Fahrenheit (205 degrees Celsius). Using nonstick cooking spray, coat two muffin pans.
Whisk together egg whites, water, and salt in a small bowl until well blended.
Fill each muffin cup with just enough egg white mixture to just cover the bottom. On each egg white, a small amount of Parmesan cheese should be sprinkled.
Bake for 10 to 15 minutes, or until dark brown around the edges, being careful not to burn them.
Allow to cool for 3 to 4 minutes in the pans before transferred to a small bowl and lightly drizzling with truffle oil.
Toss in the parsley and ½ tablespoon Parmesan. Serve.
Nutritional Information: Calories 47; Total Carbs 0g; Net Carbs 0g; Protein 18.1g; Fat 3.0g; Sugar 0g; Fiber 0 g

39

Stir-Fried Tofu Broccoli with Brown Rice

Prep time: 08 minutes | Cook time: 08 minutes | Serves 4

Ingredients:
3 tablespoons extra-virgin olive oil
12 ounces (340 g) firm tofu, cut into ½-inch pieces
4 cups broccoli, broken into florets
4 scallions, sliced
1 teaspoon peeled and grated fresh ginger
4 garlic cloves, minced
2 tablespoons soy sauce (use gluten-free soy sauce if necessary)
¼ cup vegetable broth
1 cup cooked brown rice

Direction:
In a large skillet, heat the olive oil over medium-high heat until it begins to simmer.
Stir fry in the tofu, broccoli, and scallions for 6 minutes, or until the veggies begin to soften.
Then add garlic and ginger and cook, stirring constantly, for about 30 seconds.
Combine the soy sauce, vegetable broth, and brown rice in a mixing bowl. Cook for a further 1 to 2 minutes, stirring constantly, until the rice is well heated.
Allow 5 minutes for cooling before serving.
Nutritional Information: Calories 238; Total Carbs 21.2g; Net Carbs 8.2 g; Protein 5.2 g; Fat 13.2g; Sugar 8.8g; Fiber 4.2g

Sautéed Garlicky Cabbage

Prep time: 10 minutes | Cook time: 10 minutes | Serves 8

Ingredients:
2 tablespoons extra-virgin olive oil
1 bunch collard greens, stemmed and thinly sliced
½ small green cabbage, thinly sliced
6 garlic cloves, minced
1 tablespoon low-sodium soy sauce

Direction:
Warm the olive oil in a large skillet over medium-high heat. Cook for about 2 minutes, or until the collard greens begin to wilt in the oil.
Mix in the cabbage well. Reduce the heat to medium-low, cover, and simmer for 5 to 7 minutes, or until the greens are softened, stirring periodically.
Stir in the garlic and soy sauce until everything is well combined. Cook for another 30 seconds, or until the mixture is aromatic.
Transfer to a serving platter after removing from the heat.
Nutritional Information: Calories 73; Total Carbs 5.9g; Net Carbs 3g; Protein 14.3 g; Fat 4.1g; Sugar 0g; Fiber 2.9g

Spiced Swiss Chard with Cardamom

Prep time: 08 minutes | Cook time: 08 minutes | Serves 4

Ingredients:
2 tablespoons extra-virgin olive oil
1 pound (454 g) Swiss chard, coarse stems removed and leaves chopped
1 pound (454 g) kale, coarse stems removed and leaves chopped
½ teaspoon ground cardamom
1 tablespoon freshly squeezed lemon juice
Sea salt , to taste
Freshly ground black pepper, to taste
Direction:
Warm the olive oil in a large skillet over medium-high heat.
Stir together the Swiss chard, kale, cardamom, and lemon juice in the skillet. Cook, stirring constantly for about 10 minutes, or until the greens are wilted.
Season to taste with salt and pepper and stir thoroughly.
While the greens are still warm, serve them on a dish.
Nutritional Information: Calories 139; Total Carbs 15.8g; Net Carbs 10.9g; Protein 5.9g; Fat 6.8g; Sugar 1.0g; Fiber 3.9g

Flavorful Bok Choy with Almonds

Prep time: 15 minutes | Cook time: 7 minutes | Serves 4

Ingredients:
2 teaspoons sesame oil
2 pounds (907 g) bok choy, cleaned and quartered
2 teaspoons low-sodium soy sauce
Pinch red pepper flakes
½ cup toasted sliced almonds
Direction:
In a large skillet, heat the sesame oil over medium heat until it is hot.
Cook for about 5 minutes, stirring periodically, or until the bok choy is soft but still crisp in the hot oil.
Stir in the soy sauce and red pepper flakes until everything is well combined. Sauté for another 2 minutes.
Transfer to a serving platter and garnish with sliced almonds.
Nutritional Information: Calories 118; Total Carbs 7.9g; Net Carbs 0.8g; Protein 6.2g; Fat 7.8g; Sugar 3.0g; Fiber 4.1g

Flavorful Peppery Mushrooms

Prep time: 09 minutes | Cook time: 11 minutes | Serves 4

Ingredients:
1 tablespoon butter
2 teaspoons extra-virgin olive oil
2 pounds button mushrooms, halved
2 teaspoons minced fresh garlic
1 teaspoon chopped fresh thyme
Sea salt to taste
Freshly ground black pepper
Direction:
Add olive oil and butter in a large skillet over medium-high heat.
Then add mushrooms in the skillet and cook about 10 minutyes or until lightly caramelized and tender. While cooking, stir from time to time.
Add thyme and garlic and cook for 2 minutes or more.
Add salt and pepper to season. Serve and enjoy!
Nutritional Information: Calories 97; Total Carbs 8g; Net Carbs 2g; Protein 7g; Fat 6.0g; Sugar 4.0g; Fiber 2 g

Savory Spinach Wraps

Prep time: 10 minutes | Cook time: 50 minutes | Serves 8
Ingredients:
16 fresh spinach leaves
4 sun-dried tomatoes, rinsed, drained and diced fine
2 medium eggplants
1 green onion, diced fine
4 tablespoons fat-free cream cheese, soft
2 tablespoons fat-free sour cream
2 tablespoons lemon juice
1 teaspoon olive oil
1 clove garlic, diced fine
¼ teaspoon oregano
⅛ teaspoon black pepper
Nonstick cooking spray
Spaghetti Sauce:
½ onion, diced
½ carrot, grated
½ stalk celery, diced
½ zucchini, grated
½ (28-ounce / 794-g) Italian-style tomatoes, in puree
½ (14½-ounce / 411-g) diced tomatoes, with juice
¼ cup water
1 clove garlic, diced fine
¼ tablespoon oregano
½ teaspoon olive oil
½ teaspoon basil
½ teaspoon thyme
½ teaspoon salt
¼ teaspoon red pepper flakes
Direction:
Preheat the oven to 450 degrees Fahrenheit (235 degrees Celsius). Spray cooking spray over 2 big cookie sheets.
Remove the eggplant's ends and trim them. Cut the eggplant lengthwise into ¼-inch pieces. Throw away the ones with a lot of skin; there should be approximately 16 slices left. Arrange them in a single layer on the prepared pans.
Brush both sides of the eggplant with a mixture of lemon juice and oil whisked together in a small basin. Cook for 20 to 25 minutes, or until the eggplant begins to become golden brown. Allow to cool on a platter.
Meanwhile, prepare the spaghetti sauce as follows: In a large saucepan, heat the oil over medium heat. Toss in the veggies and garlic. Cook for about 5 minutes, or until vegetables are soft, stirring frequently.
Add the remaining Ingredients and break up the tomatoes with the back of a spoon. Bring to a simmer, then cook, partially covered, for 30 minutes over medium-low heat, stirring periodically.
Combine the remaining Ingredients, except the spinach, in a mixing dish and stir well.
To make the eggplant, distribute 1 teaspoon cream cheese mixture equally over the slices, leaving a 12-inch border around the edges. Start rolling from the little end with a spinach leaf on top. Place the rolls on a serving platter, seam side down. Warm spaghetti sauce is served on the side.

Nutritional Information: Calories 80; Total Carbs 12.1g; Net Carbs 0.1g; Protein 3.2g; Fat 3.0g; Sugar 6.0g; Fiber 6g

Zucchini Strips

Prep time: 08 minutes | Cook time: 08 minutes | Serves 4
Ingredients:
3 zucchini, slice ¼- to ⅛-inch thick
2 eggs
½ cup sunflower oil
⅓ cup sugar-free coconut flour
¼ cup reduced fat Parmesan cheese
1 tablespoon water
Direction:
In a large skillet, heat the oil over medium heat.
In a shallow basin, mix together the egg and water.
Combine flour and Parmesan in a separate shallow basin.
In a separate bowl, coat the zucchini in the egg, then in the flour mixture. Put in a thin layer in the skillet.
Cook for 2 minutes per side, or until golden brown on both sides. Place on a dish lined with paper towels. Repeat.
Serve immediately with your favourite dipping sauce.
Nutritional Information: Calories 140; Total Carbs 6.1g; Net Carbs 1.1g; Protein 6.2g; Fat 11.0g; Sugar 3.0g; Fiber 2g

Golden Onion Rings

Prep time: 5 minutes | Cook time: 15 minutes | Serves 4
Ingredients:
1 large onion, slice ½-inch thick
1 egg
¼ cup sunflower oil
2 tablespoons sugar-free coconut flour
2 tablespoons reduced fat Parmesan cheese
¼ teaspoon parsley flakes
⅛ teaspoon garlic powder
⅛ teaspoon cayenne pepper
Salt, to taste
Ketchup, for serving
Direction:
Warm the oil in a large skillet over medium-high heat.
Combine flour, Parmesan, and seasonings in a small basin.
The egg should be whisked.
Separate the onion slices into individual rings and set them in a large mixing dish. Add the beaten egg and toss thoroughly to coat. Allow 1 to 2 minutes for resting.
Coat onion in flour mixture in small batches and add to skillet. Cook for 1 to 2 minutes per side, or until golden brown on both sides.
Line a cookie sheet with paper towel. Place on the cookie sheet.
Serve with ketchup on the side.
Nutritional Information: Calories 185; Total Carbs 8.1g; Net Carbs 3.1g; Protein 3.2g; Fat 11.0g; Sugar 2.0g; Fiber 3 g

Baked Zucchini on Whole Wheat Bread

Prep time: 5 minutes | Cook time: 10 minutes | Serves 6

Ingredients:
1 large zucchini, sliced into ¼-inch circle
¼ cup reduced fat, Parmesan cheese, grated fine
3 tablespoons low-fat milk
1/3 cup whole wheat breadcrumbs
½ teaspoon garlic powder
1/8 teaspoon cayenne pepper
Nonstick cooking spray

Direction:
Using paper towels, pat zucchini dry after slicing. Allow for a 60-minute rest period before using. Then pat dry once again.

Preheat the oven to 425 degrees Fahrenheit (220 degrees Celsius). Place a wire rack on a cookie sheet and coat the rack with cooking spray.

Combine all Ingredients in a medium mixing basin, except the milk and zucchini. Fill a small basin halfway with milk.

After dipping the zucchini in the milk, coat it with the bread crumb mixture. Bake 10 to 15 minutes, or until golden and crisp, on a wire rack. Serve right away.

Nutritional Information: Calories 30; Total Carbs 3.1g; Net Carbs 2.1g; Protein 2.1g; Fat 11.0g; Sugar 1.0g; Fiber 0 g

Gingery Eggplant

Prep time: 10 minutes | Cook time: 40 minutes | Serves 4

Ingredients:
1 large eggplant, sliced into fourths
3 green onions, diced, green tips only
1 teaspoon fresh ginger, peeled and finely minced
¼ cup plus 1 teaspoon cornstarch
1½ tablespoons soy sauce
1½ tablespoons sesame oil
1 tablespoon vegetable oil
1 tablespoon fish sauce
2 teaspoons Splenda
¼ teaspoon salt

Direction:
Sprinkle salt on both sides of the eggplant and place it on paper towels. Allow 1 hour for the extra moisture to evaporate. Using extra paper towels, pat dry.

Whisk together soy sauce, sesame oil, fish sauce, Splenda, and 1 teaspoon cornstarch in a small basin.

Coat the eggplant on both sides with the ¼ cup cornstarch, adding more if necessary.

Warm the oil in a big skillet over medium-high heat. Add ½ teaspoon of ginger, and 1 green onion, and then arrange on the top with 2 slices of eggplant.

Pour half of the sauce mixture over both sides of the eggplant. Cook each side for 8 to 10 minutes. Repeat.

Serve with the leftover green onions as a garnish.

Nutritional Information: Calories 156; Total Carbs 18.1g; Net Carbs 7.1g; Protein 2.1g; Fat 9.0g; Sugar 6.0g; Fiber 5 g

Eggplant Pizzas

Prep time: 15 minutes | Cook time: 1 hour 10 minutes | Serves 4

Ingredients:
1 large peeled eggplant, sliced into 14-inch circles
½ cup reduced-fat Mozzarella cheese, grated
2 eggs
1¼ cups Italian bread crumbs
1 tablespoon water
¼ teaspoon black pepper
Nonstick cooking spray
Spaghetti Sauce:
1 onion, diced
1 carrot, grated
1 stalk celery, diced
1 zucchini, grated
1 (28-ounce / 794-g) Italian-style tomatoes, in puree
1 (14½-ounce / 411-g) diced tomatoes, with juice
½ cup water
2 cloves garlic, diced fine
½ tablespoon oregano
1 teaspoon olive oil
1 teaspoon basil
1 teaspoon thyme
1 teaspoon salt
¼ teaspoon red pepper flakes

Direction:
Preheat the oven to 350 degrees Fahrenheit (180 degrees Celsius) (180 degrees Celsius). Spray 2 big cookie sheets with cooking spray and line with foil.

Eggs, water, and pepper should be whisked together in a shallow bowl.

In a separate flat dish, place the bread crumbs.

After dipping the eggplant slices in the egg mixture, cover them completely with bread crumbs. Place on cookie sheets that have been prepped. Cook for 15 minutes after spraying the tops with cooking spray.

Spray the eggplant with cooking spray again on the other side. Bake for a further 15 minutes. Meanwhile, prepare the spaghetti sauce as follows: In a large saucepan, heat the oil over medium heat.

Toss in the veggies and garlic. Cook for about 5 minutes, or until vegetables are soft, stirring frequently.

Add the remaining Ingredients and break up the tomatoes with the back of a spoon. Bring to a simmer and cook for 30 minutes, stirring often, over medium-low heat, partially covered.

Remove the eggplant from the oven and spread 1 tablespoon spaghetti sauce over each slice. Bake for another 4 to 5 minutes, or until the cheese has melted and the sauce is bubbling. Serve immediately.

Nutritional Information: Calories 172; Total Carbs 24.1g; Net Carbs 14.1g; Protein 9.2g; Fat 5.0g; Sugar 6.0g; Fiber 4g

Baked Asparagus with Cashews

Prep time: 10 minutes | Cook time: 15 to 20 minutes | Serves 4

Ingredients:
2 pounds (907 g) asparagus, woody ends trimmed
1 tablespoon extra-virgin olive oil
Sea salt , to taste
Freshly ground black pepper, to taste
½ cup chopped cashews
Zest and juice of 1 lime

Direction:
Preheat the oven to 400 degrees Fahrenheit (200 degrees Celsius) (205 degrees Celsius). A baking pan should be lined with aluminium foil.
Toss the asparagus with the olive oil in a medium bowl. To taste, season with salt and pepper.
Arrange the asparagus on the baking sheet and bake for 15 to 20 minutes, or until tender and lightly browned.
Transfer the asparagus to a serving bowl from the oven.
Toss in the cashews, lime zest, and juice to thoroughly coat. Serve right away.
Nutritional Information: Calories 173; Total Carbs 43.7g; Net Carbs 33.8g; Protein 8g; Fat 7.8g; Sugar 5.0g; Fiber 4.9g

Butternut Fritters

Prep time: 15 minutes | Cook time: 15 minutes | Serves 6

Ingredients:
5 cup butternut squash, grated
2 large eggs
1 tablespoon fresh sage, diced fine
²/₃ cup flour
2 tablespoons olive oil
Salt and pepper, to taste

Direction:
Warm the oil in a large skillet over medium-high heat. Combine squash, eggs, sage, and salt & pepper to taste in a large mixing dish. Mix in the flour.
Place ¼ cup of the batter in the skillet, spacing fritters at least 1 inch apart.
Cook so that both sides are golden brown, around 2 minutes per side.
Place on a paper towel-lined plate. Repeat. Serve immediately with a dipping sauce of your preference.
Nutritional Information: Calories 165; Total Carbs 24.1g; Net Carbs 15.1g; Protein 4.1g; Fat 6.0g; Sugar 3.0g; Fiber 6 g

Lemony Wax Beans

Prep time: 5 minutes | Cook time: 15 minutes | Serves 4

Ingredients:
2 pounds (907 g) wax beans
2 tablespoons extra-virgin olive oil
Sea salt to taste
Freshly ground black pepper
Juice of ½ lemon

Direction:
Preheat at 400 degrees Fahrenheit (205 degrees Celsius). Line aluminium foil over a baking sheet.
Toss the beans with the olive oil in a large mixing dish. Toss with salt and pepper to taste. Place the beans on the baking pan and evenly distribute them.
Roast the beans for 10 to 12 minutes, or until they are caramelised and soft.
Serve the beans on a serving plate with a squeeze of lemon juice.
Nutritional Information: Calories 100; Total Carbs 8g; Net Carbs 0g; Protein 2g; Fat 7.0g; Sugar 4.0g; Fiber 4 g

Broiled Peppery Spinach

Prep time: 5 minutes | Cook time: 4 minutes | Serves 4

Ingredients:
8 cups spinach, thoroughly washed and spun dry
1 tablespoon extra-virgin olive oil
¼ teaspoon ground cumin
Sea salt to taste
Freshly ground black pepper to taste

Direction:
Preheat the oven to broil. Place an oven rack in the oven's upper third.
On a wide baking sheet, place a wire rack. Massage the spinach, oil, and cumin together in a large mixing bowl until all of the leaves are evenly covered.
Half of the spinach should be spread out on the rack with as little overlap as possible. Season the greens to taste with salt and pepper.
Broil the spinach for 2 minutes, or until the edges are crispy.
Remove the spinach from the baking sheet and place it in a large serving bowl.
Repeat with the rest of the spinach. Serve right away.
Nutritional Information: Calories 40; Total Carbs 2g; Net Carbs 1g; Protein 2g; Fat 4.0g; Sugar 0g; Fiber 1 g

Kale and Chard with Cardamom

Prep time: 10 minutes | Cook time: 10 minutes | Serves 4

Ingredients:
2 tablespoons extra-virgin olive oil
1 pound (454 g) kale, coarse stems removed and leaves chopped
1 pound (454 g) Swiss chard, coarse stems removed and leaves chopped
1 tablespoon freshly squeezed lemon juice
½ teaspoon ground cardamom
Sea salt to taste
Freshly ground black pepper

Direction:
In a large skillet, heat the olive oil over medium-high heat.
In a skillet, combine the kale, chard, lemon juice, and cardamom.
Toss the greens constantly with tongs until they are wilted, about 10 minutes or less.
Using salt and pepper, season the greens. Serve right away.
Nutritional Information: Calories 140; Total Carbs 16g; Net Carbs 11g; Protein 18.1g; Fat 7.0g; Sugar 1.0g; Fiber 4 g

Spiced Brussels sprouts

Prep Time: 5 minutes| Cook Time: 3 minutes| Servings: 5
Ingredients:
1 teaspoonextra-virgin olive oil
1 lb. halved Brussels sprouts
3 tablespoons apple cider vinegar
3 tablespoons gluten-free tamari soy sauce
3 tablespoons chopped sun-dried tomatoes
Directions:
Select the "Sauté" function of Instant Pot, add oil and allow the pot to get hot.
Add the Brussels sprouts and cook well.
Cook the sprouts in the residual heat for 2-3 minutes.
Add the tamari soy sauce and vinegar, and then stir.
Cover the Instant Pot, seal the pressure valve.
Select the "Manual, High Pressure" setting and cook for 3 minutes.
Once the cooking is done, quick release the pressure and then stir in the chopped sun-dried tomatoes.
Serve immediately.
Nutritional Information: Calories 62; Total Carbs 1g; Net Carbs 0g; Protein 3g; Fat 1g; Sugar 2g; Fiber 0.2g

Eggplant Spread

Prep Time: 5 minutes| Cook Time: 18 minutes| Servings: 5
Ingredients:
4 tablespoons extra-virgin olive oil
2 lbs. eggplant
4 skin-on garlic cloves
½ cup water
¼ cup pitted black olives
3 sprigs fresh thyme
Juice of 1 lemon
1 tablespoon tahini
1 teaspoon sea salt
Fresh extra-virgin olive oil
Directions:
Peel the eggplant leaving some areas with skin and some with no skin.
Slice eggplants into big chunks and layer at the bottom of Pot.
Add olive oil to the pot, and on the "Sauté" function, fry the eggplant on one side, about 5 minutes.
Add in the garlic cloves with the skin on.
Flip over the eggplant and then add in the remaining uncooked eggplant chunks, salt and water.
Close the lid, ensure the pressure release valve is set to "Sealing."
Cook for 5 minutes on the "Manual, High Pressure" setting.
Once done, quick releasing the pressure.
Discard most of the brown cooking liquid.
Remove the garlic cloves and peel them.
Add the lemon juice, tahini, cooked and fresh garlic cloves and pitted black olives to the pot.
Using a hand blender, process all the Ingredients until smooth.
Pour out the spread into a serving dish and season with fresh thyme, whole black olives and some extra-virgin olive oil and serve with toasted pita bread.

Nutritional Information: Calories 155; Total Carbs 16g; Net Carbs 12g; Protein 12g; Fat 11g; Sugar 2g; Fiber 1g

Spiced Carrots

Prep Time: 2 minutes| Cook Time: 18 minutes| Servings: 3
Ingredients:
2 tablespoons plant-based butter
1 lb. baby carrots
1 cup water
1 teaspoon fresh thyme or oregano
1 teaspoon minced garlic
Black pepper to taste
Coarse sea salt to taste
Directions:
Fill the Instant Pot inner pot with water and place it in the steamer.
Place the carrots in the steamer basket.
With the air vents in the "Sealing" position, close the cover and close.
Select the "Steam" setting and cook for 2 minutes.
Quickly release the pressure, then carefully remove the steamer basket containing the steamed carrots and drain the water.
Put the butter in the Instant Pot and melt it using the "Sauté" function.
Add the garlic and sauté for 30 minutes, then add the carrots. Mix well.
Add the fresh herbs and cook for 2-3 minutes.
Season with salt and pepper and transfer to a bowl.
Keep warm and enjoy!
Nutritional Information: Calories 112; Total Carbs 7g; Net Carbs 4g; Protein 1.04g; Fat 7g; Sugar 1g; Fiber 0.4g

Brown Rice & Lentil Salad

Prep Time: 10 minutes| Cook Time: 10 minutes| Servings: 4
Ingredients:
1 cup water
½ cup instant brown rice
2 tablespoons olive oil
2 tablespoons vinegar
1 tablespoon Dijon mustard
1 tablespoon minced onion
½ teaspoon paprika
Salt and pepper to taste
1 (15-ounce) can brown lentils, rinsed and drained
1 medium carrot, shredded
2 tablespoons fresh chopped parsley
Directions:
In a large pot, combine the water and instant brown rice.
When boiling, cover with a lid and simmer for 10 minutes.
Remove from the heat and set aside time to prepare the salad.
Place olive oil, vinegar, Dijon mustard, onion, paprika, salt, and pepper in a medium bowl.
Add the rice, lentils, carrots, and parsley and mix.
Adjust the seasoning to your liking, stir well and serve hot.
Nutritional Information: Calories 145; Total Carbs 13g; Net Carbs 10g; Protein 6g; Fat 7g; Sugar 1g; Fiber 2g

Low-Sugar Bok Choy

Prep time: 15 minutes | Cook time: 7 minutes | Serves 4
Ingredients:
2 teaspoons sesame oil
2 pounds (907 g) bok choy, cleaned and quartered
2 teaspoons low-sodium soy sauce
Pinch red pepper flakes
½ cup toasted sliced almonds
Direction:
Heat the oil in a large skillet over medium heat.
When the oil is hot, sauté the bok choy for 5 minutes, or until tender-crisp.
Sauté for another 2 minutes after adding the soy sauce and red pepper flakes.
Place the bok choy in a serving bowl with the sliced almonds on top.
Nutritional Information: Calories 119; Total Carbs 8g; Net Carbs 1g; Protein 18.1g; Fat 8.0g; Sugar 3.0g; Fiber 4 g

Carrot Hummus

Prep Time: 15 minutes| Cook Time: 10 minutes| Servings: 2
Ingredients:
1 chopped carrot
2 oz. cooked chickpeas
1 teaspoonlemon juice
1 teaspoon tahini
1 teaspoonfresh parsley
Directions:
Cook the carrots and chickpeas in instant pot for 10 minutes on "Stew" setting.
Once done place all Ingredients in the blender and blend until smooth paste.
Pour in the bowl top with olive oil and serve.
Nutritional Information: Calories 58; Total Carbs 2g; Net Carbs 1g; Protein 4g; Fat 2g; Sugar 0.1g; Fiber 0.8g

Vegetable Rice Pilaf

Prep Time: 5 minutes| Cook Time: 25 minutes| Servings: 6
Ingredients:
1 tablespoon olive oil
½ medium yellow onion, diced
1 cup uncooked long-grain brown rice
2 cloves minced garlic
½ teaspoon dried basil
Salt and pepper to taste
2 cups fat-free chicken broth
1 cup frozen mixed veggies
Directions:
Heat the oil in a large skillet over medium heat.
Add the onions and sauté for 3 minutes until translucent.
Add the rice and cook until lightly browned.
Add the garlic, basil, salt, and pepper and mix.
Pour in the chicken broth and bring to a boil.
Lower the heat, cover, and simmer for 10 minutes.
Stir in frozen vegetables, cover, and cook for another 10 minutes, until heated through.
Serve hot and enjoy.
Nutritional Information: Calories 90; Total Carbs 2.2g; Net Carbs 1.5g; Protein 7g; Fat 4g; Sugar 0.5g; Fiber 0.8g

Curry Roasted Cauliflower Florets

Prep Time: 5 minutes| Cook Time: 25 minutes| Servings: 6
Ingredients:
8 cups cauliflower florets
2 tablespoons olive oil
1 teaspoon curry powder
½ teaspoon garlic powder
Salt and pepper
Directions:
Preheat the oven to 425 ° F and place the foil on a baking sheet.
Toss with the cauliflower and olive oil and spread on a baking sheet.
Sprinkle with curry powder, garlic powder, salt, and pepper.
Bake for 25 minutes or until tender.
Serve hot and enjoy.
Nutritional Information: Calories 75; Total Carbs 7.4g; Net Carbs 4g; Protein 3g; Fat 4g; Sugar 1.4g; Fiber 3.5g

Braised Summer Squash

Prep Time: 10 minutes| Cook Time: 20 minutes| Servings: 6
Ingredients:
3 tablespoons olive oil
3 cloves minced garlic
¼ teaspoon crushed red pepper flakes
1-pound summer squash, sliced
1-pound zucchini, sliced
1 teaspoon dried oregano
Salt and pepper to taste
Directions:
Heat oil in a large skillet over medium heat.
Add the garlic and crushed red pepper in it and cook for 2 minutes.
Add the summer squash and zucchini and cook for 15 minutesuntil just tender.
Stir in the oregano and season with salt and pepper to taste.
serve hot and enjoy.
Nutritional Information: Calories 90; Total Carbs 6.2g; Net Carbs 1.8g; Protein 6g; Fat 7g; Sugar 3g; Fiber 1.8g

Lemon Garlic Green Beans

Prep Time: 5 minutes| Cook Time: 10 minutes| Servings: 6
Ingredients:
1 ½ pounds green beans, trimmed
2 tablespoons olive oil
1 tablespoon fresh lemon juice
2 cloves minced garlic
Salt and pepper to taste
Directions:
Boil the green beans in salted water. Drain when done after 3 mnutes and place thein the ice cold water.
Cool the beans completely then drain them well.
Heat the oil in a large skillet over medium-high heat and add blanched green beans.
Add the lemon juice, garlic, salt, and pepper and sauté for 3 minutes until the beans are tender-crisp then serve hot.
Nutritional Information: Calories 75; Total Carbs 8.5g; Net Carbs 4.6g; Protein 2.1g; Fat 4.8g; Sugar 1.7g; Fiber 3.9g

Mashed Butternut Squash

Prep Time: 5 minutes| Cook Time: 25 minutes| Servings: 6
Ingredients:
3 pounds whole butternut squash (about 2 medium)
2 tablespoons olive oil
Salt and pepper to taste
Directions:
Preheat the oven to 400°F and place the parchment paper on the baking sheet.
Cut the zucchini in half and remove the seeds.
Cut the pumpkin into cubes, grease it with oil, and lay it out on a baking sheet.
Bake for 25 minutes until tender, then place in a food processor.
Mix gently, then season with salt and pepper to taste.
Nutritional Information: Calories 90; Total Carbs 12g; Net Carbs 10g; Protein 1.1g; Fat 4.8g; Sugar 2.3g; Fiber 2g

Cilantro Lime Quinoa

Prep Time: 5 minutes| Cook Time: 25 minutes| Servings: 6
Ingredients:
1 cup uncooked quinoa
1 tablespoon olive oil
1 medium yellow onion, diced
2 cloves minced garlic
1 (4-ounce) can diced green chiles, drained
1 ½ cups fat-free chicken broth
¾ cup fresh chopped cilantro
½ cup sliced green onion
2 tablespoons lime juice
Salt and pepper to taste
Directions:
Rinse the quinoa thoroughly in cold water using a fine strainer.
Heat the oil in a large saucepan over medium heat.
Add the onion and sauté for 2 minutes, then add the chili and garlic and sauté
Cook for 1 minute, then stir in the quinoa and chicken broth.
When it comes to a boil, reduce the heat, cover, and simmer until the quinoa has absorbed the liquid, about 20-25 minutes.
Remove from the heat, then add the cilantro, green onions, and lemon juice and stir.
Season with salt and pepper to taste and serve hot.
Nutritional Information: Calories 150; Total Carbs 22.5g; Net Carbs 19g; Protein 6g; Fat 4.1g; Sugar 1.4g; Fiber 2.7g

Roasted Veggies

Prep Time: 5 minutes| Cook Time: 25 minutes| Servings: 6
Ingredients:
1 pound cauliflower florets
½ -pound broccoli florets
1 large yellow onion, cut into chunks
1 large red pepper, cored and chopped
2 medium carrots, peeled and sliced
2 tablespoons olive oil
2 tablespoons apple cider vinegar
Salt and pepper to taste
Directions:

Preheat the oven to 425°F and place the parchment paper on a large baking sheet.
Spread the vegetables on a baking sheet and sprinkle them with oil and vinegar.
Mix well and season with salt and pepper.
Put the vegetables in a single layer and bake for 20-25 minutes, stirring every 10 minutes, until tender.
Adjust spices as per liking and serve hot.
Nutritional Information: Calories 100; Total Carbs 12g; Net Carbs 8.2g; Protein 3.2g; Fat 5g; Sugar 5.5g; Fiber 4.2g

Parsley Tabbouleh

Prep Time: 5 minutes| Cook Time: 25 minutes| Servings: 6
Ingredients:
1 cup water
½ cup bulgur
¼ cup fresh lemon juice
2 tablespoons olive oil
2 cloves minced garlic
Salt and pepper to taste
2 cups fresh chopped parsley
2 medium tomatoes, died
1 small cucumber, diced
¼ cup fresh chopped mint
Directions:
Put the water and the bulgur in a small saucepan and bring to a boil, then remove from the heat.
Cover with a lid and let stand 25 minutes until the water is completely absorbed.
Meanwhile, whisk together lemon juice, olive oil, garlic, salt, and pepper in a medium bowl.
Toss the cooked bulger with parsley, tomato, cucumber, and mint.
Season with salt and pepper and season to taste.
Nutritional Information: Calories 110; Total Carbs 14g; Net Carbs 10g; Protein 3g; Fat 5g; Sugar 2.4g; Fiber 3.9g

Root Vegetables with Balsamic

Prep Time: 25 minutes| Cook Time: 25 minutes| Servings: 3
Ingredients:
2 Potatoes, cut into 1 ½-inch piece
2 Carrots, cut into 1 ½-inch piece
2 Parsnips, cut into 1 ½-inch piece
1 Onion, cut into 1 ½-inch piece
Pink Himalayan salt and ground black pepper, to taste
¼ teaspoon smoked paprika
1 teaspoon garlic powder
½ teaspoon dried thyme
½ teaspoon dried marjoram
2 tablespoons olive oil
2 tablespoons balsamic vinegar
Directions:
Toss all Ingredients in a large mixing bowl.
Roast the veggies in the preheated Air Fryer at 400°F for 10 minutes.
Shake the basket and cook for 7 more minutes.
Serve with some extra fresh herbs if desired.
Bon appétit!
Nutritional Information: Calories 405; Total Carbs 74g; Net Carbs 55g; Protein 7g; Fat 9g; Sugar 15g; Fiber 28g

Garlic Sautéed Spinach

Prep Time: 5 minutes| Cook Time: 10 minutes| Servings: 4

Ingredients:
1 ½ tablespoons olive oil
4 cloves minced garlic
6 cups fresh baby spinach
Salt and pepper to taste

Directions:
Heat the oil in a large saucepan over medium heat.
Add the garlic and cook for 1 minute.
Add the spinach and season with salt and pepper.
Fry for 1-2 minutes until smooth.
Serve hot.

Nutritional Information: Calories 60; Total Carbs 2.6g; Net Carbs 1.5g; Protein 1.5g; Fat 5.5g; Sugar 0.2g; Fiber 1.1g

Rosemary Potatoes

Prep Time: 5 minutes| Cook Time: 25 minutes| Servings: 2

Ingredients:
1lb red potatoes
1 cup vegetable stock
2 tablespoons olive oil
2 tablespoons rosemary sprigs

Directions:
Place potatoes in the steamer basket and add the stock into the Instant Pot.
Steam the potatoes in Instant Pot for 15 minutes.
Pour away the remaining stock.
Set the pot to sauté and add the oil, rosemary, and potatoes.
Cook until brown on top and fragrent.

Nutritional Information: Calories 195; Total Carbs 1g; Net Carbs 0.5g; Protein 7g; Fat 1g; Sugar 0g; Fiber 0g

French Lentils

Prep Time: 5 minutes| Cook Time: 25 minutes| Servings: 10

Ingredients:
2 tablespoons olive oil
1 medium onion, diced
1 medium carrot, peeled and diced
2 cloves minced garlic
5 ½ cups water
2 ¼ cups French lentils, rinsed and drained
1 teaspoon dried thyme
2 small bay leaves
Salt and pepper to taste

Directions:
Heat the oil in a large saucepan over medium heat.
Add the onions, carrots, and garlic and sauté for 3 minutes.
Add the water, lentils, thyme, and bay leaf and season with salt.
When boiling, reduce heat to low and cook until tender, about 20 minutes.
Remove the excess water and adjust the taste as desired.
Serve hot.

Nutritional Information: Calories 185; Total Carbs 27.9g; Net Carbs 14.2g; Protein 11.4g; Fat 3.3g; Sugar 1.7g; Fiber 13.7g

Coffee-Steamed Carrots

Prep Time: 10 minutes| Cook Time: 3 minutes| Servings: 4

Ingredients:
1 cup brewed coffee
1 teaspoon light brown sugar
½ teaspoon kosher salt
Freshly ground black pepper
1-pound baby carrots
Chopped fresh parsley
1 teaspoon grated lemon zest

Directions:
Pour the coffee into the coffee. Add the light brown sugar, salt, and pepper and mix. Add the carrots.
Close the pressure cooker. Set to close. Cook for a few minutes over high heat.
When done, click Cancel and quickly release.
Using a spoon, divide the carrots between bowls. Garnish with parsley and lemon zest and serve.

Nutritional Information: Calories 51; Total Carbs 12g; Net Carbs 8g; Protein 3g; Fat 3g; Sugar 4g; Fiber 4g

Corn on the Cob

Prep Time: 10 minutes| Cook Time: 5 minutes| Servings: 12

Ingredients:
6 ears corn

Directions:
Take off husks and silk from the corn. Cut or break each ear in half.
Pour 1 cup water into the bottom of the pressure cooker.
Insert a wire rack in it.
Place the corn on the rack, cut-side down. Seal lid of the pressure cooker.
Cook on high pressure for 5 minutes.
When its complete, Quickly release the pressure.
Pull out the corn from the pot.
Season with your favorite seasoning as desired and serve immediately.

Nutritional Information: Calories 62; Total Carbs 14g; Net Carbs 10g; Protein 6g; Fat 3g; Sugar 1.5g; Fiber 1g

Spiced Avocado Dip

Prep Time: 5 minutes| Cook Time: 0 minutes| Servings: 4

Ingredients:
1 avocado, cut into cubes
Juice of ½ limes
2 tablespoons finely chopped red onion
2 tablespoons chopped fresh cilantro
1 garlic clove, minced
¼ teaspoon sea salt
1 cup sliced jicama

Direction:
In a small bowl, combine the avocado, lime juice, onion, cilantro, garlic, and salt. Mash them lightly with a fork.
Serve with the jicama for dipping.

Nutritional Information: Calories 74; Total Carbs 7.9g; Net Carbs 4g; Protein 1g; Fat 5g; Sugar 3g; Fiber 4.9g

Japanese Tempura Bowl

Prep Time: 20 minutes| Cook Time: 10 minutes| Servings: 3

Ingredients:
1 cup all-purpose flour
Kosher salt and ground black pepper, to taste
½ teaspoon paprika
2 Eggs
3 tablespoons soda water
1 cup panko crumbs
2 tablespoons olive oil
1 cup green beans
1 Onion, cut into rings
1 Zucchini, cut into slices
2 tablespoons gluten-free tamari soy sauce
1 tablespoon mirin
1 teaspoon dashi granule

Directions:
In a shallow bowl, combine the flour, salt, pepper, and paprika.
In a bowl, whisk together the eggs and soda.
In other shallow bowls, combine the panko breadcrumbs and olive oil.
Dip the vegetables in the flour mixture, then in the egg mixture. Finally, roll over the Panco mixture to ensure a smooth layer.
Shake the basket while cooking for 10 minutes at 400 ° F in a preheated air fryer.
Combine the soy sauce, mirin, and dashi granules to make the sauce.
Serve hot and enjoy.

Nutritional Information: Calories 446; Total Carbs 63.5g; Net Carbs 45g; Protein 14.6g; Fat 14g; Sugar 3.8g; Fiber 12g

Braised Winter Vegetable

Prep Time: 25 minutes| Cook Time: 10 minutes| Servings: 2

Ingredients:
4 Potatoes, peeled and cut into 1-inch pieces
1 Celery root, peeled and cut into 1-inch pieces
1 Cup winter squash
2 tablespoons unsalted butter, melted
½ Cup chicken broth
¼ Cup tomato sauce
1 teaspoon parsley
1 teaspoon rosemary
1 teaspoon thyme

Directions:
Preheat the air fryer to 370 ° F.
Add all the Ingredients to a small, greased casserole dish.
Stir to combine well.
In a preheated air fryer, gently stir the vegetables for 10 minutes, then increase the temperature to 400 ° F. Cook for another 10 minutes. Serve hot top with lemon juice on top and enjoy.

Nutritional Information: Calories 358; Total Carbs 55g; Net Carbs 45g; Protein 7g; Fat 12g; Sugar 7g; Fiber 22g

Spiced Button Mushrooms

Prep Time: 10 minutes| Cook Time: 12 minutes| Servings: 4

Ingredients:
1 tablespoon butter
2 teaspoons extra-virgin olive oil
2 pounds (907 g) button mushrooms, halved
2 teaspoons minced fresh garlic
1 teaspoon chopped fresh thyme
Sea salt and freshly ground black pepper, to taste

Directions:
Heat butter and olive oil in a large skillet over medium heat.
Add the mushrooms and sauté for 10 minutes until the mushrooms are lightly browned and cooked through.
Add the garlic and thyme and cook for another 2 minutes.
Season with salt and pepper and place on a plate.

Nutritional Information: Calories 96; Total Carbs 8.2g; Net Carbs 4g; Protein 6.9g; Fat 6.1g; Sugar 3.9g; Fiber 1.7g

Peppery Bok Choy with Almonds

Prep Time: 15 minutes| Cook Time: 7 minutes| Servings: 4

Ingredients:
2 teaspoons sesame oil
2 pounds (907 g) bok choy, cleaned and quartered
2 teaspoons low-sodium soy sauce
Pinch red pepper flakes
½ cup toasted sliced almonds

Directions:
Add sesame oil to a large saucepan and heat over medium heat until hot.
Fry the bok choy in hot oil for 5 minutes. Stir-fry them until tender and still crisp.
Add soy sauce and red pepper powder and stir to combine evenly. Continue frying for 2 minutes.
Transfer to a plate and garnish with toasted almonds.

Nutritional Information: Calories 118; Total Carbs 7.9g; Net Carbs 4g; Protein 6.2g; Fat 7.8g; Sugar 3g; Fiber 4.1g

Spicy Baked Asparagus with Cashews

Prep Time: 10 minutes| Cook Time: 20 minutes| Servings: 4

Ingredients:
2 pounds (907 g) asparagus, woody ends trimmed
1 tablespoon extra-virgin olive oil
Sea salt and freshly ground black pepper, to taste
½ cup chopped cashews
Zest and juice of 1 lime

Directions:
Preheat the oven to 400 ºF. Place the baking sheet with foil.
Toss asparagus with olive oil in a medium bowl. Season with salt and pepper.
Place the asparagus on a baking sheet and bake for 15 to 20 minutes, or until lightly browned and soft.
Remove the asparagus in a bowl from the oven.
Add the cashews, lemon zest, and juice and mix well.
Serve immediately.

Nutritional Information: Calories 173; Total Carbs 43g; Net Carbs 20g; Protein 8g; Fat 11g; Sugar 5g; Fiber 4g

Gingery Eggplant with Green Onions

Prep Time: 10 minutes| Cook Time: 40 minutes| Servings: 4

Ingredients:
1 large eggplant, sliced into 4ths
3 green onions, diced, green tips only
1 teaspoon fresh ginger, peeled and diced fine
¼ cup plus 1 teaspoon cornstarch
1½ tablespoons gluten-free tamari soy sauce
1½ tablespoons sesame oil
1 tablespoon vegetable oil
1 tablespoon fish sauce
2 teaspoons Splenda
¼ teaspoon salt

Directions:
Place the eggplant on a paper towel and sprinkle with salt on both sides.
Wait an hour to remove excess moisture.
Pat dry with several paper towels.
In a small bowl, add soy sauce, sesame oil, fish sauce, Splenda, and 1 teaspoon of cornstarch and mix.
Use ¼ cup of cornstarch on both sides of the eggplant.
Heat the oil in a large skillet over medium heat.
Add ½ ginger and 1 green onion and place 2 eggplants on top.
Gently shake both sides of the eggplant using ½ the sauce mixture. Cook 8 to 10 minutes per side.
Repeat.
Serve garnished with remaining green onions.
Nutritional Information: Calories 156; Total Carbs 18.1g; Net Carbs 15g; Protein 2g; Fat 9g; Sugar 6g; Fiber 5g

Peppery Butternut Fritters

Prep Time: 15 minutes| Cook Time: 15 minutes| Servings: 6

Ingredients:
5 cup butternut squash, grated
2 large eggs
1 tablespoon fresh sage, diced fine
⅔ cup flour
2 tablespoons olive oil
Salt and pepper, to taste

Directions:
Heat the oil in a large saucepan over medium heat.
In a large bowl, combine squash, eggs, sage, salt, and pepper to taste. Stir in the flour.
Put ¼ cup of mixture in the pan and fry at least 1 inch. Cook until golden brown on both sides, about 2 minutes per side.
Transfer to a plate lined with a tissue. repeat.
Serve immediately with your favorite dip.
Nutritional Information: Calories 165; Total Carbs 24g; Net Carbs 20g; Protein 4g; Fat 6g; Sugar 3g; Fiber 3g

Cauliflower Tater Tots

Prep Time: 25 minutes| Cook Time: 10 minutes| Servings: 4

Ingredients:
1 lb. cauliflower floret
2 Eggs
1 tablespoon olive oil
2 tablespoons scallions, chopped
1 Garlic clove, minced

1 Cup low-fat Colby cheese, shredded
½ Cup breadcrumbs
Sea salt and ground black pepper, to taste
¼ teaspoon dried dill weed
1 teaspoon paprika

Directions:
Blanch the cauliflower in salted boiling water for 3 to 4 minutes until al dente.
Drain well and grind in a food processor.
Add more Ingredients. Mix well. Shape the cauliflower mixture into small skewers.
Spray the Airfryer basket with cooking spray.
Bake in preheated 375 ° F Airfryer for 16 minutes, shaking halfway.
Use your favorite sauce to serve and Bon appétit!
Nutritional Information: Calories 267; Total Carbs 9.6g; Net Carbs 4g; Protein 14g; Fat 19g; Sugar 2.9g; Fiber 3g

Sweet Corn Fritters with Avocado

Prep Time: 20 minutes| Cook Time: 10 minutes| Servings: 3

Ingredients:
2 Cups sweet corn kernels
1 Small-sized onion, chopped
1 Garlic clove, minced
2 Eggs, whisked
1 teaspoon baking powder
2 tablespoons fresh cilantro, chopped
Sea salt and ground black pepper, to taste
1 Avocado, peeled, pitted, and diced
2 tablespoons sweet chili sauce

Directions:
In a bowl, mix together the corn, onion, garlic, egg, baking powder, cilantro, salt, and pepper.
Transfer the corn mixture into 6 patties and slowly transfer to an Airfryer basket.
Bake 8 minutes in an air fryer to 370 ° F. Flip and cook for another 7 minutes.
Serve the fritters with avocado and chili sauce.
Nutritional Information: Calories 383; Total Carbs 42g; Net Carbs 20g; Protein 12g; Fat 21g; Sugar 9.2g; Fiber 4g

Sautéed Mushrooms

Prep Time: 10 minutes| Cook Time: 10 minutes| Servings: 4

Ingredients:
1 tablespoon plant-based butter
2 teaspoons extra-virgin olive oil
2 pounds button mushrooms, halved
2 teaspoons minced fresh garlic
1 teaspoon chopped fresh thyme
Sea salt to taste
Freshly ground black pepper

Directions:
Put the pan on medium heat and add the butter and olive oil.
Sauté mushrooms, stirring occasionally, for 10 minutes until mushrooms are lightly caramelized and tender.
Add the garlic and thyme and sauté for another 2 minutes.
Season the mushrooms with salt and pepper before serving.
Nutritional Information: Calories 97; Total Carbs 7g; Net Carbs 4g; Protein 6g; Fat 6g; Sugar 4g; Fiber 2g

Greek-Style Vegetable Bake

Prep Time: 35 minutes| Cook Time: 10 minutes| Servings: 4
Ingredients:
1 Eggplant, peeled and sliced
2 Bell peppers, seeded and sliced
1 Red onion, sliced
1 teaspoonfresh garlic, minced
4 tablespoons olive oil
1 teaspoon mustard
1 teaspoon dried oregano
1 teaspoon smoked paprika
Salt and ground black pepper, to taste
1 Tomato, sliced
6 oz. halloumi cheese, sliced lengthways
Directions:
First, preheat the air fryer to 370 ° F.
Spray the roasting pan with nonstick spray.
Place the eggplant, peppers, onions, and garlic in the bottom of the roasting pan.
Add olive oil, mustard, and spices.
Transfer to a cooking basket and cook for 14 minutes.
Garnish with tomatoes and cheese.
Reduce heat to 390 ° F and cook for another 5 minutes until frothy.
Cool for 10 minutes before eating.
Bon appétit!
Nutritional Information: Calories 296; Total Carbs 22g; Net Carbs 15g; Protein 9.3g; Fat 22g; Sugar 9.9g; Fiber 2g

Spiced Tofu with Spinach

Prep Time: 15 minutes| Cook Time: 1 hour 25 minutes| Servings: 4
Ingredients:
1 package extra firm tofu, pressed 15 minutes and cut into cubes
1 package fresh baby spinach
2 limes
1 tablespoon plant-based butter
½ cup plant-based butter
2 tablespoons lite soy sauce
3 cloves garlic, chopped fine
½ teaspoon ginger
¼ teaspoon red pepper flakes
Directions:
Melt the plant-based butter in a large saucepan.
Add the tofu and garlic and cook, stirring occasionally, for 5 to 10 minutes or until the beans are golden brown.
Add the remaining spinach and bring to a boil.
Lower the heat, cover, and cook, stirring occasionally, for 30 to 35 minutes.
Add the spinach and cook for another 15 minutes.
Serve hot and enjoy.
Nutritional Information: Calories 326; Total Carbs 15g; Net Carbs 10g; Protein 18g; Fat 24g; Sugar 5g; Fiber 5g

Cauliflower Soup

Prep Time: 10 minutes| Cook Time: 15 minutes| Servings: 6
Ingredients:
2½ pounds (1.1 kg) cauliflower florets
½ leek, white and pale green part, halved
4 tablespoons plant-based butter
2 teaspoons fresh parsley, diced
2 tablespoons low sodium chicken broth
2 teaspoons extra virgin olive oil
4 cloves garlic, diced fine
¼ teaspoon salt
¼ teaspoon pepper
Directions:
Place the cauliflower in a steamer basket over boiling water. Cover and cook for 10 to 15 minutes or until the pork is tender.
Rinse the leek with water and pat dry. Cut into thin slices.
Heat the oil in a large saucepan over medium heat. Add the chives and cook for 2-3 minutes until tender.
Add the garlic and cook for another 1 minute.
Put everything in a food processor and pulse until almost tender. Keep warm or store in the refrigerator for later use.
Nutritional Information: Calories 147; Total Carbs 14g; Net Carbs 10g; Protein 5g; Fat 9g; Sugar 6g; Fiber 6g

Classic Brussels Sprouts

Prep Time: 10 minutes| Cook Time: 20 minutes| Servings: 4
Ingredients:
1 pound (454 g) Brussels sprouts
2 tablespoons avocado oil, divided
1 cup chicken bone broth
1 tablespoon minced garlic
½ teaspoon kosher salt
Freshly ground black pepper, to taste
½ medium lemons
½ tablespoon poppy seeds
Direction:
Trim the Brussels sprouts stem and removing any loose outer leaves.
Cut each in ½ lengthwise.
Set the electric pressure cooker to the Sauté setting.
When the pot is hot, pour in 1 tablespoon the avocado oil.
Add ½ of the Brussels sprouts to the pot, cut-side down, and let them brown for 3 to 5 minutes without disturbing.
Transfer to a bowl and add the remaining tablespoon avocado oil and the remaining Brussels sprouts to the pot.
Add the broth, garlic, salt, and a few grinds of pepper. Stir to distribute the seasonings.
Close and lock the lid of the pressure cooker.
Seal the pressure cooker. Cook on high pressure for 2 minutes.
While the Brussels sprouts are cooking, zest the lemon, then cut it into quarters.
When the cooking is complete, quick release the pressure. Using a slotted spoon, transfer the Brussels sprouts to a serving bowl.
Toss with the lemon zest, a squeeze of lemon juice, and the poppy seeds.
Serve immediately.
Nutritional Information: Calories 126; Total Carbs 12g; Net Carbs 10g; Protein 4g; Fat 8.1g; Sugar 3g; Fiber 4g

Cheese Coated Muffins

Prep Time: 10 minutes| Cook Time: 20 minutes| Servings: 4

Ingredients:
4 egg whites
½ teaspoon fresh parsley, diced fine
3 tablespoons reduced fat Parmesan cheese, divided
2 teaspoons water
½ teaspoon salt
Truffle oil to taste
Nonstick cooking spray

Directions:
Preheat the oven to 400 ºF (205 ºC). Grease two cups of muffins with cooking spray.
In a small bowl, combine the egg whites, water, and salt until blended.
In each muffin cup, pour the egg white mixture almost to the bottom.
Sprinkle a little Parmesan cheese on each egg white.
Cook for 10 to 15 minutes or until the edges are dark brown.
Let cool in the pan for 3 to 4 minutes, then transfer to a small bowl and drizzle with truffle oil.
Add parsley and ½ tablespoon Parmesan and toss to coat.
Serve.
Nutritional Information: Calories 47; Total Carbs 0g; Net Carbs 0g; Protein 4g; Fat 3g; Sugar 0g; Fiber 0g

Low Sugar Bok Choy Bowl

Prep Time: 15 minutes| Cook Time: 7 minutes| Servings: 4

Ingredients:
2 teaspoons sesame oil
2 pounds (907 g) bok choy, cleaned and quartered
2 teaspoons low-sodium soy sauce
Pinch red pepper flakes
½ cup toasted sliced almonds

Directions:
Place a large saucepan over medium heat and add the oil.
Once the oil is hot, fry the bok choy for about 5 minutes until tender.
Add the sauce and red pepper and sauté for another 2 minutes.
Place the bok choy in a bowl and garnish with flaked almonds.
Nutritional Information: Calories 119; Total Carbs 8g; Net Carbs 4g; Protein 6g; Fat 8g; Sugar 3g; Fiber 4g

Zucchini Tahini with Pepper Dip

Prep Time: 10 minutes| Cook Time: 0 minutes| Servings: 4

Ingredients:
2 zucchinis, chopped
3 garlic cloves
2 tablespoons extra-virgin olive oil
2 tablespoons tahini
Juice of 1 lemon
½ teaspoon sea salt
1 red bell pepper, seeded and cut into sticks

Direction:
In a food processor, combine the zucchini, garlic, olive oil, tahini, lemon juice, and salt. Blend until smooth puree formed.
Serve with the red bell pepper and carrots for dipping.
Nutritional Information: Calories 120; Total Carbs 6.9g; Net Carbs 3g; Protein 2.1g; Fat 11g; Sugar 4g; Fiber 2g

Acorn Squash with Parmesan

Prep Time: 10 minutes| Cook Time: 20 minutes| Servings: 4

Ingredients:
1 acorn squash (about 1 pound / 454 g)
1 tablespoon extra-virgin olive oil
1 teaspoon dried sage leaves, crumbled
¼ teaspoon freshly grated nutmeg
⅛ Teaspoon kosher salt
⅛ Teaspoon freshly ground black pepper
2 tablespoons freshly grated low-fat Parmesan cheese

Direction:
Cut the acorn squash in half lengthwise and remove the seeds. Cut them into 4 wedges. Snap the stem off.
In a small bowl, combine the olive oil, sage, nutmeg, salt, and pepper.
Wipe down the cut sides of the pumpkin with the olive oil mixture.
Pour 1 cup of water into the electric oven and put on a wire on it.
Place the squash in a layer, skin inside, on the tripod.
Close the pressure cooker lid. Adjust the valve to close.
Cook 20 minutes over high heat. When cooking is complete, click Cancel and release pressure immediately.
Carefully remove the squash from the pan, sprinkle with Parmesan, and serve.
Nutritional Information: Calories 208; Total Carbs 10g; Net Carbs 5g; Protein 2.1g; Fat 10g; Sugar 0g; Fiber 2g

Wochestershire Turkey Meatballs

Prep Time: 10 minutes| Cook Time: 20 minutes| Servings: 4
Ingredients:
¼ cup tomato paste
1 tablespoon honey
1 tablespoon Worcestershire sauce
½ cup milk
½ cup whole-wheat bread crumbs
1 pound (454 g) ground turkey
1 onion, grated
1 tablespoon Dijon mustard
1 teaspoon dried thyme
½ teaspoon sea salt
Directions:
Preheat the oven to 375 ºF (190 ºC). Line the baking sheets with parchment paper.
In a small saucepan over medium-low heat, combine the tomato paste, honey, and Worcestershire sauce. Bring to a boil and remove from heat.
In a large bowl, combine the milk and breadcrumbs. Rest for 5 minutes.
Add the ground turkey, onion, mustard, thyme, and salt. Mix well by hand without overdoing it.
Make 1-inch meatballs and place them on a baking sheet.
Brush the top with tomato paste. Bake in the oven until meatballs reach 165 ºF (74 ºC), about 15 minutes.
Nutritional Information: Calories 286; Total Carbs 21g; Net Carbs 17g; Protein 24g; Fat 11g; Sugar 13.6g; Fiber 2.1g

Spatchcock with Lime Aioli

Prep time: 15 minutes | Cook time: 45 minutes | Serves 6
Ingredients:
4 pounds (1.8 kg) chicken, spatchcocked
3 tablespoons blackened seasoning
2 tablespoons olive oil
Lime Aioli:
½ cup lite mayonnaise
Juice and zest of 1 lime
¼ teaspoon kosher salt
¼ teaspoon ground black pepper
Directions:
Heat the grill to a medium-high heat in advance.
Rub the chicken with blackened seasoning and olive oil on a clean work surface.
Cook the chicken for 45 minutes on a hot grill, skin side up, or until the internal temperature reaches 165°F (74°C).
Meanwhile, in a small mixing bowl, add all of the aioli Ingredients and swirl well to combine.
Transfer the chicken to a large platter and baste with the lime aioli after it's finished grilling.
Allow to cool before serving.
Serving Tip: Serve this dish with roasted Brussels sprouts or radish soup to make it a complete dinner.
Nutritional Information: Calories 436; Total Carbs 6.8g; Net Carbs 4.6g; Protein 61.1g; Fat 8.0g; Sugar 1.5g; Fiber 0.7 g

Turkey Burgers

Prep Time: 10 minutes| Cook Time: 20 minutes| Servings: 4
Ingredients:
1½ pounds (680 g) lean ground turkey
½ cup bread crumbs
½ sweet onion, chopped
1 carrot, peeled, grated
1 teaspoon minced garlic
1 teaspoon chopped fresh thyme
Sea salt and freshly ground black pepper, to taste
Nonstick cooking spray
Directions:
In a large bowl, combine the turkey, breadcrumbs, onion, carrot, garlic and thyme until well combined.
Season gently with salt and pepper.
Make the turkey mixture into 4 equal patties.
Place a large saucepan over medium heat and spray lightly with cooking spray.
Cook the turkey patties until golden brown, about 10 minutes per side.
Serve with a white burger or top with your favorite whole grain toppings.
Nutritional Information: Calories 320; Total Carbs 11g; Net Carbs 7g; Protein 32g; Fat 15g; Sugar 2g; Fiber g

Stuffed Chicken Breasts

Prep Time: 15 minutes| Cook Time: 30 minutes| Servings: 4
Ingredients:
1 cup chopped roasted red pepper
2 ounces (57 g) low-fat goat cheese
4 Kalamata olives, pitted, finely chopped
1 tablespoon chopped fresh basil
4 (5-ounce / 142-g) boneless, skinless chicken breasts
1 tablespoon extra-virgin olive oil
Directions:
Preheat the oven to 400 ºF.
In a small bowl, combine the peppers, goat cheese, olives, and basil until blended.
Put the container in the refrigerator for 15 minutes to harden.
Cut the chicken breast horizontally and make a pocket in the middle.
Distribute the filling evenly between the chicken breast pouches and secure with a wooden toothpicks.
Place a large saucepan over medium-high heat and pour in the olive oil.
Cook chicken for a total of 10 minutes on both sides.
Transfer to the oven. Cook the chicken until cooked through, about 20 minutes.
Let the chicken sit for 10 minutes, then remove the toothpicks before eating.
Nutritional Information: Calories 246; Total Carbs 3g; Net Carbs 2g; Protein 35g; Fat 9g; Sugar 2g; Fiber 1g

Ribeye with Mushrooms and Onions

Prep time: 10minutes | Cook time: 25 minutes | Serves 4

Ingredients:
4 (5 oz) rib-eye steaks, room temperature
Sea salt, ground
Black pepper, ground
2 tbsp. olive oil, divided
4 tbsp. plant-based butter
3 tsp. garlic, crushed
4 cups button mushrooms, sliced
1 medium red onion, thinly sliced
1 tbsp. Worcestershire sauce

Directions:
Season the steaks with ground sea salt and ground black pepper after drying them with paper towels.

In a large grill pan, heat 1 tablespoon olive oil over medium-high heat until hot. Cook for 2 minutes on each side, until the steaks are browned.

Raise the heat to medium and add the plant-based butter, allowing it to thoroughly melt. Cook the steaks in the melted plant-based butter until done to your liking. Place the cooked steaks on a dish and drizzle with butter. Allow 10 minutes for rest.

Cook the remaining 1 tbsp. olive oil and crushed garlic in the same pan over medium-high heat until fragrant. Cook for about 8 minutes, until the sliced mushrooms and onions are soft and caramelised. Cook for 2 minutes after adding the Worcestershire sauce. Add a bit of salt and black pepper to taste.

Serve the steaks with onions and mushrooms that have been fried.

Nutritional Information: Calories: 579; Total Fat: 49g; Protein: 28g; Total Carbs: 6g; Net Carbs: 5g

Low-Fat Pork Shoulder Slaw

Prep time: 15 minutes | Cook time: 5 hours | Serves 4

Ingredients:
1½ tbsp. chili powder, divided
2 tbsp. ground cumin, divided
1½ tsp. salt, divided
2½ tsp. black pepper, divided
2 tbsp. orange zest, divided
3–4 lbs. pork shoulder, fat trimmed
6 tsp. chopped garlic, divided
Juice of 2 oranges, divided
4 cups green or red cabbage, julienned
½ tbsp. extra-virgin olive oil

Directions:
Mix up 1 tbsp. chilli powder, 1 tbsp. cumin, 1 tsp. salt, 2 tsp. black pepper, and 1 tbsp. orange zest in a small bowl. Season the pork shoulder with the seasoning. Remove from the equation.

Add 5 tsp. chopped garlic and 1 orange's juice to a slow cooker and stir to combine. Cook on low heat for 8 hours or high for 5 hours after placing the seasoned pork shoulder inside. Remove the cooked pork shoulder from the pan and set it aside in a dish that will gather the juices.

Return the shredded meat to the slow cooker, along with the liquids. Toss with salt and pepper to taste.

Preheat the broiler in the oven.

Place the shredded pork on a baking pan and broil for 3 to 4 minutes, or until crispy.

Combine the remaining orange juice, chilli powder, cumin, garlic, salt, black pepper, and orange zest in a large mixing bowl. Mix in the julienned cabbage and olive oil until thoroughly mixed.

Serving Tip: Substitute any protein of your choosing for the protein.

Tip: If you don't like the citrus flavour, step 2 can be replaced with sliced apples.

Nutritional Information: Calories: 920; Total Fat: 72g; Protein: 59g; Net Carbs: 5g; Total Carbs: 9g

Lettuce Wraps with Pickled Onions and Pork

Prep time: 14 minutes | Cook time: 16 minutes | Serves 4

Ingredients:
½ red onion, thinly sliced
2 tbsp. red wine vinegar
Pinch of sea salt
1 tbsp. olive oil
1 tbsp. fresh ginger, minced
1 tbsp. garlic, minced
¼ tsp. chili flakes
1½ lb. ground pork
1 red bell pepper, in thin slices
1 green bell pepper, in thin slices
Fresh black pepper
4–8 lettuce leaves
2 carrots, julienned
1 cup cilantro, coarsely chopped

Directions:
Toss the thinly sliced red onion, red wine vinegar, and sea salt together in a small bowl.

In a heavy bottom pan, heat the olive oil over medium-high heat until it is hot; add the minced ginger, garlic, and chilli flakes and cook for 30 seconds, or until aromatic.

As for the ground pork, cook it for 7 to 8 minutes, breaking up the ground pork with a fork as it cooks. Place the bell pepper slices on top. Toss with salt and pepper to taste.

Place the lettuce leaves flat on your work area and evenly distribute the pork filling on each leaf. Add the julienned carrots, cilantro, and pickled onion to the top of the salad.

Fold the bottom of the lettuce leaf over the filling, then draw the edges over and roll. Serve and enjoy.

Substitution Tip: Substitute cabbage leaves for lettuce leaves by cooking the cabbage for 2 to 3 minutes, or until al dente.

Nutritional Information: Calories: 413; Net Carbs: 7g; Protein: 31g; Total Fat: 12g; Total Carbs: 9g

Cauliflower Shepherd's Pie

Prep time: 15 minutes | Cook time: 20 minutes | Serves 4

Ingredients:
1 cauliflower head, cored and cut into florets
1 tbsp. sea salt
2 tbsp. unsalted butter
1 tbsp. canola oil
1 onion, diced
2 carrots, cut into small cubes
1 celery stalk, diced
1 tbsp. fresh rosemary, minced
1 tsp. fresh thyme, minced
1 lb. ground beef
1 tbsp. tomato paste
¼ cup red wine
Salt and pepper

Directions:
Preheat the oven to broil and position the oven rack at the top.

In a large pot, add the salt, cauliflower, water that is enough to cover the cauliflower, boil them and cook for 15 minutes until the cauliflower is tender.

Place the cauliflower in a food processor after draining it and allowing most of the liquid to drain. Purée in the butter until it is completely smooth. Remove from the equation.

In a heavy-bottomed pan, heat the canola oil over medium-high heat.

Stir in the chopped onions, carrots, celery, rosemary, thyme, and salt, and simmer for another 5 minutes, or until the veggies soften. Remove the pan from the heat.

Add the ground beef and cook for 5 minutes, breaking up the ground beef with a fork as it cooks, or until no pink remains.

Bring the vegetables, tomato paste, and wine to a low boil, then reduce to a low heat and cook for another 2 minutes to let the alcohol evaporate.

To taste, mix with salt and pepper.Spread the cauliflower mash on top of the meat mixture in an oven-safe dish. Cook for 2 to 3 minutes under the broiler, or until browned.

When done, serve and enjoy.

Nutritional Information: Calories 337; Total Carbs 19g; Net Carbs 11g; Protein 18.1g; Fat 17.0g; Sugar 4.0g; Fiber 4 g

Tortillas with Steak and Guacamole

Prep time: 10minutes | Cook time: 15 minutes | Serves 4

Ingredients:
For The Guacamole
4 ripe avocados, peeled and pitted
Pinch of salt
1 tsp. garlic, minced
1 shallot or onion, minced
1 tomato chopped, remove the pulp
¼ tsp. chili flakes (optional)
1 tbsp. fresh lime juice
For The Filling
3 tbsp. olive oil, divided
1 tbsp. chili powder
2 tsp. ground coriander
2 tsp. ground cumin
1 tsp. salt
1 lb. frying steak, thinly sliced
1 onion, thinly sliced
1 finely sliced red and green bell pepper
8 lettuce leaves or low-carb tortillas
1 cup guacamole

Directions:
To make the guacamole, mash the ripe avocados with a fork in a medium basin until slightly lumpy. Mix in the minced garlic, onion, diced tomato, chilli flakes (if using), and lime juice until everything is well combined. Salt & pepper to taste. Refrigerate until ready to use.

Filling Ingredients

In a medium bowl, whisk together 2 tablespoons olive oil, chilli powder, coriander, cumin, and 1 teaspoon salt. Add the thinly sliced steak and toss to coat.

Heat a heavy-bottomed skillet over medium-high heat until it is smoking hot, then add the seasoned steak pieces and cook for 4 minutes. Take the object out of the room and put it away.

Add the chopped onions and bell peppers to the pan with the remaining 1 tbsp. olive oil and sauté for 5 minutes, until lightly browned. To taste, mix with salt and pepper..

Place the thinly cut steaks and vegetables in the centre of the lettuce leaves or low-carb tortillas and top with homemade guacamole.

Nutritional Information: Calories 547; Total Carbs 19g; Net Carbs 10g; Protein 18.1g; Fat 42.0g; Sugar 4.0g; Fiber 5 g

Baked Basil Meatballs

Prep time: 09 minutes | Cook time: 12minutes | Serves 4

Ingredients:
Non-stick cooking spray
½ lb. ground pork, lean
½ lb. ground beef, lean
1 onion, finely chopped
¼ cup breadcrumbs
2 tbsp. basil, chopped
2 tsp. garlic, minced
1 egg
Pinch Himalayan pink salt, ground
Pinch black pepper, ground
Marinara sauce
Vegetable of your choice

Directions:
Preheat the oven to 350 degrees Fahrenheit (180 degrees Celsius).

Set aside a baking tray that has been sprayed with nonstick cooking spray.

Toss the ground pork, ground beef, chopped onion, breadcrumbs, chopped basil, minced garlic, egg, ground Himalayan pink salt, and ground black pepper together in a large mixing basin.

Make medium-sized meatballs out of the ground beef.

Place the meatballs on a baking pan and bake for 15 minutes, or until browned and well cooked.

Serve the meatballs with marinara sauce and cooked green beans (or any other vegetable).

Ingredient Tip:Serve with spaghetti squash or courgette noodles.

Nutritional Information: Calories: 332; Net Carbs: 3g; Protein: 24g; Total Carbs: 13g; Total Fat: 19g

Aubergine with Lamb and Pine Nuts

Prep time: 10minutes | Cook time: 25 minutes | Serves 4

Ingredients:
2 medium aubergines, cut into thick slices
5 tbsp. olive oil, divided
Sea salt
Black pepper
1 small onion, minced
1 lb. ground lamb or pork
1 tbsp. tomato paste
1 tsp. garlic, minced
⅛ tsp. ground allspice
½ cup plain yogurt
¼ cup pine nuts
¼ cup parsley, minced

Directions:
Preheat the oven to 375 degrees Fahrenheit.
Toast the pine nuts in a small heavy bottom pan over medium heat until brown and aromatic. Remove from the equation.
Toss the aubergine slices with 4 tablespoons olive oil in a large mixing bowl and spread them out on a baking sheet. Season with salt and pepper, then bake for 25 minutes, or until tender and gently browned.
Meanwhile, heat the remaining 1 tablespoon olive oil in a large pan over medium-high heat; add the onion and cook for 3 minutes, or until the onion is gently browned.
Add the ground lamb or pork and cook for about 5 minutes, breaking it up with a fork as it cooks, then add the tomato paste. Cook for 2 minutes, or until the paste's acidity has dissipated.
Season the meat mixture to taste with the minced garlic and spices. Cook for another minute to fully integrate the Ingredients.
On each plate, arrange the cooked aubergine slices and top with the ground lamb or beef mixture. Drizzle with yoghurt and top with parsley and toasted pine nuts.
Substitution Tip: Put a can of coconut cream in the fridge overnight to substitute the yoghurt with a dairy-free alternative. Skim the cream that has developed on top and use it in place of the yoghurt when ready to use.
Nutritional Information: Calories: 625; Net Carbs: 9g; Protein: 24g; Total Fat: 60g; Total Carbs: 20g

Lamb Lettuce Cups with Garlic Yogurt

Prep time: 08 minutes | Cook time: 14 minutes | Serves 4

Ingredients:
1 lb. ground lamb
1 tbsp. garlic, chopped and divided
½ tbsp. oregano, finely chopped
1 lemon, juiced and divided
3 tsp. olive oil, divided
¾ tsp. sea salt, ground
¾ tsp. black pepper, ground
½ cup low-fat yogurt, plain
8 crisp lettuce leaves
2 cups romaine lettuce, shredded
½ cup ricotta cheese, crumbled

Directions:
Mix the ground lamb, ½ tablespoons chopped garlic, chopped oregano, half of the lemon juice, 2 teaspoons of olive oil, ground sea salt, and ground black pepper in a large mixing basin.
In a heavy bottomed pan, heat the remaining olive oil until it is hot.
Add the ground lamb and cook for 8 minutes, or until the ground lamb mixture is browned. Turn off the heat.
Combine the plain yoghurt, the remaining minced garlic, and the lemon juice in a small mixing bowl, and season with ground sea salt and ground black pepper.
Place 2 crisp lettuce leaves on each plate and create the lettuce cup according to the following order: ground lamb, shredded lettuce, crumbled ricotta cheese, yoghurt, and garlic sauce.
Nutritional Information: Calories: 463; Total Fat: 35g; Protein: 31; Total Carbs: 6g; Net Carbs: 5g

Roasted Pork Tenderloin & Apple Slaw

Prep time: 10minutes | Cook time: 20 minutes | Serves 4

Ingredients:
2 tbsp. avocado oil, divided
1 (1¼ lb.) pork tenderloin, boneless and patted dry
Himalayan pink salt, ground
Black pepper, ground
1 tbsp. rosemary, chopped
1 Granny Smith apple, cored, seeded cut into wedges
½ red cabbage, thinly sliced and core removed
½ red onion, thinly sliced
1 tbsp. apple cider vinegar
½ cup parsley, roughly chopped
1 tbsp. mint, chopped

Directions:
Preheat the oven to 425 degrees F.
In a large cast-iron pan, heat 1 tablespoon avocado oil over medium heat until hot.
Rub the ground Himalayan pink salt, ground black pepper, and finely chopped rosemary all over the dried pork.
Place the pork in the pan and sear for about 10 minutes, or until both sides are browned.
Combine the apple wedges, sliced cabbage, and sliced onion in a large mixing bowl with the remaining 1 tablespoon avocado oil. In the cast iron pan, scatter the mixture around the meat.
Arrange the pan to the oven and roast the pan for 10 minutes, or until the pork is fully cooked and the vegetables are soft.
Set aside the cooked pork on a chopping board to cool.
Mix the apple wedges and cabbage with the apple cider vinegar, chopped mint, and chopped parsley in the pan.
Serve the pork slices with the slaw.
Nutritional Information: Calories: 263; Net Carbs: 10g; Protein: 28g; Total Carbs: 15g; Total Fat: 11g

Filet Mignon with Mushrooms and Peppercorns

Prep time: 10minutes | Cook time: 25 minutes | Serves 4

Ingredients:
4 (5 oz) filet mignon steaks, room temperature
Sea salt, ground
Black pepper, ground
2 tbsp. avocado oil, divided
1 lb. portobello mushrooms, sliced
½ medium yellow onion, sliced
3 tsp. garlic, finely chopped
4 tbsp. plant-based butter
6 sage leaves, finely chopped

Directions:
Using paper towels, pat the fillet mignon steaks dry Add a pinch of salt and black pepper to taste.
1 tbsp. avocado oil, heated in a big heavy bottom pan over medium-high heat Cook the steaks on both sides until they are cooked to your satisfaction. Remove the steaks from the pan and lay them aside on a platter.
Reduce the heat to medium-low and stir in the remaining 1 tablespoon avocado oil. Cook for 5 to 7 minutes after adding the sliced mushrooms and onions. Cook for 2 minutes after adding the chopped garlic. Add it to the platter with the steaks and season with ground sea salt and ground black pepper.
Add the plant-based butter and chopped sage leaves and cook for 3 to 5 minutes, until the plant-based butter has melted and browned. Remove the sage leaves and toss them out.
Serve the steaks with the fried mushrooms and onions on top, drizzling the sage brown butter over top.

Nutritional Information: Calories: 420; Total Fat: 28g; Protein: 36g; Total Carbs: 6g; Net Carbs: 4g

Roasted Beef with Sherry and Pepper Sauce

Prep time: 10minutes | Cook time: 1 hr. 40 minutes | Serves 4

Ingredients:
1½ lb. rump beef roast
Himalayan pink salt, fine
Black pepper, ground
3 tsp. olive oil, divided
3 small onions, minced
2 tsp. garlic, minced
1 tbsp. green peppercorns
2 tbsp. sherry
2 tbsp. almond flour
1 cup beef broth, no salt

Directions:
Preheat the oven to 300 degrees Fahrenheit, gas mark 2.
Season the beef roast liberally with fine Himalayan pink salt and freshly ground black pepper.
Cook 2 tsp. olive oil in a cast-iron pan over medium-high heat until hot.
Brown the beef on all sides for about 10 minutes, then transfer to a baking dish.
Roast the meat until it's done to your liking, about 1½ hours for medium. Begin the pepper sauce after the roast has been in the oven for 1 hour.
Fry the minced onion in the remaining 1 tsp. olive oil in the same skillet over medium-high heat for 4 minutes, or until tender.
Cook for 1 minute after adding the minced garlic and green peppercorns. To deglaze the pan, whisk in the sherry.
Cook for 1 minute, stirring frequently, after whisking in the almond flour to produce a thick paste.
Whisk in the no-salt beef broth for 4 minutes, or until the sauce thickens and becomes glossy.
Fine Himalayan pink salt and ground black pepper are used to season the sauce.
Carve the steak and serve it with a large dollop of sauce.

Nutritional Information: Calories: 330; Total Fat: 18g; Total Carbs: 4g; Net Carbs: 1g; Protein: 36g

Jerked Chicken Breasts

Prep time: 4 hours 10 minutes | Cook time: 15 minutes | Serves 4

Ingredients:
2 habanero chile peppers, halved lengthwise, seeded
½ sweet onion, cut into chunks
1 tablespoon minced garlic
1 tablespoon ground allspice
2 teaspoons chopped fresh thyme
¼ cup freshly squeezed lime juice
½ teaspoon ground nutmeg
¼ teaspoon ground cinnamon
1 teaspoon freshly ground black pepper
2 tablespoons extra-virgin olive oil
4 (5-ounce / 142-g) boneless, skinless chicken breasts
2 cups fresh arugula
1 cup halved cherry tomatoes

Directions:
In a blender, combine the habanero peppers, onion, garlic, allspice, thyme, lime juice, nutmeg, cinnamon, black pepper, and olive oil. Toss everything into the blender and give it a good pulsing.
Place the mixture in a large mixing basin or two medium mixing bowls, then submerge the chicken in the bowl and press to thoroughly coat it.
Place the bowl in the refrigerator for at least 4 hours to marinate.
Preheat the oven to 400 degrees Fahrenheit (205 degrees Celsius) before beginning.
Take the bowl out of the fridge and toss out the marinade.
Place the chicken on a baking sheet and roast for 15 minutes, or until golden brown and faintly charred in the oven. Midway through the cooking time, rotate the chicken.
Allow 5 minutes after removing the baking sheet from the oven.
Serve the chicken with arugula and cherry tomatoes on a big platter.
Tip: To serve with the chicken, replace the arugula with the same amount of blanched spinach.

Nutritional Information: Calories 226; Total Carbs 3g; Net Carbs 2g; Protein 33.0g; Fat 9.0g; Sugar 1g; Fiber 0 g

Lamb Chops with Lime

Prep time: 10minutes | Cook time: 10 minutes | Serves 4

Ingredients:
¼ cup olive oil
¼ cup lime juice
2 tbsp. lime zest
2 tbsp. mint, chopped
2 tbsp. parsley, chopped
Pinch of Himalayan pink salt, ground
Pinch black pepper, ground
12 lamb chops

Directions:
Combine the olive oil, lime juice, lime zest, chopped parsley, chopped mint, ground Himalayan pink salt, and ground black pepper in a small mixing dish.
Pour the mixture into a lidded marinating dish. Cover the marinating dish with the lid and add the lamb chops. To blend, stir everything together.
Refrigerate the dish with the marinated lamb for 4 hours, flipping it many times.
Preheat the broiler in the oven.
Remove the chops from the dish and place them on a baking sheet lined with aluminium foil. Remove the rest of the marinade and discard it.
Cook the lamb chops for 4 minutes on each side under the broiler.
Before serving, let the lamb chops rest for 5 minutes.
Ingredient tip: Mint pairs well with lamb. You may thicken the remaining marinade by cooking it down.
Nutritional Information: Calories: 413; Net Carbs: 0g; Protein: 31g; Total Carbs: 1g; Total Fat: 29g

Spiced Lamb Vegetable Casserole

Prep time: 10minutes | Cook time: 2 hr. 15 minutes | Serves 4

Ingredients:
2 tbsp. canola oil
1½ lb. organic lamb shoulder, cut into chunks
½ sweet onion, finely chopped
1 tbsp. ginger, grated
2 tsp. garlic, minced
1 tsp. cinnamon, ground
1 tsp. cumin, ground
¼ tsp. cloves, ground
2 white sweet potatoes, peeled and diced
2 cups beef broth, low sodium
Himalayan pink salt, fine
Black pepper, ground
2 tsp. parsley, chopped for garnish
2 tsp. mint, finely chopped

Directions:
Preheat the oven to 300 degrees Fahrenheit.
Heat the canola oil in a big heavy-bottomed pan over medium-high heat.
Cook for 6 minutes, tossing periodically, until the lamb chunks are browned.
Fry for 5 minutes with the chopped onion, grated ginger, minced garlic, ground cinnamon, ground cumin, and ground cloves.
Bring the stew to a boil with the diced sweet potatoes and low sodium beef stock.

Place the lamb mixture in an oven-safe casserole dish and cover with a lid or aluminium foil before baking. Cook for 2 hours, stirring occasionally, or until the meat is cooked.
Remove the stew from the oven and season with ground black pepper and fine Himalayan pink salt.
Garnish with chopped parsley.and serve hot.
Ingredient Tip: Mint goes well with almost any lamb dish. Mint can also assist with dyspepsia.
Nutritional Information: Calories: 545; Total Fat: 35g; Total Carbs: 16g; Net Carbs: 4g; Protein: 32g

Carrots and Kale with Chicken

Prep time: 15 minutes | Cook time: 27 minutes | Serves 2

Ingredients:
½ cup couscous
1 cup water, divided
⅓ cup basil pesto
3 teaspoons olive oil, divided
3 (2-ounce / 57-g) whole carrots, rinsed, thinly sliced
Salt and ground black pepper, to taste
1 (about 6-ounce / 170-g) bunch kale, rinsed, stems removed, chopped
2 cloves garlic, minced
2 tablespoons dried currants
1 tablespoon red wine vinegar
2 (6-ounce / 170-g) boneless, skinless chicken breasts, rinsed
1 tablespoon Italian seasoning

Directions:
In a pot, combine the couscous and ¾ cup of water. On high heat, bring to a boil. Reduce the heat to a low setting. Cook for 7 minutes, or until the liquid has almost completely evaporated.Mix in the basil pesto and fluff with a fork.
In a nonstick skillet, heat 1 teaspoon olive oil over medium-high heat until it shimmers. Season with salt and pepper after adding the carrots Sauté the vegetables for 3 minutes, or until they are tender. Sauté the kale and garlic for 2 minutes, or until the kale has wilted somewhat.
Add the currents and the remaining water to the pan and cook for 3 minutes, or until most of the liquid has evaporated.
Remove the pan from the heat and add the red wine vinegar, stirring constantly. Place them in a large mixing bowl and cover with plastic wrap to keep warm.
Rub the chicken with Italian seasoning, salt, and pepper on a clean work surface.
Clean the skillet and heat 2 teaspoons olive oil until it shimmers over medium-high heat.
Sear the chicken for 12 minutes, or until it is thoroughly browned. Rotate the chicken midway through the cooking time.
Place the chicken on a big platter with the vegetables and couscous on top.
To serve, cut into slices.
Tip: Serve with beef stew or a leafy green salad to make it a complete dinner.
Nutritional Information: Calories 461; Total Carbs 9g; Net Carbs 0g; Protein 57.0g; Fat 5.0g; Sugar 5g; Fiber 6.5 g

Baked Fruity Bacon & Veggies

Prep time: 10minutes | Cook time: 15 minutes | Serves 4

Ingredients:
Non-stick cooking spray
6 cups brussels sprouts, halved
¼ lb. bacon, chopped
1 onion, sliced
½ red apple, peeled, cored, and chopped
4 tsp. garlic, chopped
2 tbsp. olive oil, divided
2½ tsp. sea salt, ground and divided
1½ tsp. black pepper, ground and divided
2–2½ lb. pork tenderloin

Directions:
Preheat the oven to 425°F.
Using nonstick cooking spray, coat a roasting pan.
Combine the brussels sprout halves, chopped bacon, sliced onion, diced apple, chopped garlic, and 1 tbsp. olive oil in a large mixing bowl and mix well. Mix in the 12 tsp. ground sea salt and ½ tsp. ground black pepper.
Rub the remaining ground sea salt, ground black pepper, and olive oil into the pork tenderloin. Place it in the roasting pan's centre. Surround the pork with the fruit and vegetable combination.
Bake for 30 minutes, or until the pork is fully cooked.
Serve immediately.
You can use any vegetables you wish in this recipe as a substitute.
Nutritional Information: Calories: 544; Net Carbs: 12g; Protein: 63g; Total Carbs: 19g; Total Fat: 24g

Chicken Breast with Artichoke Hearts

Prep time: 08 minutes | Cook time: 18 minutes | Serves 4

Ingredients:
2 tablespoons olive oil, divided
4 boneless, skinless chicken breast halves (6 oz / 170-g)
½ teaspoon dried thyme, divided
1 teaspoon crushed dried rosemary, divided
½ teaspoon ground black pepper, divided
2 (14-ounce/397-g) cans water-packed, low-sodium artichoke hearts, drained and quartered
½ cup low-sodium chicken broth
2 garlic cloves, chopped
1 medium onion, coarsely chopped
¼ cup shredded low-fat Parmesan cheese
1 lemon, cut into 8 slices
2 green onions, thinly sliced

Directions:
Preheat the oven at 375 degrees Fahrenheit (190 degrees Celsius) before beginning.
Oil the baking sheet with 1 teaspoon of the olive oil.
Rub ¼ teaspoon thyme, ½ teaspoon rosemary, 14 teaspoon black pepper, and 1 tablespoon olive oil into the chicken breasts on the baking sheet.
Combine the artichoke hearts, chicken broth, garlic, onion, and the rest of the thyme, rosemary, black pepper, and olive oil in a large mixing bowl. Toss well to coat.
Arrange the artichokes around the chicken breasts, then top with Parmesan cheese and lemon wedges.
Place the baking sheet in a preheated oven and roast for 20 minutes, or until the chicken breasts reach an internal temperature of 165°F (74°C).
Take the baking sheet out of the oven. Allow 10 minutes to cool before serving with green onions on top.
Tip: You can use the same quantity of white wine in place of the chicken broth.
Nutritional Information: Calories 339; Total Carbs 18g; Net Carbs 15g; Protein 42.0g; Fat 9.0g; Sugar 2g; Fiber 1 g

Strawberry and Peach Chicken

Prep Time: 20 minutes| Cook Time: 40 minutes| Servings: 4

Ingredients:
For the barbecue sauce:
1 cup frozen peaches
1 cup frozen strawberries
¼ cup tomato purée
½ cup white vinegar
1 tablespoon yellow mustard
1 teaspoon mustard seeds
1 teaspoon turmeric
1 teaspoon sweet paprika
1 teaspoon garlic powder
½ teaspoon cayenne pepper
½ teaspoon onion powder
½ teaspoon freshly ground black pepper
1 teaspoon celery seeds
For the Chicken:
4 boneless, skinless chicken thighs

Directions:
To Make the Barbecue Sauce
In a saucepan, combine the peaches, strawberries, tomato puree, vinegar, mustard, mustard seeds, turmeric, paprika, garlic powder, cayenne pepper, onion powder, black pepper, and celery seeds.
Cook over low heat for 15 minutes or until the flavors are well mixed.
Remove the sauce from the heat and let cool for 5 minutes.
Transfer the sauce to a blender and blend to a smooth puree.
To Make the Chicken
Preheat the oven to 350 ºF (180 ºC).
Place chicken in a medium bowl. Coat well with ½ cup of BBQ sauce.
Place the chicken on a rimmed baking sheet.
Place a baking sheet on the rack in the middle of the oven and bake for 20 minutes (depending on the thickness of the chicken) or until the juice runs out.
Pour the sauce over the chicken, return to the oven and cook over high heat for 3 to 5 minutes or until the crust is light brown.
Serve immediately.
Nutritional Information: Calories 190; Total Carbs 11g; Net Carbs 8g; Protein 23g; Fat 5g; Sugar 7g; Fiber 3g

Roasted Chicken Breats with Vegetables

Prep time: 08 minutes | Cook time: 20 minutes | Serves 4

Ingredients:
1 seeded red bell pepper, cut into 1-inch-wide strips
½ small eggplant, cut into ¼-inch-thick slices
½ small red onion, sliced
1 medium zucchini, cut lengthwise into strips
1 tablespoon extra-virgin olive oil
Salt, to taste
Feshly ground black pepper, to taste
4 whole-wheat tortilla wraps
2 (8-ounce / 227-g) cooked chicken breasts, sliced

Directions:
Preheat the oven to 400 degrees Fahrenheit (205 degrees Celsius) before beginning. A baking pan should be lined with aluminium foil.
In a large mixing bowl, combine the bell pepper, eggplant, red onion, zucchini, and olive oil. Toss well to coat.
Sprinkle salt and pepper over the vegetables before placing them on the baking pan.
Roast for 20 minutes or until tender and browned in a preheated oven.
On a clean work area, unfold the tortillas and divide the vegetables and chicken slices among them.
Wrap and serve right away.
Tip: Cooking Instructions for Chicken Breasts: Preheat the oven to 400 degrees Fahrenheit (205 degrees Celsius) before beginning. 1 tablespoon olive oil is used to grease a baking sheet. Place the chicken on the baking pan and bake for 24 minutes, or until the internal temperature of the chicken reaches 165 degrees Fahrenheit (74 degrees Celsius). Allow for cooling time before utilising the combination.
Nutritional Information: Calories 483; Total Carbs 9g; Net Carbs 2g; Protein 20.0g; Fat 25.0g; Sugar 4g; Fiber 3 g

Turkey Meatball and Vegetable Kabobs

Prep time: 50 minutes | Cook time: 20 minutes | Serves 6

Ingredients:
20 ounces (567 g) lean ground turkey (93% fat-free)
2 egg whites
2 tablespoons grated low-fat cheese
2 cloves garlic, minced
½ teaspoon salt, or to taste
¼ teaspoon ground black pepper
1 tablespoon olive oil
8 ounces (227 g) fresh cremini mushrooms, cut in half to make 12 pieces
24 cherry tomatoes
1 medium onion, cut into 12 pieces
¼ cup balsamic vinegar
Special Equipment:
12 bamboo skewers, soaking for at least 30 minutes in water

Directions:
In a large mixing bowl, combine the ground turkey, egg whites, Parmesan, garlic, salt, and pepper. Stir everything together thoroughly.

Make 12 meatballs out of the mixture and lay them on a baking sheet. At the very least, chill for 30 minutes.
Preheat the oven to 375 degrees Fahrenheit (190 degrees Celsius) before beginning. 1 tablespoon olive oil is used to grease a second baking sheet.
Take the meatballs out of the fridge. Alternate between 2 meatballs, 1 mushroom, 2 cherry tomatoes, and 1 onion piece on the bamboo skewers.
Brush the kabobs with balsamic vinegar and place them on a prepared baking sheet.
Grill for 20 minutes in a preheated oven, or until an instant-read thermometer placed in the centre of the meatballs registers 165°F (74°C). Halfway during the cooking period, flip the kabobs.
Allow 10 minutes for the kabobs to cool before serving heated.
Tips:Grape tomatoes can be used in place of cherry tomatoes.
When brushing the kabobs, set aside half of the balsamic vinegar; when turning, brush the kabobs with the reserved balsamic vinegar and extra olive oil. This will aid in evenly grilling the kabobs.
Nutritional Information: Calories 200; Total Carbs 7g; Net Carbs 2g; Protein 22.0g; Fat 8.0g; Sugar 4g; Fiber 1 g

Turkey Stuffed Red Bell Peppers

Prep Time: 15 minutes| Cook Time: 50 minutes| Servings: 4

Ingredients:
1 teaspoon extra-virgin olive oil, plus more for greasing the baking dish
1 pound (454 g) ground turkey breast
½ sweet onion, chopped
1 teaspoon minced garlic
1 tomato, diced
½ teaspoon chopped fresh basil
Sea salt and freshly ground black pepper, to taste
4 red bell peppers, tops cut off, seeded
2 ounces (57 g) low-sodium feta cheese

Directions:
Preheat the oven to 350 ºF (180 ºC).
Grease a baking dish with a little olive oil and set it aside.
Put a large saucepan over medium heat and add 1 teaspoon of olive oil.
Place the turkey in the pan and cook until it is not red. Shred the meat, stirring occasionally, and simmer for about 6 minutes until evenly browned.
Add onion and garlic and sauté until tender and translucent, about 3 minutes. Combine the tomatoes and basil. Season with salt and pepper.
Place the chopped peppers on a baking sheet. Divide the meat filling into 4 equal parts and fill in the peppers.
Sprinkle feta cheese over the filling. Add ¼ cup of water to the plate and cover with foil.
Bake for about 40 minutes until the peppers are tender and hot.
Nutritional Information: Calories 282; Total Carbs 14g; Net Carbs 10g; Protein 24g; Fat 14g; Sugar 9g; Fiber 4g

Yogurt Chicken Salad Sandwiches

Prep Time: 10 minutes| Cook Time: 10 minutes| Servings: 4
Ingredients:
2 (4-ounce / 113-g) boneless, skinless chicken breasts
⅛ teaspoon freshly ground black pepper
1½ tablespoons plain low-fat Greek yogurt
¼ cup halved purple seedless grapes
¼ cup chopped pecans
2 tablespoons chopped celery
4 whole-wheat sandwich thins
Avocado oil cooking spray
Directions:
Heat a small saucepan over medium-low heat. When hot, shake the sides with cooking spray. Sprinkle pepper on the chicken. Put the chicken in a pan and cook for 6 minutes.
Flip and cook for another 3 to 5 minutes, or until cooked through. Remove the chicken from the pan and let it cool for 5 minutes.
Chop or mash the chicken.
Serve with chicken, yogurt, berries, pecans, and celery.
Cut the sandwich in half finely so that it is on the top and bottom.
Divide the chicken salad into 4 equal parts and thinly pour half of the sandwiches, then cover with the top half.
Nutritional Information: Calories 251; Total Carbs 23g; Net Carbs 15g; Protein 23g; Fat 8g; Sugar 4g; Fiber 6g

Chicken Sandwiches with Caesar Dressing

Prep Time: 5 minutes| Cook Time: 0 minutes| Servings: 4
Ingredients:
For the Dressing:
4 tablespoons plain low-fat Greek yogurt
4 teaspoons Dijon mustard
4 teaspoons freshly squeezed lemon juice
4 teaspoons shredded reduced-fat Parmesan cheese
¼ teaspoon freshly ground black pepper
⅛ teaspoon garlic powder
For the Sandwiches:
2 cups shredded rotisserie chicken
1½ cups chopped romaine lettuce
12 cherry tomatoes, halved
4 whole-wheat sandwich thins
¼ cup thinly sliced red onion (optional)
Directions:
To Make the Dressing
In a small bowl, combine the yogurt, mustard, lemon juice, Parmesan, pepper, and garlic powder.
To Make the Sandwiches
In a large bowl, combine the chicken, lettuce, and tomatoes. Add dressing and toss until evenly coated.
Divide the filling into 4 equal parts.
Cut the sandwiches thinly so that the top and bottom are ½ for each. Put some of the fillings in each of the bottom halves and cover with the top half.
Nutritional Information: Calories 243; Total Carbs 24g; Net Carbs 1g; Protein 28g; Fat 5g; Sugar 4g; Fiber 8g

Chicken with Balsamic Kale

Prep Time: 5 minutes| Cook Time: 15 minutes| Servings: 4
Ingredients:
4 (4-ounce / 113-g) boneless, skinless chicken breasts
¼ teaspoon salt
1 tablespoon freshly ground black pepper
2 tablespoons unsalted butter
1 tablespoon extra-virgin olive oil
8 cups stemmed and roughly chopped kale, loosely packed (about 2 bunches)
½ cup balsamic vinegar
20 cherry tomatoes, halved
Directions:
Season both sides of the chicken breast with salt and pepper.
Heat a large saucepan over medium heat. Heat the butter and oil.
Add the chicken and cook for 8 to 10 minutes, turning halfway through cooking. When finished cooking, remove the chicken from the pan and set it aside.
Increase the heat to medium-high heat. Place the peppers in the pan and cook for 3 minutes, stirring every minute.
Add the vinegar and tomatoes and cook for another 3 minutes to 5 minutes.
Combine kale and tomatoes into 4 equal pieces and place 1 chicken breast in each.
Nutritional Information: Calories 294; Total Carbs 17g; Net Carbs 12g; Protein 31g; Fat 11g; Sugar 4g; Fiber 3g

Asian Chicken and Edamame Stir-Fry

Prep Time: 10 minutes| Cook Time: 10 minutes| Servings: 4
Ingredients:
3 tablespoons extra-virgin olive oil
1 pound (454 g) chicken breasts or thighs, cut into ¾-inch pieces
2 cups edamame or pea pods
3 garlic cloves, chopped
1 tablespoon peeled and grated fresh ginger
2 tablespoons reduced-sodium soy sauce
Juice of 2 limes
1 teaspoon sesame oil
2 teaspoons toasted sesame seeds
1 tablespoon chopped fresh cilantro
Directions:
Heat olive oil in a large saucepan over medium-high heat until cooked through.
Add the chicken to the oil and cook, stirring occasionally, until opaque, about 5 minutes.
Add the peas and cook, stirring occasionally, until tender and crisp, 3 to 5 minutes.
Add the garlic and ginger and cook for 30 seconds, stirring constantly.
Combine soy sauce, lemon juice, and sesame oil in a small bowl. Add the sauce mixture to the pan. Bring to a boil over low heat, stirring, and simmer for 2 minutes.
Remove from heat and garnish with sesame seeds and cilantro.
Nutritional Information: Calories 332; Total Carbs 10g; Net Carbs 5g; Protein 31.1g; Fat 17.1g; Sugar 5g; Fiber 5g

Chicken Thighs with Dandelion Greens

Prep Time: 10 minutes| Cook Time: 30 minutes| Servings: 4

Ingredients:
4 boneless, skinless chicken thighs
Juice of 1 lime
½ cup white vinegar
2 garlic cloves, smashed
1 cup frozen peaches
½ cup water
Pinch ground cinnamon
Pinch ground cloves
Pinch ground nutmeg
⅛ teaspoon vanilla extract
½ cup low-sodium chicken broth
1 bunch dandelion greens, cut into ribbons
1 medium onion, thinly sliced

Directions:
Preheat your oven to get ready for broil.
In a bowl, put the chicken, lime juice, vinegar, and garlic to coat the chicken well.
Meanwhile, prepare the peach frosting by mixing the peach, water, cinnamon, cloves, nutmeg, and vanilla in a small saucepan.
Cook over medium heat, stirring frequently, for 10 minutes or until the peaches are tender.
In a large cast-iron skillet, bring the broth to a boil over medium heat. Add the dandelion greens and sauté for 5 minutes or until the vegetables are tender.
Add the onions and cook for 3 minutes or until soft, stirring occasionally.
Add the chicken and cover with the peach frosting.
Transfer the pan to the oven and cook for 10 to 12 minutes or until the chicken is golden brown.
Nutritional Information: Calories 201; Total Carbs 13g; Net Carbs 9g; Protein 24g; Fat 4.9g; Sugar 6g; Fiber 4.1g

Turkey Taco

Prep Time: 10 minutes| Cook Time: 20 minutes| Servings: 4

Ingredients:
3 tablespoons extra-virgin olive oil
1 pound (454 g) ground turkey
1 onion, chopped
1 green bell pepper, seeded and chopped
½ teaspoon sea salt
1 small head cauliflower, grated
1 cup corn kernels
½ cup prepared salsa
1 cup shredded pepper Jack cheese

Directions:
In a large non-stick skillet, heat over medium-high heat until the olive oil is shiny.
Add the turkey. Mix with a spoon until browned, about 5 minutes.
Add the onion, pepper, and salt. Cook, stirring occasionally, for 4 to 5 minutes, until the vegetables are tender.
Add the cauliflower, corn, and salsa. Cook, stirring constantly, until the cauliflower rice is tender, about 3 minutes more.
Sprinkle with cheese. Reduce the heat to low, cover, and let the cheese melt for 2-3 minutes.
Nutritional Information: Calories 449; Total Carbs 17g; Net Carbs 12g; Protein 30g; Fat 30g; Sugar 8.7g; Fiber 4.1g

Golden Chicken Tenders

Prep Time: 10 minutes| Cook Time: 15 minutes| Servings: 4

Ingredients:
1 cup whole-wheat bread crumbs
1 tablespoon dried thyme
1 teaspoon garlic powder
1 teaspoon paprika
½ teaspoon sea salt
3 large eggs, beaten
1 tablespoon Dijon mustard
1 pound (454 g) chicken, cut into ½-inch-thick pieces and pounded to even thickness

Directions:
Preheat the oven to 375 ºF (190 ºC). Line the baking pan with parchment paper edges.
In a large bowl, combine the breadcrumbs, thyme, garlic powder, paprika, and salt.
Beat together eggs and mustard in another bowl.
Put each chicken in the egg mixture and then in the breadcrumb mixture. Place on a prepared baking sheet.
Bake for 15 minutes until the chicken has reached a temperature of 165ºF (74ºC) and the breadcrumbs are golden brown.
Nutritional Information: Calories 277; Total Carbs 16.9g; Net Carbs 12g; Protein 34.1g; Fat 6.1g; Sugar 8g; Fiber 3g

Sesame Chicken and Cucumber Soba

Prep Time: 10 minutes| Cook Time: 15 minutes| Servings: 6

Ingredients:
8 ounces (227 g) soba noodles
2 boneless, skinless chicken breasts, halved lengthwise
¼ cup tahini
1 tablespoon tamari
1 (1-inch) piece fresh ginger, finely grated
2 tablespoons rice vinegar
1 teaspoon toasted sesame oil
⅓ cup water
1 large cucumber, deseeded and diced
1 scallions bunch, green parts only, cut into 1-inch segments
1 tablespoon sesame seeds

Directions:
Preheat the broiler to a high setting.
Add the soba noodles to the salted boiling water and cook for 5 minutes or until al dente.
Transfer to a plate and pat dry with a paper towel.
Place the chicken in a layer on a baking sheet. Cook on preheated grill for 6 to 7 minutes or until chicken is tender. Transfer the chicken to a bowl and finely chop with a fork.
In a small bowl, put the tahini, tamari, ginger, rice vinegar, sesame oil, and water. Stir to combine well.
Place soba, chicken, cucumber, and scallions in a large bowl. Sprinkle with tahini sauce and toss to combine. Put the sesame seeds on it.
Nutritional Information: Calories 253; Total Carbs 34.8g; Net Carbs 28g; Protein 16.1g; Fat 7.8g; Sugar 1.8g; Fiber 2.2g

Ritzy Chicken Cacciatore

Prep Time: 20 minutes| Cook Time: 1 hour|
Servings: 6
Ingredients:
¼ cup all-purpose flour
1 (2-pound / 907-g) chicken, cut into 4 breasts,
2 drumsticks, 2 wings, and 2 thighs
Salt and freshly ground black pepper, to taste
2 tablespoons olive oil
3 slices bacon, chopped
4 ounces (113 g) button mushrooms, halved
1 sweet onion, chopped
2 teaspoons garlic, minced
½ cup red wine
1 (15-ounce / 425-g) can low-sodium stewed
tomatoes
Pinch red pepper flakes
2 teaspoons fresh oregano, chopped
Directions:
In a large bowl, put the flour, dip all the chicken
in the flour and sprinkle with salt and pepper.
Heat olive oil in a large skillet over medium-
high heat.
Place the chicken in the pan and cook for 20
minutes or until both sides are golden brown.
Turn the chicken halfway through the cooking
time. Transfer the grilled chicken to a plate.
Place the bacon in the pan and cook for 5
minutes, until curls. Stir from time to time while
cooking. Transfer the bacon to the same plate.
Add the mushrooms, onion, and garlic to the
pan and sauté for 4 minutes until tender.
Combine red wine, tomatoes, pepper flakes,
and oregano. Stir to mix. Bring to a boil.
Return the chicken and bacon to the pan.
Reduce heat and simmer for 30 minutes or until
chicken is 74ºC (165ºF).
Pour them into a large bowl. Cool 10 minutes,
then serve.
Nutritional Information: Calories 232; Total
Carbs 13.7g; Net Carbs 9g; Protein 8.2g; Fat
16.8g; Sugar 4.8g; Fiber 2.2g

Chicken and Veggies Roast

Prep Time: 10 minutes| Cook Time: 40
minutes| Servings: 6
Ingredients:
¼ cup olive oil, divided
½ head cabbage, cut into 2-inch chunks
1 sweet potato, peeled and cut into 1-inch
chunks
1 onion, peeled and cut into eighths
4 garlic cloves, peeled and lightly crushed
2 teaspoons fresh thyme, minced
Salt and freshly ground black pepper, to taste
2½ pounds (1.1 kg) bone-in chicken thighs and
drumsticks
Directions:
Preheat the oven to 450 ºF (235 ºC). Grease 1
tablespoon of olive oil in a roasting pan.
Place the cabbage, potatoes, onions, and garlic
in a roasting pan. Sprinkle with thyme, salt, and
pepper and pour 1 tablespoon of olive oil on
top. Separate. On a clean work surface, rub the
chicken with salt and pepper.
Heat 2 tablespoons of olive oil in a large skillet
over medium heat.
Place the chicken in the pan and cook for 10
minutes or until lightly browned on both sides.

Turn the chicken halfway through the cooking
time.
Place the chicken over the vegetables in a
roasting pan and bake in a preheated oven for
30 minutes until the internal temperature of the
chicken reaches 165 ºF (74 ºC).
Remove from the oven and serve hot on a large
plate.
Nutritional Information: Calories 542; Total
Carbs 13g; Net Carbs 8g; Protein 43g; Fat 33g;
Sugar 4g; Fiber 4.1g

Indian Creamy Curry Chicken

Prep Time: 15 minutes| Cook Time: 35
minutes| Servings: 4
Ingredients:
2 teaspoons olive oil
3 (5-ounce / 142-g) boneless, skinless chicken
breasts, cut into 1-inch chunks
1 tablespoon garlic, minced
2 tablespoons curry powder
1 tablespoon fresh ginger, grated
1 cup unsweetened coconut milk
2 cups low-sodium chicken broth
1 sweet potato, diced
1 carrot, peeled and diced
2 tablespoons fresh cilantro, chopped
Directions:
Heat olive oil in a saucepan over medium-high
heat.
Place the chicken in the saucepan and sauté for
10 minutes until all sides are golden.
Add the garlic, curry powder, and ginger to the
pan and sauté for 3 minutes until fragrant.
Pour the coconut milk and the chicken into the
pot and add the sweet potatoes and carrots to
the pot. Stir to combine well. Bring to a boil.
Reduce heat to low and simmer for 20 minutes
until tender. Stir from time to time.
Pour it into a large bowl and sprinkle cilantro
over it before eating.
Nutritional Information: Calories 328; Total
Carbs 14g; Net Carbs 9g; Protein 29g; Fat
16.9g; Sugar 3.9g; Fiber 1.1g

Greek Chicken Sandwiches

Prep Time: 10 minutes| Cook Time: 0 minutes|
Servings: 3
Ingredients:
3 slices 100% whole-wheat bread, toasted
3 tablespoons red pepper hummus
3 cups arugula
¾ cup cucumber slices
1 cup rotisserie chicken, shredded
¼ cup sliced red onion
Oregano, for garnish (optional)
Directions:
Place the toast on a clean baking sheet and
sprinkle 1 tablespoon of red pepper hummus on
each slice of bread.
Place each arugula, cucumber slices, chicken,
and red onion evenly on each slice of bread.
Garnish with oregano, if desired, and serve.
Nutritional Information: Calories 227; Total
Carbs 24g; Net Carbs 19g; Protein 23g; Fat
6.1g; Sugar 4.1g; Fiber 4g

Turkey and Cabbage Broth

Prep Time: 15 minutes| Cook Time: 30 minutes| Servings: 4
Ingredients:
1 tablespoon olive oil
2 celery stalks, chopped
2 teaspoons fresh garlic, minced
1 sweet onion, chopped
1 sweet potato, peeled, diced
4 cups green cabbage, finely shredded
8 cups low-sodium chicken broth
2 bay leaves
1 cup cooked turkey, chopped
2 teaspoons fresh thyme, chopped
Salt and freshly ground black pepper, to taste
Directions:
Place olive oil in a large saucepan and heat over medium heat.
Add the celery, garlic, and onion to the pot and sauté for 3 minutes until the onions are translucent.
Put the sweet potatoes and cabbage in the pan and cook for 3 minutes until the vegetables are slightly soft.
Pour the chicken broth into the pan and add the bay leaves. Bring to a boil. Reduce the heat to low and simmer for 20 minutes until the vegetables are tender.
Add the turkey and thyme to the pan and cook for 4 minutes until the turkey is heated through.
Pour the chicken broth into a large bowl and discard the leafy greens.
Season with salt and pepper to taste before cooking.
Nutritional Information: Calories 328; Total Carbs 29.8g; Net Carbs 18.8g; Protein 24.1g; Fat 10g; Sugar 12g; Fiber 4.2g

Turkey Zoodles with Spaghetti Sauce

Prep Time: 5 minutes| Cook Time: 20 minutes| Servings: 4
Ingredients:
1 (10-ounce / 284-g) package zucchini noodles, rinsed and patted dry
2 tablespoons olive oil, divided
1 pound (454 g) 93% lean ground turkey
½ teaspoon dried oregano
2 cups low-sodium spaghetti sauce
½ cup low-fat Cheddar cheese, shredded
Directions:
Preheat the broiler to a high temperature.
Heat 1 tablespoon of olive oil in an ovenproof skillet over medium heat.
Place the noodles in the pan and cook for 3 minutes until tender. Stir the noodles several times.
Drizzle with additional olive oil, then add the ground turkey and oregano to the pan. Cook 8 minutes until the turkey is golden brown.
Pour the spaghetti sauce over the turkey and stir to combine.
Spread cheddar cheese on top and cook in preheated grills for 5 minutes until cheese is melted and foamy.
Remove from the grill and serve hot.
Nutritional Information: Calories 337; Total Carbs 20g; Net Carbs 18g; Protein 27g; Fat 20g; Sugar 3.8g; Fiber 3.2g

Herbed Turkey and Vegetable Roast

Prep Time: 20 minutes| Cook Time: 2 hours| Servings: 6
Ingredients:
1 tablespoon fresh parsley, chopped
1 teaspoon fresh rosemary, chopped
1 teaspoon fresh thyme, chopped
2 teaspoons garlic, minced
Salt and freshly ground black pepper, to taste
2 pounds (907 g) boneless, skinless whole turkey breast
3 teaspoons extra-virgin olive oil, divided
2 carrots, peeled and cut into 2-inch chunks
1 sweet onion, peeled and cut into eighths
2 parsnips, peeled and cut into 2-inch chunks
2 sweet potatoes, peeled and cut into 2-inch chunks
Directions:
Preheat the oven to 350 ºF (180 ºC).
Combine parsley, rosemary, thyme, garlic, salt, and pepper in a bowl.
Arrange the chicken breasts in a roasting pan with foil.
Take 1 teaspoon of olive oil on each side. Rub with the parsley mixture. Bake in preheated oven for 30 minutes.
Meanwhile, pour additional olive oil into a large bowl.
Place the carrots, onions, parsnips, and sweet potatoes in a bowl. Mix well.
Place the vegetables around the turkey, return the pan to the oven and cook for another half hour until the turkey has reached a temperature of 165 ºF (74 ºC).
Serve hot and enjoy.
Nutritional Information: Calories 274; Total Carbs 19.7g; Net Carbs 12g; Protein 38g; Fat 2.8g; Sugar 5.8g; Fiber 4.2g

Blackened Spatchcock with Lime Aioli

Prep Time: 15 minutes| Cook Time: 45 minutes| Servings: 6
Ingredients:
4 pounds (1.8 kg) chicken, spatchcocked
3 tablespoons blackened seasoning
2 tablespoons olive oil
Lime Aioli:
½ cup mayonnaise
Juice and zest of 1 lime
¼ teaspoon kosher salt
¼ teaspoon ground black pepper
Directions:
Preheat the grill to medium high heat.
Rub the chicken with the blackened seasoning and olive oil on a clean work surface.
Place the chicken in a preheated oven and bake on the skin side up for 45 minutes or until the chicken is 74ºC (165ºF).
Meanwhile, put the Ingredients for the aioli in a small bowl and stir to combine well.
When the chicken is completely browned, transfer it to a large plate and sprinkle with lime aioli. Cool and help.
Nutritional Information: Calories 436; Total Carbs 6.8g; Net Carbs 2g; Protein 61.7g; Fat 16.3g; Sugar 1.4g; Fiber 0.7g

Coconut-Encrusted Chicken

Prep Time: 10 minutes| Cook Time: 20 minutes| Servings: 6
Ingredients:
4 chicken breasts, each cut lengthwise into 3 strips
½ teaspoon salt
¼ teaspoon freshly ground black pepper
2 eggs
2 tablespoons unsweetened plain almond milk
½ cup coconut flour
1 cup unsweetened coconut flakes
Directions:
Preheat the oven to 400 ºF (205 ºC).
On a clean work surface, rub the chicken with salt and pepper.
Combine the eggs and almond milk in a bowl. Put the coconut powder in another bowl. Place the coconut flakes in the third bowl. Place the chicken in a bowl of flour, then dredge the egg mixture and dip it in the coconut flakes. Shake excess off.
Arrange the chicken well coated in an ovenproof dish lined with parchment paper.
Bake in preheated oven for 16 minutes. Turn the chicken for half the cooking time or until golden brown.
Take the chicken out of the oven and place it on a plate.
Nutritional Information: Calories 218; Total Carbs 8.8g; Net Carbs 4g; Protein 20g; Fat 12g; Sugar 1.8g; Fiber 6.1g

Chicken Leg Roast

Prep Time: 10 minutes| Cook Time: 35 minutes| Servings: 6
Ingredients:
1 teaspoon ground paprika
1 teaspoon garlic powder
½ teaspoon ground coriander
½ teaspoon ground cumin
½ teaspoon salt
¼ teaspoon ground cayenne pepper
6 chicken legs
1 teaspoon extra-virgin olive oil
Directions:
Preheat the oven to 400 ºF (205 ºC).
In a bowl, put the cilantro, cumin, paprika, garlic powder, salt, and cayenne pepper.
Dip the chicken thighs in the mixture to coat them well.
Heat olive oil in a pan over medium heat.
Add the chicken and cook for 9 minutes or until golden brown and crisp.
Turn the thighs halfway through cooking.
Place the skillet in the oven and bake for 14 minutes or until the chicken reaches a temperature of 165 ºF (74 ºC).
Take the chicken out of the oven and serve hot.
Nutritional Information: Calories 278; Total Carbs 0.8g; Net Carbs 0.1g; Protein 30g; Fat 15g; Sugar 0g; Fiber 0g

Creamy Chicken with Quinoa and Broccoli

Prep Time: 5 minutes| Cook Time: 15 minutes| Servings: 4
Ingredients:
½ cup uncooked quinoa
4 (4-ounce / 113-g) boneless, skinless chicken breasts
1 teaspoon garlic powder, divided
¼ teaspoon salt
¼ teaspoon freshly ground black pepper
1 tablespoon avocado oil
3 cups fresh or frozen broccoli, cut into florets
1 cup half-and-half
Directions:
Put the quinoa in a saucepan with salted water. Bring to a boil. Reduce the heat and simmer for 15 minutes or until the quinoa is tender and the "tails" are white. Leave it for 5 minutes.
In a clean area, rub the chicken with ½ teaspoon of garlic powder, salt, and pepper.
Heat avocado oil in a nonstick skillet over medium-low heat.
Place the chicken and broccoli in a skillet and cook for 9 minutes or until the chicken is golden brown and the broccoli is tender.
Turn the chicken over and shake the pan halfway through cooking.
Pour half-and-half into the pan and sprinkle with added garlic powder. Increase heat and simmer until creamy, about 2 minutes.
Serve hot with rice, chicken breast, and florets of broccoli with the rest of the sauce.
Nutritional Information: Calories 305; Total Carbs 21.8g; Net Carbs 15g; Protein 33g; Fat 9.8g; Sugar 3.9g; Fiber 9.8g

Herbed Chicken and Artichoke Hearts

Prep Time: 10 minutes| Cook Time: 20 minutes| Servings: 4
Ingredients:
2 tablespoons olive oil, divided
4 (6-ounce / 170-g) boneless, skinless chicken breast halves
½ teaspoon dried thyme, divided
1 teaspoon crushed dried rosemary, divided
½ teaspoon ground black pepper, divided
2 (14-ounce / 397-g) cans water-packed, low-sodium artichoke hearts, drained and quartered
½ cup low-sodium chicken broth
2 garlic cloves, chopped
1 medium onion, coarsely chopped
¼ cup low-fat shredded Parmesan cheese
1 lemon, cut into 8 slices
2 green onions, thinly sliced
Directions:
Preheat the oven to 375 ºF (190 ºC). Use 1 teaspoon of olive oil on a baking sheet.
Place the chicken on a baking sheet and toss with ¼ teaspoon of thyme, ½ teaspoon of rosemary, 1 teaspoon of pepper and 1 teaspoon of olive oil.
Add the artichoke heart, chicken broth, garlic, onion, remaining thyme, rosemary, black pepper and olive oil. Mix well.
Use artichokes around the chicken breast and sprinkle with Parmesan and lemon slices.
Place the baking sheet in a preheated oven and bake for 20 minutes or until the chicken breast has reached a temperature of 165 ºF (74 ºC).
Take the form out of the oven. Let cool for 10 minutes, then place the green onions on top.
Nutritional Information: Calories 339; Total Carbs 18g; Net Carbs 12g; Protein 42g; Fat 9g; Sugar 2g; Fiber 1g

Ritzy Jerked Chicken Breasts

Prep Time: 4 hours 10 minutes| Cook Time: 15 minutes| Servings: 4
Ingredients:
2 habanero chile peppers, halved lengthwise, seeded
½ sweet onion, cut into chunks
1 tablespoon minced garlic
1 tablespoon ground allspice
2 teaspoons chopped fresh thyme
¼ cup freshly squeezed lime juice
½ teaspoon ground nutmeg
¼ teaspoon ground cinnamon
1 teaspoon freshly ground black pepper
2 tablespoons extra-virgin olive oil
4 (5-ounce / 142-g) boneless, skinless chicken breasts
2 cups fresh arugula
1 cup halved cherry tomatoes
Directions:
Combine the habanero, onion, garlic, allspice, thyme, lemon juice, nutmeg, cinnamon, pepper, and olive oil in a blender. Mix well in a blender.
Transfer mixture to 2 large or medium bowls, place chicken in a bowl, and coat well.
Put the chicken in the refrigerator and let marinate for at least 4 hours.
Preheat the oven to 400 ºF (205 ºC). Take the bowl out of the refrigerator and discard the marinade.
Place the chicken on a baking sheet and bake in a preheated oven for 15 minutes or until golden brown and lightly charred. Turn the chicken halfway through the cooking time.
Remove the foil from the oven and let stand for 5 minutes. Transfer the chicken to a large plate and serve with arugula and tomatoes.
Nutritional Information: Calories 226; Total Carbs 3g; Net Carbs 1g; Protein 33g; Fat 9g; Sugar 1g; Fiber 0g

Roasted Vegetable and Chicken Tortillas

Prep Time: 10 minutes| Cook Time: 20 minutes| Servings: 4
Ingredients:
1 red bell pepper, seeded and cut into 1-inch-wide strips
½ small eggplant, cut into ¼-inch-thick slices
½ small red onion, sliced
1 medium zucchini, cut lengthwise into strips
1 tablespoon extra-virgin olive oil
Salt and freshly ground black pepper, to taste
4 whole-wheat tortilla wraps
2 (8-ounce / 227-g) cooked chicken breasts, sliced
Directions:
Preheat the oven to 400 ºF (205 ºC). Prepare the baking sheet with foil.
In a large bowl, put the bell peppers, eggplant, red onion, zucchini, and olive oil. Mix well.
Pour the vegetables on the baking sheet and sprinkle with salt and pepper.
Bake in preheated oven for 20 minutes or until tender and charred.
Spread the tortillas out on a clean surface, then divide the vegetables and chicken into tortillas.Wrap and serve immediately.

Nutritional Information: Calories 483; Total Carbs 45g; Net Carbs 28g; Protein 20g; Fat 25g; Sugar 4g; Fiber 4g

Mexican Turkey Sliders

Prep Time: 15 minutes| Cook Time: 6 minutes| Servings: 7
Ingredients:
1 pound (454 g) lean ground turkey
1 tablespoon chili powder
½ teaspoon garlic powder
¼ teaspoon ground black pepper
7 mini whole-wheat hamburger buns
7 tomato slices
3½ slices reduced-fat pepper Jack cheese, cut in ½
½ mashed avocado
Directions:
Preheat the grill to high heat.
Place turkey, pepper, garlic powder, chili powder, and black pepper in a large bowl. Stir to combine well.
Divide the mixture into 7 patties evenly, then place the patties on a preheated grill.
Bake for 6 minutes or until golden brown. Turn the patties in half.
Place the patties with the buns, tomato slices, cheese slices, and mashed avocado in sliders, then serve immediately.
Nutritional Information: Calories 225; Total Carbs 21g; Net Carbs 18g; Protein 17g; Fat 9g; Sugar 6g; Fiber 4g

Arroz Con Pollo

Prep Time: 10 minutes| Cook Time: 25 minutes| Servings: 4
Ingredients:
1 onion, diced
1 red pepper, diced
2 cup chicken breast, cooked and cubed
1 cup cauliflower, grated
1 cup peas, thaw
2 tablespoons cilantro, diced
½ teaspoon lemon zest
14½ ounces (411 g) low-sodium chicken broth
¼ cup black olives, sliced
¼ cup sherry
1 clove garlic, diced
2 teaspoons olive oil
¼ teaspoon salt
¼ teaspoon cayenne pepper
Directions:
Heat the oil in a large saucepan over medium-high heat. Add the pepper, onion, and garlic and cook for 1 minute.
Add the cauliflower and cook, stirring frequently, until light brown, 4 to 5 minutes.
Stir in the broth, sherry, zest, and seasonings. Bring to a boil.
Lower the heat, cover, and simmer for 15 minutes.
Stir in the chicken, peas, and olives. Cover and simmer for 3 to 6 minutes or until completely heated through.
Garnish with cilantro and serve.
Nutritional Information: Calories 162; Total Carbs 13g; Net Carbs 9g; Protein 14g; Fat 5g; Sugar 5g; Fiber 4.2g

Chicken with Couscous

Prep Time: 15 minutes| Cook Time: 27 minutes| Servings: 2

Ingredients:

½ cup couscous
1 cup water, divided
⅓ cup basil pesto
3 teaspoons olive oil, divided
3 (2-ounce / 57-g) whole carrots, rinsed, thinly sliced
Salt and ground black pepper, to taste
1 (about 6-ounce / 170-g) bunch kale, rinsed, stems removed, chopped
2 cloves garlic, minced
2 tablespoons dried currants
1 tablespoon red wine vinegar
2 (6-ounce / 170-g) boneless, skinless chicken breasts, rinsed
1 tablespoon Italian seasoning

Directions:

Pour the couscous and ¾ cup of water into the pot. Bring to a boil over high heat.
Reduce the heat to low. Boil for 7 minutes or until most of the water is absorbed. Crisp with a fork and stir in the basil pesto.
Add 1 teaspoon of olive oil to a nonstick skillet and heat over medium-high heat until cooked through.
Add the carrots, then season with salt and pepper. Cook for 3 minutes or until tender.
Add kale and garlic and sauté for 2 minutes or until onions are lightly wilted.
Add water and sauté for 3 minutes or until most of the water is cooked through.
Lower the heat and stir in the red wine vinegar. Transfer them to a large bowl and cover to keep warm.
On a clean surface, sauté the chicken with Italian seasoning, salt, and pepper.
Clean the pan and heat over medium-high heat until 2 teaspoons of olive oil boil.
Add the chicken and cook for 12 minutes or until golden brown. Turn the chicken halfway through the cooking time.
Transfer the chicken to a large plate and sprinkle with vegetables and couscous.

Nutritional Information: Calories 461; Total Carbs 26g; Net Carbs 18g; Protein 57g; Fat 14g; Sugar 5g; Fiber 6g

Cashew Chicken

Prep Time: 10 minutes| Cook Time: 10 minutes| Servings: 4

Ingredients:

1 pound (454 g) skinless boneless chicken breast, cut in cubes
½ onion, sliced
2 tablespoons green onion, diced
½ teaspoon fresh ginger, peeled and grated
1 cup whole blanched cashews, toasted
1 clove garlic, diced fine
4 tablespoons oil
2 tablespoons dark soy sauce
2 tablespoons hoisin sauce
2 tablespoons water
2 teaspoons cornstarch
2 teaspoons dry sherry
1 teaspoon Splenda
1 teaspoon sesame seed oil

Directions:

Place the chicken in a large bowl and add the cornstarch, sherry, and ginger. Stir until well mixed.
In a small bowl, combine the sauce, hoisin, Splenda, and water and stir until smooth.
Heat the oil in a wok or large saucepan over high heat. Add the garlic and onion and simmer until the garlic sizzles, about 30 seconds.
Add the chicken and cook, stirring frequently, until the chicken is almost cooked through, about 2 minutes.
Reduce the heat to medium and stir in the sauce. Continue to cook and stir until combined.
Add the cashews and cook for 30 seconds. Drizzle with sesame oil and cook for another 30 seconds, stirring constantly.
Garnish with green onions.

Nutritional Information: Calories 484; Total Carbs 19g; Net Carbs 15g; Protein 33g; Fat 32g; Sugar 6.1g; Fiber 2.2g

Chicken Pappardelle

Prep Time: 15 minutes| Cook Time: 15 minutes| Servings: 4

Ingredients:

¾ pound (340 g) chicken breast, sliced lengthwise into ⅛-inch strips
1 small onion, sliced thin
8 cups spinach, chopped fine
4 cups low sodium chicken broth
1 cup fresh basil
2 quarts water
¼ cup reduced fat Parmesan cheese, divided
6 cloves garlic, diced
1 tablespoon walnuts, chopped
¼ teaspoon cinnamon
¼ teaspoon paprika
¼ teaspoon red pepper flakes
Salt, to taste
Olive oil cooking spray

Directions:

Boil 2 liters of water in a medium saucepan.
Sprinkle cooking spray lightly on a medium frying pan and place over medium-high heat.
Add the garlic and cook until golden brown. Add the cinnamon, paprika, red pepper flakes, basil leaves, and onion. Simmer until onion is tender, about 2 minutes.
Add the spinach and cook for another 2 minutes, until wilted and tender. Add the broth and bring to a boil, cover and cook until tender, about 5 minutes.
Now add a pinch of salt to the boiling water. Turn the heat off, add the chicken and stir to separate all the strips. Cook until the strips turn white. They will be half cooked. Using a spoon, transfer the strips to a plate to cool.
Check the spinach mixture. Boil until the broth is almost evaporated.
Add ½ cheese, mix, and season with salt. Add the chicken and toss into the batter and cook until the chicken strips are all cooked through about 90 seconds.
Divide the mixture among 4 plates, top with cheese and serve.

Nutritional Information: Calories 175; Total Carbs 7.1g; Net Carbs 4g; Protein 24.2g; Fat 5g; Sugar 2g; Fiber 2g

Cheesy Chicken Casserole

Prep Time: 10 minutes| Cook Time: 40 minutes| Servings: 6
Ingredients:
4 slices bacon, cooked and crumbled
3 cups cauliflower
3 cups chicken, cooked and chopped
3 cups broccoli florets
2 cups reduced fat cheddar cheese, grated
1 cup fat free sour cream
4 tablespoons olive oil
1 teaspoon salt
½ teaspoon black pepper
½ teaspoon garlic powder
½ teaspoon paprika
Nonstick cooking spray
Directions:
Put 4 to 5 cups of water in a large saucepan and bring to a boil. Add the cauliflower and drain well, then cook 4 to 5 minutes or until tender. Repeat with the broccoli.
Preheat the oven to 350 ºF (180 ºC). Spray the baking dish with cooking spray.
In a large bowl, mash the cauliflower with olive oil, sour cream, and seasonings. Add ½ more cheese and mix well.
Spread the mixture on a prepared baking sheet and sprinkle with the rest cheese. Bake for 20-25 minutes or until heated through and cheese is melted.
Nutritional Information: Calories 345; Total Carbs 10g; Net Carbs 8g; Protein 28.7g; Fat 15g; Sugar 4g; Fiber 2.2g

Cheesy Chicken and Spinach

Prep Time: 10 minutes| Cook Time: 45 minutes| Servings: 6
Ingredients:
3 chicken breasts, boneless, skinless and halved lengthwise
6 ounces (170 g) low fat cream cheese, soft
2 cup baby spinach
1 cup low-fat Mozzarella cheese, grated
2 tablespoons olive oil, divided
3 cloves garlic, diced fine
1 teaspoon Italian seasoning
Nonstick cooking spray
Directions:
Preheat the oven to 350 ºF (180 ºC). Spray cooking spray on a baking sheet.
Place the chicken cutlets on the baking sheet.
Pour 1 tablespoon of cooking oil over the chicken. Sprinkle evenly with garlic and Italian seasoning. Spread cream cheese over the chicken.
Heat the remaining oil in a saucepan over medium heat.
Add the spinach and simmer until the spinach is wilted, for about 3 minutes. Spread evenly over the layer of cream cheese.
Sprinkle the top with mozzarella.
Bake for 35-40 minutes or until the chicken is cooked through. provided.
Nutritional Information: Calories 362; Total Carbs 3.1g; Net Carbs 1.8g; Protein 31g; Fat 25g; Sugar 0g; Fiber 0g

Chicken Tuscany

Prep Time: 10 minutes| Cook Time: 15 minutes| Servings: 4
Ingredients:
1½ pounds (680 g) chicken breasts, boneless, skinless and sliced thin
1 cup spinach, chopped
1 cup half-and-half
½ cup reduced fat Parmesan cheese
½ cup low sodium chicken broth
½ cup sun dried tomatoes
2 tablespoons olive oil
1 teaspoon Italian seasoning
1 teaspoon garlic powder
Directions:
Heat the oil in a large saucepan over medium-high heat. Add the chicken and cook for 3 to 5 minutes for each side or until golden brown and cooked through. Transfer to a plate.
Add half and half, broth, cheese, and seasoning to the pan. Continue until the sauce begins to thicken.
Add the spinach and tomatoes and cook, stirring frequently, until the spinach begins to wilt, about 2-3 minutes.
Return the chicken to the pan and cook long enough to heat through.
Nutritional Information: Calories 463; Total Carbs 6.1g; Net Carbs 4g; Protein 55g; Fat 23g; Sugar 0g; Fiber 1.0g

Chicken Zucchini Patties with Salsa

Prep Time: 10 minutes| Cook Time: 10 minutes| Servings: 8
Ingredients:
2 cup chicken breast, cooked, divided
1 zucchini, cut in ¾-inch pieces
¼ cup cilantro, diced
⅓ cup bread crumbs
⅓ cup lite mayonnaise
2 teaspoons olive oil
½ teaspoon salt
¼ teaspoon pepper
Roasted Tomato Salsa:
6 plum tomatoes
1¼ cups cilantro
2 teaspoons olive oil
1 teaspoon adobo sauce
½ teaspoon salt, divided
Nonstick cooking spray
Directions:
Place 1½ cups of chicken and zucchini in a food processor. Cover and mix until coarsely chopped. Add the breadcrumbs, mayonnaise, pepper, cilantro, remaining chicken, and salt. Cover and pulse until chunky.
Heat the oil in a large saucepan over medium-high heat. Shape the chicken into 8 patties and cook 4 minutes for each side or until golden brown.
Meanwhile, combine the salsa Ingredients in a small bowl.
Serve the patties topped with salsa.
Nutritional Information: Calories 147; Total Carbs 10g; Net Carbs 6g; Protein 12.2g; Fat 7g; Sugar 5g; Fiber 2g

Creole Chicken

Prep Time: 15 minutes| Cook Time: 25 minutes| Servings: 2
Ingredients:
2 chicken breast halves, boneless and skinless
1 cup cauliflower rice, cooked
1/3 cup green bell pepper, julienned
¼ cup celery, diced
¼ cup onion, diced
14½ ounces (411 g) stewed tomatoes, diced
1 teaspoon sunflower oil
1 teaspoon chili powder
½ teaspoon thyme
⅛ teaspoon pepper
Directions:
Heat the oil in a small skillet over medium heat. Add the chicken and cook 5 to 6 minutes per side or until cooked through. Transfer to a plate and keep warm.
Add the bell pepper, celery, onion, tomato, and seasoning. Bring to a boil. Reduce the heat, cover, and simmer for 10 minutes or until the vegetables start to soften.
Return the chicken to the pan and heat through. Serve over cauliflower rice.
Nutritional Information: Calories 361; Total Carbs 14g; Net Carbs 10g; Protein 45.2g; Fat 14g; Sugar 8g; Fiber 4g

Pecan Chicken Enchiladas

Prep Time: 20 minutes| Cook Time: 45 minutes| Servings: 12
Ingredients:
1 onion, diced
4 cups chicken breast, cooked and cubed
1 cup fat free sour cream
1 cup skim milk
4 ounces (113 g) low fat cream cheese
½ cup reduced fat cheddar cheese, grated
2 tablespoons cilantro, diced
12 (6-inch) flour tortillas, warm
1 can low fat condensed cream of chicken soup
¼ cup pecans, toasted
2 tablespoons green chilies, diced
1 tablespoon water
1 teaspoon cumin
¼ teaspoon pepper
⅛ teaspoon salt
Nonstick cooking spray
Directions:
Preheat the oven to 350 ºF (180 ºC). Spray the baking dish with cooking spray.
Sprinkle a little cooking spray on a nonstick skillet and place it over medium heat.
Add the onions and cook until tender.
In a large bowl, whisk cream cheese, water, cumin, salt, and pepper until smooth. Stir in the onions, chicken, and pecans.
Place 1/3 cup of the chicken mixture in the center of each tortilla. Roll it in a baking dish and lay it seam-side down.
In a medium bowl, combine the soup, sour cream, milk, and pepper and pour over the enchiladas.
Cover with foil and bake for 40 minutes. Open the lid, sprinkle the cheese on top, and cook for another 5 minutes until the cheese is melted.
Sprinkle with cilantro and serve.

Nutritional Information: Calories 321; Total Carbs 2g; Net Carbs 18g; Protein 21.2g; Fat 13g; Sugar 4g; Fiber 2g

Baked Spiced Chicken

Prep Time: 20 minutes| Cook Time: 1 hour 20 minutes| Servings: 4
Ingredients:
11 (3 ounces of) chicken breast, boned & skinned
2 tablespoons (any brand) bottled diet Italian dressing
Directions:
Marinate chicken in dressing overnight in a covered casserole in a refrigerator.
Bake the marinated chicken for one hour at 350 ºF.
After baking, it will be very tender and juicy. Serve and enjoy!
Nutritional Information: Calories 240; Total Carbs 1.8g; Net Carbs 0.2g; Protein 29.5g; Fat 12.2g; Sugar 8.2g; Fiber 0.3g

Duck Breasts with Grilled Plums

Prep Time: 10 minutes| Cook Time: 20 minutes| Servings: 6
Ingredients:
4 (12- to 14-ounce / 340- to 397-g) boneless duck breast halves, trim off excess fat
6 firm purple plums, halved, pitted
4 teaspoons fresh thyme, chopped.
1 tablespoon extra-virgin olive oil
2 teaspoons fresh ground black pepper, divided
1½ teaspoons salt, divided
½ teaspoon Splenda
Directions:
Heat the grill over medium-high heat.
Cut the duck skin in a cross shape with a sharp knife, being careful not to cut the meat.
Sprinkle 1 teaspoon of thyme, 1 teaspoon of pepper, and 1 teaspoon of salt on both sides. Cover and cool.
In a large bowl, put olive oil, Splenda, 1 teaspoon of thyme, add black pepper and ½ teaspoon of salt and mix with the plums.
Cut the plums one side at a time on the grill and cook until the grill marks appear and the plums begin to soften about 4 minutes. Flip and cook another 4 minutes until tender. Transfer to a bowl and cover with foil.
Heat 2 large saucepans over medium-high heat. Add 2 breasts to a saucepan, skin side down. Cook for about 7 minutes until the skin is crisp and most of the fat is gone.
Turn and cook until desired. Cook the ducks to rare, about 6-8 minutes.
Transfer the duck to a cutting board and let stand for 5 minutes. Cut the duck into thin slices and place them on a plate.
Place 2 plum halves next to the duck. Sprinkle the juice from the bowl over the duck and sprinkle with the added thyme. Serve.
Nutritional Information: Calories 345; Total Carbs 9.1g; Net Carbs 4g; Protein 50.7g; Fat 12g; Sugar 7g; Fiber 1.2g

Roasted Duck Legs with Balsamic Mushrooms

Prep Time: 15 minutes| Cook Time: 1 hour| Servings: 4

Ingredients:
4 bone-in, skin-on duck legs
½ pound (227 g) cremini mushrooms, remove stems and cut caps into thick slices
1 green onion, sliced thin
1 small shallot, sliced thin
3 to 4 fresh thyme sprigs, crushed lightly
5 tablespoons extra-virgin olive oil
5 tablespoons balsamic vinegar
2 cloves garlic, sliced thin
½ teaspoon fresh thyme, chopped
Kosher salt and freshly ground pepper

Directions:
Rinse the duck and dry it with a paper towel.
In a shallow bowl large enough for the ducks, put 3 tablespoons of oil, 3 tablespoons of vinegar, garlic, shallots, thyme sprigs, ½ teaspoon of salt and a little pepper.
Add the ducks and toss to coat. Cover the lid and turn the thighs 1 to 2 times to cool for 3 to 4 hours.
Remove the duck from the marinade. Pour the marinade into a saucepan and bring to a boil over high heat.
Place the rack with the base at the bottom of the pot large enough that your duck feet stand 2 inches off the ground. Add about 1 inch of water. Place the ducks on the grill, skin side down. Cover with a lid and cook over medium-high heat. Steam until the skin is translucent, about 20 minutes.
While the duck cooks, preheat the oven to 450 ºF (235 ºC). Line a skillet large enough to hold the duck in foil. Place the counter flat on the platter.
When the duck is ready, transfer it to a ready-to-use oven, skin side down. Glaze the skin and bake for 20 minutes until the skin is golden and crisp. Take out of the oven and reglaze the duck. Rest for 5 minutes.
Heat the oil in a large saucepan over medium-high heat. Add the mushrooms and green onions and simmer for 2 minutes, stirring frequently.
Add the remaining vinegar, minced thyme, salt and pepper to taste. Cook until mushrooms are tender and most of the liquid has evaporated.
To serve, place the duck legs on a plate and spoon in the mushrooms.
Nutritional Information: Calories 375; Total Carbs 4.1g; Net Carbs 2g; Protein 26.7g; Fat 28.2g; Sugar 1g; Fiber 1g

Broiled Garlicky Chicken

Prep Time: 15 minutes| Cook Time: 30 minutes| Servings: 4

Ingredients:
2 ½ pounds chicken, quartered
6 cloves garlic
¾ teaspoon powdered rosemary
Salt & pepper to taste
Chicken bouillon
Directions:

Rub the chicken with 2 cloves of garlic and rosemary. Also add pepper and salt. Rest the chicken for 30 minutes.
Place the chicken on the grill pan and coat with the bouillon.
Add a little broth to the pan. When half cooked, turn over and cook.
Add the broth and add 2 or more garlic cloves to cover the top. Season with leftover sauce.Serve and enjoy!
Nutritional Information: Calories 324; Total Carbs 7.7g; Net Carbs 4.8g; Protein 27g; Fat 22g; Sugar 6.1g; Fiber 2g

Chicken Casserole

Prep Time: 20 minutes| Cook Time: 20 minutes| Servings: 12

Ingredients:
¼ cup margarine
⅓ cup flour
1 cup turkey
2 cups skim milk
1 ½ teaspoon salt
½ cup blanched almonds, slivered & toasted
1 cup brown rice
2 ½ cups diced, cooked turkey
1 (3 or 4 ounces of) can mushroom, drained
½ cup chopped pimiento
⅓ cup chopped green pepper

Directions:
Melt the margarine in a large saucepan and stir in the flour. Mix the broth and the milk.
Cook over low heat until thickened, stirring constantly.
Combine all the Ingredients except the almonds.
Pour into 9 "x 13" mold.
Garnish with almonds and bake at 350 degrees F uncovered. You can eliminate salt for no-salt, less cholesterol diet.
Serve and enjoy!
Nutritional Information: Calories 324; Total Carbs 19g; Net Carbs 12g; Protein 32g; Fat 21g; Sugar 7g; Fiber 3g

Lemon Pepper Wings

Prep Time: 25 minutes| Cook Time: 35 minutes| Servings: 4

Ingredients:
2 tablespoons grated lemon zest
2 tablespoons freshly squeezed lemon juice
1 tablespoon freshly ground black pepper
Large baking sheet, lined with foil, with a wire rack set on top
2 pounds of free-range chicken wings
1 teaspoon sea salt

Directions:
Preheat the oven to 375 degrees ° F.
Pat the chicken with a paper towel.
Bake in preheated oven for 30 to 35 minutes, flipping halfway when chicken is pierced and juices are translucent.
Meanwhile, in a large bowl, combine the lemon juice, pepper, lemon zest and salt.
Add the wings to the lemon juice. Coat evenly in juices.
Serve hot and enjoy!
Nutritional Information: Calories 286; Total Carbs 2.2g; Net Carbs 1.8g; Protein 27g; Fat 15g; Sugar 2.8g; Fiber 1g

Chicken Stew

Prep Time: 10 minutes| Cook Time: 1 hour 15 minutes | Servings: 4
Ingredients:
4 chicken breasts, stewed
1 (6 ounces of) can mushrooms
½ medium head cabbage, chopped
2 medium onions, chopped
Salt, pepper, and garlic to taste
1 (12 ounces of) tomato juice
Directions:
To cook the chicken, cover with water and pressure for 15 minutes.
Remove the chicken from the water and add the cabbage, mushrooms and onions.
Add pepper, salt and garlic to taste.
Add tomato juice and shredded chicken.
Simmer for about 1 hour. Serve.
Nutritional Information: Calories 284; Total Carbs 18g; Net Carbs 10g; Protein 17g; Fat 4g; Sugar 5g; Fiber 1g

Onion Fried Chicken

Prep Time: 15 minutes| Cook Time: 30 minutes| Servings: 12
Ingredients:
1 broiler (2 ½ to 3 pounds cut up)
1 teaspoon salt
½ teaspoon pepper
2 onions, peeled and sliced
½ cup water
Directions:
Place the chicken in a nonstick skillet.
Sprinkle with salt and pepper and put the onions on top.
Cover with a lid and cook over low heat for 30 minutes.
Tilt the lid so that the liquid evaporates.
Continue cooking for 20 minutes or until tender.
Place the chicken on a plate.
Return the onions, add water and cook until thickened.
Serve warm and enjoy.
Nutritional Information: Calories 280; Total Carbs 13.5g; Net Carbs 13.5g; Protein 25g; Fat 9g; Sugar 1.5g; Fiber 1g

Sweet 'n Sour Chicken

Prep Time: 25 minutes| Cook Time: 30 minutes| Servings: 12
Ingredients:
½ cup chopped green pepper
½ cup chopped carrots
½ cup chopped onion
¾ cup lite ketchup
2 tablespoons Vinegar
2 tablespoons low sodium soy sauce
1 cup pineapple juice
1 teaspoon brown Sugar Twin
½ teaspoon garlic powder
¼ teaspoon freshly ground pepper
Dash ground ginger
1 cup pineapple chunks, drained
Directions:
Heat the margarine in a large saucepan until it melts. Add the green peppers, carrots and onions. Cook for 5 minutes and stir.

Add the ketchup, pineapple juice, vinegar, soy sauce, Sugar twin, garlic powder, black pepper and ginger.
Stir and cook until boiling. Add the pineapple pieces.
Prepare the chicken meat in a 9 "x 13" dish.
Pour the sauce over it. Cover tightly with foil.
Bake at 400 degrees F for 45 minutes.
Open the lid and bake for 30 minutes or until cooked through.
Serve with rice.
Nutritional Information: Calories 298; Total Carbs 48g; Net Carbs 28g; Protein 2g; Fat 15g; Sugar 6g; Fiber 12g

Kung Pao Chicken

Prep Time: 20 minutes| Cook Time: 15 minutes| Servings: 4
Ingredients:
Sauce:
1 tablespoon rice vinegar
1 tablespoon hoisin sauce
1 teaspoon chili sauce
1 tablespoon cornstarch
1 tablespoon tamari or soy sauce
1 tablespoon ketchup
½ cup low-sodium chicken or vegetable broth (chilled in the refrigerator for at least 1 hour)
Chicken:
1 tablespoon dry sherry
1 red bell pepper (seeded and cut into 1-inch chunks)
2 scallions (white part thinly sliced and green part cut into 1-inch lengths)
2 tablespoons roasted cashews
2 boneless chicken breasts (about 1 pound)
ground white pepper
1 tablespoon peanut oil (can use coconut or canola oil)
4 dried red chilies
Directions:
Put the cornstarch and cold broth in a glass jar with a lid. Shake vigorously until the corn is mixed.
Add the ketchup, vinegar, hoisin sauce, tamari or soy sauce and gravy to the jar. Replace the cover. Shake again until well combined.
Cut each chicken breast in half lengthwise, then into ½ inch pieces horizontally. Place the chicken in a bowl and season with white pepper.
Heat a large pot or skillet over medium heat and add the oil.
Season with pepper and sauté for a few minutes, then add the chicken. Sauté for 2-3 minutes or until the chicken is opaque, then add the sherry and mix well.
Shake the sauce bottle and pour it into the pan. Bring everything to a boil, then add the pepper.
Fry another 2 to 3 minutes until the chicken is cooked through and the sauce thickens.
Remove from the heat and stir in the green onions and cashews.
Serve and enjoy.
Nutritional Information: Calories 154; Total Carbs 14.1g; Net Carbs 10g; Protein 31.7g; Fat 8g; Sugar 6g; Fiber 3.9g

Curried Apple Chicken

Prep Time: 15 minutes| Cook Time: 30 minutes| Servings: 4
Ingredients:
1 pound (454 g) chicken breasts, boneless, skinless, cut in 1-inch cubes
2 tart apples, peel and slice
1 sweet onion, cut in ½ and slice
1 jalapeno, seeded and diced
2 tablespoons cilantro, diced
½ teaspoon ginger, grated
14½ ounces (411 g) tomatoes, diced and drained
½ cup water
3 cloves garlic, diced
2 tablespoons sunflower oil
1 teaspoon salt
1 teaspoon coriander
½ teaspoon turmeric
¼ teaspoon cayenne pepper
Directions:
Heat oil in a large skillet over medium-high heat. Add chicken and onion, and cook until onion is tender. Add garlic and cook 1 more minute.
Add apples, water and seasonings and stir to combine. Bring to a boil. Reduce heat and simmer 12 to 15 minutes, or until chicken is cooked through, stirring occasionally.
Stir in tomatoes, jalapeno, and cilantro and serve hot.
Nutritional Information: Calories 372; Total Carbs 23.1g; Net Carbs 18g; Protein 34.2g; Fat 16.0g; Sugar 15g; Fiber 2g

Turkey Stuffed Zucchini

Prep Time: 25 minutes| Cook Time: 15 minutes| Servings: 4
Ingredients:
4 medium zucchini, halved lengthwise
1 pound ground turkey
¼ cup onion, chopped
1 garlic clove, minced
1 tablespoon olive oil
1 small tomato, chopped (½ cup)
1 tablespoon chopped parsley
½ teaspoon salt
¼ teaspoon basil
⅛ teaspoon pepper
½ cup crunchy nut (cereal nuggets or Grape nuts)
1 (8 ounces of) container plain low-fat yogurt
Directions:
Remove the pulp from the zucchini. Cut and set aside.
Inmmerse the zuicchini shells in boiling water to blanch, for 2 minutes.
Remove and place in a shallow bowl.
In a skillet with the margarine, brown the turkey, onion and garlic for 2 minutes.
Add the chopped pulp, parsley, tomatoes, salt, basil and pepper. Cook for 5 minutes or more, or until zucchini is tender.
Add the cereal and ½ cup yogurt. Fill the filling in the zucchini shells with a spoon.
Bake at 350 degrees F for 10-15 minutes or until the skin is soft.
Serve with the rest of the yogurt. If desired, add to sprinkle with chopped parsley.

Nutritional Information: Calories 214; Total Carbs 11g; Net Carbs 6g; Protein 31.7g; Fat 4.6g; Sugar 3.6g; Fiber 2.9g

Turkey Chili

Prep Time: 10 minutes| Cook Time: 45 minutes| Servings: 4
Ingredients:
1 pound (454 g) lean ground turkey
2 carrots, peeled and diced
2 stalks of celery, diced
1 onion, diced
1 zucchini, diced
1 red pepper, diced
1 (14-ounce / 397-g) can tomato sauce
1 can black beans, drained and rinsed
1 can kidney beans, drained and rinsed
3 cups water
3 garlic cloves, diced fine
1 tablespoon chili powder
1 tablespoon olive oil
2 teaspoons salt
1 teaspoon pepper
1 teaspoon cumin
1 teaspoon coriander
1 bay leaf
Directions:
Heat the oil in a heavy-bottomed pan over medium-high heat. Add the turkey and onions and cook, 5 to 10 minutes, until they are no longer pink.
Add the vegetables and cook for 5 minutes, stirring occasionally. Add the garlic and spices and cook, stirring, for 2 minutes.
Add the leftovers and bring them to a boil.
Lower the heat to low and simmer for 30 minutes.
Nutritional Information: Calories 220; Total Carbs 14.1g; Net Carbs 14g; Protein 25.2g; Fat 9g; Sugar 6g; Fiber 4g

Roll from Mexico

Prep Time: 10 minutes| Cook Time: 0 minutes| Servings: 2
Ingredients:
1 teaspoon olive oil
2 large heads 2 romaine lettuce leaves, large ribs removed
2 (8 inches) whole wheat 96% fat-free heart-healthy tortillas, such as Mission brand
8 ounces extra-lean ground beef (95% lean)
⅓ cup chopped tomato (1 small)
⅓ cup chopped red sweet pepper
1 tablespoon red wine vinegar
1 teaspoon ground cumin
Directions:
In a skillet, cook ground beef over medium-high heat until golden brown, using a spoon to break up meat as it cooks.
Drain off the fat. Stir the vinegar, tomato, cumin, sweet pepper, and oil into the meat in the skillet.
Place a turbot leaf on each tortilla.
Spoon ½ of the cooked ground meat mixture onto each lettuce leaf. Completely roll up each filled tortilla.
If desired, secure roll-ups with skewers.
Nutritional Information: Calories 296; Total Carbs 28g; Net Carbs 18g; Protein 28g; Fat 9g; Sugar g; Fiber 4g

Hungarian Pork Goulash

Prep Time: 35 minutes| Cook Time: 3 hours | Servings: 6

Ingredients:
2 stalks celery, thinly sliced (1 cup)
2 medium carrots, thinly sliced (1 cup)
2 medium parsnips, halved lengthwise if large & thinly sliced (1 cup)
1 large onion, chopped (1 cup)
1 (14.5 ounces) can no-salt-added diced tomatoes, undrained
½ cup water
4 ounces dried wide whole-grain noodles (2 cups dried)
6 tablespoons light sour cream
1 pinch of Paprika
1 ½ to 2-pound pork sirloin roast
1 tablespoon Hungarian paprika or Spanish paprika
1 teaspoon caraway seeds, crushed
½ teaspoon garlic powder
½ teaspoon black pepper
¼ teaspoon salt
1 tablespoon canola oil

Directions:
Trim the fat from the roast. Cut roast into 2-inch (5cm) cubes.
In a bowl, combine cumin seeds, paprika, garlic powder, pepper, and salt. Add pork cubes and toss to coat.
In another skillet, cook pork, ½ at a time, in hot oil over medium heat until golden brown, turning occasionally.
Transfer pork to a saucepan over low heat. Add onion, parsnips, carrots, celery, and tomatoes. Pour the total water into the pot.
Cover and cook on low heat for about 5-6 hours or for 2-3 hours.
Stir the noodles into the pork mixture in the pot. Cover and cook over high heat until noodles are tender for about 30 minutes, stirring once halfway through cooking.
Add 1 tablespoon sour cream to each serving. If desired, sprinkle each serving with paprika. Serve

Nutritional Information: Calories 224; Total Carbs 23g; Net Carbs 20g; Protein 27g; Fat 7.6g; Sugar 6g; Fiber 5.3g

Sweet & Sour Pork with Cabbage

Prep Time: 35 minutes| Cook Time: 20 minutes| Servings: 4

Ingredients:
2 teaspoons rice vinegar
4 teaspoons canola oil
1 medium green sweet pepper, seeded & cut into 1-inch pieces
1 (8 ounces) can bamboo shoots, drained
1 tablespoon packed brown sugar or brown sugar substitute equivalent to 1 tablespoon brown sugar
1 tablespoon cornstarch
12 ounces boneless pork loin, bias-sliced across the grain into strips
4 cups shredded Napa cabbage
1 large red sweet pepper, quartered and seeded
1 teaspoon water
1 (8 ounces) can pineapple chunks (juice pack)
2 tablespoons reduced-sodium soy sauce
2 teaspoons grated fresh ginger
2 cloves garlic

Directions:
Place red sweet pepper quarters, cut sides down, in a microwave-safe dish. Add the water. Cover with plastic wrap—microwave on 100 percent power (high) for 4 to 5 minutes or until tender.
Let stand for about 10 minutes or until the skin easily peels from the flesh; remove and discard skin.
Place red sweet pepper in a food processor—cover & process until smooth.
Drain pineapple chunks, reserving ⅓ cup the juice. Set pineapple chunks aside.
Add the reserved ⅓ cup pineapple juice, cornstarch, ginger, garlic, soy sauce, brown sugar, and rice vinegar to red sweet pepper in a food processor. Cover & process until combined; set aside.
In a skillet, heat 1 teaspoon the oil over medium-high heat.
Add sweet green pepper. Stir-fry for about 2 minutes or until crisp-tender.
Add bamboo shoots—Stir-fry for 30 seconds. Remove vegetables from skillet.
Add the 3 teaspoons oil to the pan with the pork strips and sauté for 2-3 minutes
Next, add the red bell pepper mixture, cook, and stir for about 30 seconds.
Cook and stir for an additional 2 minutes. Add the pineapple chunks and green bell pepper mixture; heat through.
Serve over Napa cabbage and enjoy!

Nutritional Information: Calories 256; Total Carbs 23g; Net Carbs 18g; Protein 21g; Fat 10g; Sugar 11g; Fiber 3.6g

Parmesan Golden Pork Chops

Prep Time: 10 minutes| Cook Time: 25 minutes| Servings: 4

Ingredients:
Nonstick cooking spray
4 bone-in, thin-cut pork chops
2 tablespoons butter
½ cup grated low-fat Parmesan cheese
3 garlic cloves, minced
¼ teaspoon salt
¼ teaspoon dried thyme
Freshly ground black pepper, to taste

Directions:
Preheat the oven to 400ºF (205ºC). Line a baking sheet with parchment paper and spray with nonstick cooking spray.
Arrange the pork chops on the prepared baking sheet so they do not overlap.
In a small bowl, combine the butter, cheese, garlic, salt, thyme, and pepper. Press 2 tablespoons the cheese mixture onto the top of each pork chop.
Bake for 18 to 22 minutes until the pork is cooked through and its juices run clear. Set the broiler to high, then broil for 1 to 2 minutes to brown the tops.

Nutritional Information: Calories 333; Total Carbs 1.1g; Net Carbs 0.9g; Protein 44g; Fat 16.1g; Sugar 0g; Fiber 0g

Asparagus & Beef Rolls

Prep Time: 20 minutes| Cook Time: 20 minutes| Servings: 4

Ingredients:
1 bunch scallions, trimmed & halved crosswise
1 tablespoon canola oil
¼ teaspoon salt
¼ teaspoon freshly ground pepper
1 ¼ pounds of skirt steak, trimmed
2 teaspoons toasted sesame seeds
3 tablespoons hoisin sauce
3 tablespoons water
1 tablespoon tomato paste
1 tablespoon rice vinegar
1 teaspoon toasted sesame oil
½ teaspoon crushed red pepper
1 bunch asparagus (about 1 pound), trimmed

Directions:
Preheat one side of the grill to medium-high. Leave the other side unheated.
Mix the vinegar, hoisin, sesame oil, water, tomato paste, and crushed red pepper in a bowl until smooth.
Spoon 2 tablespoons the mixture into a small bowl. Set the rest aside.
Place the canola oil, scallions, salt, asparagus, and pepper in a large bowl.
Cut the steak in ½ lengthwise, then cut each long strip in ½ crosswise to make 4 2-by-6-inch (15cm) pieces
Brush the top side of the steak pieces with the 2 tablespoons sauce.
Divide the asparagus and scallions among the steak pieces, placing the bundles in the center.
Fold and roll the steak over the top of the bundles
Thread a skewer through the overlapping ends of the steak and hold the rolls together through the bundle.
Place the rolls seam side down on the hot side of the grill for 5-7 minutes. Turn and grill until the second side begins to char, about 5 minutes longer.
Move the rolls to the unheated side, cover, and cook for about 5 more minutes.
Remove from grill. Brush steak with some of the reserved sauce and sprinkle with sesame seeds.
Serve with the remaining sauce for dipping.
Nutritional Information: Calories 220; Total Carbs 11.6g; Net Carbs 8g; Protein 35.2g; Fat 13.8g; Sugar 5g; Fiber 2.5g

Beef Mushroom Stew

Prep Time: 40 minutes| Cook Time: 4 hours| Servings: 8

Ingredients:
2 tablespoons mild-flavored molasses
½ teaspoon salt
½ teaspoon celery salt
¼ teaspoon ground black pepper
¼ a teaspoon ground ginger
12 ounces assorted fresh mushrooms, halved
¼ cup raisins
4 cups hot cooked noodles, rice, or mashed potatoes (Optional)
2 pounds of boneless beef chuck steak, trimmed and cut into 1-inch cubes
3 tablespoons all-purpose flour
2 tablespoons cooking oil
6 medium carrots, cut into ½ -inch-thick slices
2 medium onions, chopped
1 (14.5 ounces) can diced tomatoes, undrained
¼ cup cider vinegar

Directions:
Mix the meat cubes with the flour in a bowl.
Heat oil in an extra-large skillet over medium-high heat. Brown the meat cubes, ½ at a time, in the hot oil.
Place the onions and carrots in a saucepan over low heat. Add the browned meat cubes.
Combine the undrained tomatoes, pepper, celery salt, vinegar, molasses, salt, and ginger in a medium bowl. Pour over the meat.
Cover and cook on low for 8 hours or on high for 4 hours.
Add raisins and mushrooms, cover, and cook for 1 hour more over medium-high heat.
Serve over hot cooked noodles, rice, or mashed potatoes, if desired. Enjoy!
Nutritional Information: Calories 242; Total Carbs 21g; Net Carbs 15g; Protein 28.8g; Fat 8.5g; Sugar 8.9g; Fiber 2.6g

Savory Bread Pudding

Prep Time: 15 minutes| Cook Time: 20 minutes| Servings: 6

Ingredients:
2 cups low-fat (1%) milk
3 large egg whites
1 cup diced onion
9 small links (6 ounces) fully cooked chicken, apple, and maple breakfast sausage, thinly sliced
8 slices of whole wheat or multigrain bread, cut into 1-inch squares
1 tablespoon olive or vegetable oil
1 red bell pepper, diced
½ cup low-fat sharp Cheddar cheese, shredded

Directions:
Preheat the oven to 350 ° F.
Coat a 11 by 7-inch baking dish or shallow pan with nonstick spray.
Heat a large saucepan over medium heat until heated through.
Add the oil, pepper and onion. Stir occasionally, for 6 to 8 minutes or until tender. Remove from the heat and set aside.
Meanwhile, combine the milk and egg whites in a large bowl.
Combine sausage and bread. Mix well.
Add the cooked vegetables. Mix again.
Transfer the mixture to the prepared baking dish and press gently.
Bake for 40 to 45 minutes, or until puffed and centered.
Remove from the oven. Sprinkle cheese over the pudding.
Return to the oven; Bake for about 2 minutes or until the cheese is slightly melted. Cut into 6 equal parts. Help yourself and enjoy!
Nutritional Information: Calories 215; Total Carbs 22g; Net Carbs 14g; Protein 14g; Fat 7g; Sugar 2g; Fiber 3g

Lentil Shepherd's Pie with Lamb

Prep Time: 25 minutes| Cook Time: 3 hours| Servings: 8
Ingredients:
1 can reduced-fat and reduced-sodium condensed tomato soup
1 cup dry brown lentils, rinsed and drained
¼ teaspoon crushed red pepper
2-⅔ cups prepared mashed potatoes
1 sprig Snipped fresh mint
1 pound lean ground lamb or beef
1 large onion, chopped (1 cup)
1 package frozen mixed vegetables
1 can lower-sodium beef broth
1 can no-salt-added diced tomatoes with basil, garlic, and oregano, undrained
Directions:
In a large skillet, cook ground lamb and onion until meat is brown & onion is tender. Drain off fat.
In a 3 ½ or 4-quart slow cooker, combine the meat mixture, frozen vegetables, tomato soup, lentils, broth, tomatoes, and crushed red pepper.
Cover and cook on a low-heat setting for about 6 to 8 hours or on a high-heat setting for about 3 to 4 hours.
Serve meat and lentil mixture over potatoes.
If desired, sprinkle each serving with snipped fresh mint.
Nutritional Information: Calories 317; Total Carbs 43g; Net Carbs 28g; Protein 24g; Fat 6g; Sugar 8g; Fiber 1g

Lamb Tagine from Morocco

Prep Time: 40 minutes| Cook Time: 4 hours| Servings: 6
Ingredients:
2 tablespoons quick-cooking tapioca
2 tablespoons finely shredded lemon peel
½ teaspoon lemon zest
1 tablespoon lemon juice
2 cloves of garlic, minced
1 (14.5 ounces) can reduced-sodium chicken broth
2 cups hot, cooked whole-wheat couscous
¼ cup sliced almonds, toasted
¼ teaspoon ground cinnamon
1-½ pounds of boneless lamb shoulder or lamb stew meat, cut into 1-inch pieces
1-½ cups coarsely chopped, peeled sweet potato
1 medium of plum tomato, chopped
2 medium carrots, cut into 1-inch pieces
1 medium of onion, chopped
½ teaspoon ground ginger
½ teaspoon ground cumin
½ teaspoon salt
¼ teaspoon ground turmeric
¼ cup pitted dates, quartered
¼ cup green olives, halved
Directions:
In a large bowl, combine salt, turmeric, ginger, cumin, and cinnamon.
Add lamb to the bowl. Toss to coat in spices.
In a 3 ½ to a 4-quart slow cooker, place the lamb, sweet potato, tomato, carrots, tapioca, lemon peel, lemon juice, onion, dates, olives, and garlicup.

Pour broth over all.
Cover; cook on low-heat setting for about 8 to 10 hours or on high-heat setting for about 4 to 5 hours.
Serve over couscous and top with almonds.
Nutritional Information: Calories 343; Total Carbs 39.5g; Net Carbs 25g; Protein 28g; Fat 8.5g; Sugar 11g; Fiber 5.8g

Mustard Pork Chops

Prep Time: 5 minutes| Cook Time: 25 minutes| Servings: 4
Ingredients:
¼ cup Dijon mustard
1 tablespoon pure maple syrup
2 tablespoons rice vinegar
4 bone-in, thin-cut pork chops
Directions:
Preheat the oven to 400ºF (205ºC).
In a small saucepan, combine the mustard, maple syrup, and rice vinegar. Stir to mix and bring to a simmer over medium heat. Cook for about 2 minutes until just slightly thickened.
In a baking dish, place the pork chops and spoon the sauce over them, flipping to coat.
Bake, uncovered, for 18 to 22 minutes until the juices run clear.
Nutritional Information: Calories 258; Total Carbs 6.9g; Net Carbs 4g; Protein 39g; Fat 7.1g; Sugar 4g; Fiber 0g

Oven Barbecued Pork Chops

Prep Time: 15 minutes| Cook Time: 20 minutes| Servings: 4
Ingredients:
1 clove garlic, minced
⅓ cup orange juice
½ cup barbecue sauce
1 ½ -1 ¾ pounds of bone-in, ¾-inch-thick pork rib chops, trimmed of fat
¼ teaspoon salt
¼ teaspoon freshly ground pepper
3 teaspoons canola oil, divided
1 medium onion, diced
Directions:
Preheat oven to 425 º F.
Sprinkle pork chops with pepper and salt.
Heat 2 teaspoons oil in an ovenproof skillet over high heat.
Add pork chops and cook until they begin to brown, 1 to 2 minutes per side. Transfer to a plate.
Add 1 teaspoon oil to the skillet. Add onion and cook, stirring, until softened, 3 to 4 minutes.
Add the garlic and cook, stirring, until fragrant, 30 seconds.
Add orange juice and cook until most of the liquid has evaporated, 30 seconds to 1 minute.
Add the barbecue sauce. Return the pork chops to the skillet, turning several times to coat them with the sauce.
Transfer the skillet to the oven and bake until the pork chops are pink in the center, about 8 to 10 minutes.
Serve the sauce over the pork chops and enjoy!
Nutritional Information: Calories 196; Total Carbs 15.1g; Net Carbs 10g; Protein 20g; Fat 9.9g; Sugar 9g; Fiber 0.22g

Lamb and Mushroom Cheese Burgers

Prep Time: 15 minutes| Cook Time: 15 minutes| Servings: 4
Ingredients:
8 ounces (227 g) grass-fed ground lamb
8 ounces (227 g) brown mushrooms, finely chopped
¼ teaspoon salt
¼ teaspoon freshly ground black pepper
¼ cup crumbled goat cheese
1 tablespoon minced fresh basil
Directions:
In a large mixing bowl, combine the lamb, mushrooms, salt, and pepper, and mix well.
In a small bowl, mix the goat cheese and basil.
Form the lamb mixture into 4 patties, reserving about ½ cup the mixture in the bowl. In each patty, make an indentation in the center and fill with 1 tablespoon the goat cheese mixture. Use the reserved meat mixture to close the burgers. Press the meat firmly to hold together.
Heat the barbecue or a large skillet over medium-high heat. Add the burgers and cook for 5 to 7 minutes on each side, until cooked through.
Serve.
Nutritional Information: Calories 172; Total Carbs 2.9g; Net Carbs 1.8g; Protein 11.7g; Fat 13.1g; Sugar 1g; Fiber g

Autumn Pork Chops

Prep Time: 15 minutes| Cook Time: 30 minutes| Servings: 4
Ingredients:
¼ cup apple cider vinegar
2 tablespoons granulated sweetener
4 (4-ounce / 113-g) pork chops, about 1 inch thick
Sea salt and freshly ground black pepper, to taste
1 tablespoon extra-virgin olive oil
½ red cabbage, finely shredded
1 sweet onion, thinly sliced
1 apple, peeled, cored, and sliced
1 teaspoon chopped fresh thyme
Directions:
In a small bowl, whisk together the vinegar and sweetener. Set it aside.
Season the pork with salt and pepper.
Place a large skillet over medium-high heat and add the olive oil.
Cook the pork chops until no longer pink, turning once, about 8 minutes per side.
Transfer the chops to a plate and set aside.
Add the cabbage and onion to the skillet and sauté until the vegetables have softened, about 5 minutes.
Add the vinegar mixture and the apple slices to the skillet and bring the mixture to a boil.
Reduce the heat to low and simmer, covered, for 5 additional minutes.
Return the pork chops to the skillet, along with any accumulated juices and thyme, cover, and cook for 5 more minutes.
Nutritional Information: Calories 224; Total Carbs 12g; Net Carbs 8g; Protein 26g; Fat 8g; Sugar 8g; Fiber 3.1g

Herbed meatballs

Prep Time: 10 minutes| Cook Time: 15 minutes| Servings: 4
Ingredients:
½ pound (227 g) lean ground pork
½ pound (227 g) lean ground beef
1 sweet onion, finely chopped
¼ cup bread crumbs
2 tablespoons chopped fresh basil
2 teaspoons minced garlic
1 egg
Pinch sea salt
Pinch freshly ground black pepper
Directions:
Preheat the oven to 350ºF (180ºC).
Line a baking tray with parchment paper and set it aside.
In a large bowl, mix together the pork, beef, onion, bread crumbs, basil, garlic, egg, salt, and pepper until very well mixed.
Roll the meat mixture into 2-inch meatballs.
Transfer the meatballs to the baking sheet and bake until they are browned and cooked through, about 15 minutes.
Serve the meatballs with your favorite marinara sauce and some steamed green beans.
Nutritional Information: Calories 33; Total Carbs 12g; Net Carbs 12g; Protein 24.7g; Fat 19g; Sugar 2.9g; Fiber 0.9g

Pulled Pork Sandwiches with Apricot Jelly

Prep Time: 5 minutes| Cook Time: 15 minutes| Servings: 4
Ingredients:
Avocado oil cooking spray
8 ounces (227 g) store-bought pulled pork
½ cup chopped green bell pepper
2 slices reduced fat provolone cheese
4 whole-wheat sandwich thins
2½ tablespoons apricot jelly
Directions:
Heat the pulled pork according to the package instructions.
Heat a medium skillet over medium-low heat. When hot, coat the cooking surface with cooking spray.
Put the bell pepper in the skillet and cook for 5 minutes. Transfer to a small bowl and set aside.
Meanwhile, tear each slice of cheese into 2 strips, and halve the sandwich thins so you have a top and bottom.
Reduce the heat to low, and place the sandwich thins in the skillet cut-side down to toast, about 2 minutes.
Remove the sandwich thins from the skillet.
Spread one-quarter of the jelly on the bottom ½ of each sandwich thin, then place one-quarter of the cheese, pulled pork, and pepper on top. Cover with the top ½ of the sandwich thin.
Nutritional Information: Calories 250; Total Carbs 34.1g; Net Carbs 20.8g; Protein 16.1g; Fat 8.1g; Sugar 8g; Fiber 6g

Beef and Mushroom Cauliflower Wraps

Prep Time: 5 minutes| Cook Time: 20 minutes|
Servings: 4
Ingredients:
Avocado oil cooking spray
½ cup chopped white onion
1 cup chopped portobello mushrooms
1 pound (454 g) 93% lean ground beef
½ teaspoon garlic powder
Pinch salt
1 (10-ounce / 283-g) bag frozen cauliflower rice
12 iceberg lettuce leaves
¾ cup shredded low-fat Cheddar cheese
Directions:
Heat a large skillet over medium heat. When
hot, coat the cooking surface with cooking
spray and add the onion and mushrooms. Cook
for 5 minutes, stirring occasionally.
Add the beef, garlic powder, and salt, stirring
and breaking apart the meat as needed. Cook
for 5 minutes.
Stir in the frozen cauliflower rice and increase
the heat to medium-high. Cook for 5 minutes
more, or until the water evaporates.
For each portion, use 3 lettuce leaves. Spoon
one-quarter of the filling onto the lettuce
leaves, and top with one-quarter of the cheese.
Then, working from the side closest to you, roll
up the lettuce to close the wrap. Repeat with
the remaining lettuce leaves and filling.
Nutritional Information: Calories 290; Total
Carbs 7.1g; Net Carbs 6g; Protein 31.1g; Fat
15g; Sugar 4g; Fiber 3.1g

Steak and Broccoli Bowls

Prep Time: 10 minutes| Cook Time: 15
minutes| Servings: 4
Ingredients:
2 tablespoons extra-virgin olive oil
1 pound (454 g) sirloin steak, cut into ¼-inch-
thick strips
2 cups broccoli florets
1 garlic clove, minced
1 teaspoon peeled and grated fresh ginger
2 tablespoons reduced-sodium soy sauce
¼ cup beef broth
½ teaspoon Chinese hot mustard
Pinch red pepper flakes
Directions:
In a large skillet over medium-high heat, heat
the olive oil until it shimmers. Add the beef.
Cook, stirring, until it browns, 3 to 5 minutes.
With a slotted spoon, remove the beef from the
oil and set it aside on a plate.
Add the broccoli to the oil. Cook, stirring, until it
is crisp-tender, about 4 minutes.
Add the garlic and ginger and cook, stirring
constantly, for 30 seconds.
Return the beef to the pan, along with any
juices that have collected.
In a small bowl, whisk together the soy sauce,
broth, mustard, and red pepper flakes.
Add the soy sauce mixture to the skillet and
cook, stirring, until everything warms through,
about 3 minutes.
Nutritional Information: Calories 230; Total
Carbs 4.9g; Net Carbs 4g; Protein 27g; Fat
11g; Sugar 3g; Fiber 1g

Chipotle Chili Pork

Prep Time: 4 hours 20 minutes| Cook Time: 20
minutes| Servings: 4
Ingredients:
4 (5-ounce / 142-g) pork chops, about 1 inch
thick
1 tablespoon chipotle chili powder
Juice and zest of 1 lime
2 teaspoons minced garlic
1 teaspoon ground cinnamon
1 tablespoon extra-virgin olive oil
Pinch sea salt
Lime wedges, for garnish
Directions:
Combine all the Ingredients, except for the
lemon wedges, in a large bowl. Toss to combine
well.
Wrap the bowl in plastic and refrigerate to
marinate for at least 4 hours.
Preheat the oven to 400ºF (205ºC). Set a rack
on a baking sheet.
Remove the bowl from the refrigerator and let
sit for 15 minutes. Discard the marinade and
place the pork on the rack.
Roast in the preheated oven for 20 minutes or
until well browned. Flip the pork halfway
through the cooking time.
Serve immediately with lime wedges.
Nutritional Information: Calories 204; Total
Carbs 1g; Net Carbs 0g; Protein 30g; Fat 9g;
Sugar 1g; Fiber g

Lamb Kofta with Cucumber Salad

Prep Time: 10 minutes| Cook Time: 15
minutes| Servings: 4
Ingredients:
¼ cup red wine vinegar
Pinch red pepper flakes
1 teaspoon sea salt, divided
2 cucumbers, peeled and chopped
½ red onion, finely chopped
1 pound (454 g) ground lamb
2 teaspoons ground coriander
1 teaspoon ground cumin
3 garlic cloves, minced
1 tablespoon fresh mint, chopped
Directions:
Preheat the oven to 375ºF (190ºC). Line a
rimmed baking sheet with parchment paper.
In a medium bowl, whisk together the vinegar,
red pepper flakes, and ½ teaspoon salt. Add the
cucumbers and onion and toss to combine. Set
aside.
In a large bowl, mix the lamb, coriander,
cumin, garlic, mint, and remaining ½ teaspoon
salt. Form the mixture into 1-inch meatballs
and place them on the prepared
baking sheet.
Bake until the lamb reaches 140ºF (60ºC)
internally, about 15 minutes.
Serve with the salad on the side.
Nutritional Information: Calories 346; Total
Carbs 6g; Net Carbs 3g; Protein 20g; Fat 27g;
Sugar 5g; Fiber 1.1g

Steak Sandwich

Prep Time: 10 minutes| Cook Time: 10 minutes| Servings: 4

Ingredients:
2 tablespoons balsamic vinegar
2 teaspoons freshly squeezed lemon juice
1 teaspoon fresh parsley, chopped
2 teaspoons fresh oregano, chopped
2 teaspoons garlic, minced
2 tablespoons olive oil
1 pound (454 g) flank steak, trimmed of fat
4 whole-wheat pitas
1 tomato, chopped
1 ounce (28 g) low-sodium feta cheese
2 cups lettuce, shredded
1 red onion, thinly sliced

Directions:
Combine the balsamic vinegar, lemon juice, parsley, oregano, garlic, and olive oil in a bowl. Dunk the steak in the bowl to coat well, then wrap the bowl in plastic and refrigerate for at least 1 hour.
Preheat the oven to 450ºF (235ºC).
Remove the bowl from the refrigerator. Discard the marinade and arrange the steak on a baking sheet lined with aluminum foil.
Broil in the preheated oven for 10 minutes for medium. Flip the steak halfway through the cooking time.
Remove the steak from the oven and allow to cool for 10 minutes. Slice the steak into strips. Assemble the pitas with steak, tomato, feta cheese, lettuce, and onion to make the sandwich, and serve warm.
Nutritional Information: Calories 345; Total Carbs 21g; Net Carbs 18g; Protein 28g; Fat 15g; Sugar 2g; Fiber 3g

Pork Carnitas

Prep Time: 15 minutes| Cook Time: 4 hours | Servings: 6

Ingredients:
2 teaspoons finely shredded lime peel
2 tablespoons lime juice
12 (16 inches) crisp corn tortillas
2 scallions, thinly sliced
⅓ cup light dairy sour cream (Optional)
⅓ cup purchased salsa (Optional)
1 (2 pounds) boneless pork shoulder roast, cut into 2-inch pieces
¼ teaspoon salt
¼ teaspoon ground pepper
1 tablespoon whole black peppercorns
2 teaspoons cumin seeds
4 cloves garlic, minced
1 teaspoon dried oregano, crushed
3 bay leaves
2 (14 ounces) cans of reduced-sodium chicken broth

Directions:
Sprinkle pork with salt & pepper—place in a 3 ½ - or 4-quart slow cooker.
To make a bouquet garni, cut a 6-inch square from a double thickness of cheesecloth.
Place the garlic, peppercorns, cumin seeds, oregano, and bay leaves in the center of the cheesecloth square.

Pull up the corners of the cheesecloth and tie it with kitchen twine. Add to the pot over low heat. Add the broth.
Cover and cook on low for 10-12 hours or on High for 4-5 hours.
Remove meat from the pot.
Discard the bouquet and cooking liquid.
Using 2 forks, coarsely shred the meat. Discard fat.
Sprinkle meat with lime juice and lime zest. Toss to mix.
Serve over tortillas. Top with scallions and, if not cooked, sour cream and salsa. Enjoy!
Nutritional Information: Calories 318; Total Carbs 24g; Net Carbs 15g; Protein 32g; Fat 10g; Sugar 1g; Fiber 4g

Ritzy Beef Stew

Prep Time: 20 minutes| Cook Time: 2 hours| Servings: 6

Ingredients:
2 tablespoons all-purpose flour
1 tablespoon Italian seasoning
2 pounds (907 g) top round, cut into ¾-inch cubes
2 tablespoons olive oil
4 cups low-sodium chicken broth, divided
1½ pounds (680 g) cremini mushrooms, rinsed, stems removed, and quartered
1 large onion, coarsely chopped
3 cloves garlic, minced
3 medium carrots, peeled and cut into ½-inch pieces
1 cup frozen peas
1 tablespoon fresh thyme, minced
1 tablespoon red wine vinegar
½ teaspoon freshly ground black pepper

Directions:
Combine the flour and Italian seasoning in a large bowl. Dredge the beef cubes in the bowl to coat well.
Heat the olive oil in a pot over medium heat until shimmering.
Add the beef to the single layer in the pot and cook for 2 to 4 minutes or until golden brown on all sides. Flip the beef cubes frequently.
Remove the beef from the pot and set aside, then add ¼ cup chicken broth to the pot.
Add the mushrooms and sauté for 4 minutes or until soft. Remove the mushrooms from the pot and set aside.
Pour ¼ cup chicken broth in the pot. Add the onions and garlic to the pot and sauté for 4 minutes or until translucent.
Put the beef back to the pot and pour in the remaining broth. Bring to a boil.
Reduce the heat to low and cover. Simmer for 45 minutes. Stir periodically.
Add the carrots, mushroom, peas, and thyme to the pot and simmer for 45 more minutes or until the vegetables are soft.
OPEN THE LID, DRIZZLE WITH RED WINE VINEGAR AND SEASON WITH BLACK PEPPER. STIR AND SERVE IN A LARGE BOWL.
Nutritional Information: Calories 250; Total Carbs 24g; Net Carbs 18g; Protein 25g; Fat 7g; Sugar 5g; Fiber 3g

Alfredo Sausage and Vegetables

Prep Time: 10 minutes| Cook Time: 15 minutes| Servings: 6
Ingredients:
1 package smoked sausage, cut in ¼-inch slices
1 cup half-and-½
½ cup zucchini, cut in matchsticks
½ cup carrots, cut in matchsticks
½ cup red bell pepper, cut in matchsticks
½ cup peas, frozen
¼ cup plant-based butterplant-based butter
¼ cup onion, diced
2 tablespoons fresh parsley, diced
1 cup whole-wheat pasta, cooked and drained
⅓ cup reduced fat Parmesan cheese
1 clove garlic, diced fine
Salt and ground black pepper, to taste
Directions:
Melt plant-based butterbutter in a large skillet over medium heat. Add onion and garlic and cook, stirring occasionally, 3 to 4 minutes or until onion is soft.
Increase heat to medium-high. Add sausage, zucchini, carrots, and red pepper. Cook, stirring frequently, 5 to 6 minutes, or until carrots are tender crisp.
Stir in peas and half-and-half, cook for 1 to 2 minutes until heated through. Stir in cheese, parsley, salt, and pepper. Add pasta and toss to mix. Serve.
Nutritional Information: Calories 285; Total Carbs 18g; Net Carbs 12g; Protein 21g; Fat 15g; Sugar 8g; Fiber 4g

Tuscan Pork Loin

Prep Time: 5 minutes| Cook Time: 1 hour| Servings: 6
Ingredients:
2 tablespoons chopped fresh rosemary
1 tablespoon freshly grated lemon zest
¾ cup dry vermouth or white wine
2 tablespoons white wine vinegar
1 3-pound pork loin, trimmed
1 teaspoon kosher salt
3 cloves garlic, crushed and peeled
2 tablespoons extra-virgin olive oil
Directions:
Tie kitchen string around pork in 3 places so it doesn't flatten while roasting.
Place salt & garlic in a small bowl & mash with the back of a spoon to form a paste.
Stir in oil, rosemary & lemon zest. Rub the mixture into the pork. Refrigerate, uncovered, for about an hour.
Preheat oven to 375 degrees F.
Place pork in a roasting pan. Roast, turning from time to time, 40 to 50 minutes.
Transfer to a cutting board. Let rest for about 10 mins.
Meanwhile, add vermouth (or wine) and vinegar to the roasting pan and place over medium-high heat.
Bring to a simmer and cook, scraping up any browned bits, until the sauce is reduced by half, 2 to 4 minutes.
Remove the string and slice the roast.
Add any accumulated juices to the sauce and serve with the pork.

Nutritional Information: Calories 182; Total Carbs 0.6g; Net Carbs 0g; Protein 20.7g; Fat 8.3g; Sugar 1.4g; Fiber 0.1g

Sloppy Joes

Prep Time: 10 minutes| Cook Time: 15 minutes| Servings: 4
Ingredients:
1 tablespoon extra-virgin olive oil
1 pound (454 g) 93% lean ground beef
1 medium red bell pepper, chopped
½ medium yellow onion, chopped
2 tablespoons low-sodium Worcestershire sauce
1 (15-ounce / 425-g) can low-sodium tomato sauce
2 tablespoons low-sodium, sugar-free ketchup
4 whole-wheat sandwich thins, cut in ½
1 cup cabbage, shredded
Directions:
Heat the olive oil in a nonstick skillet over medium heat until shimmering.
Add the beef, bell pepper, and onion to the skillet and sauté for 8 minutes or until the beef is browned and the onion is translucent.
Pour the Worcestershire sauce, tomato sauce, and ketchup in the skillet. Turn up the heat to medium-high and simmer for 5 minutes.
Assemble the sandwich thin halves with beef mixture and cabbage to make the sloppy Joes, then serve warm.
Nutritional Information: Calories 329; Total Carbs 35g; Net Carbs 20g; Protein 31.7g; Fat 8.9g; Sugar 10g; Fiber 7g

Coffeed and Herbed Steak

Prep Time: 10 minutes| Cook Time: 10 minutes| Servings: 4
Ingredients:
¼ cup whole coffee beans
2 teaspoons fresh rosemary, chopped
2 teaspoons fresh thyme, chopped
2 teaspoons garlic, minced
1 teaspoon freshly ground black pepper
2 tablespoons apple cider vinegar
2 tablespoons olive oil
1 pound (454 g) flank steak, trimmed of fat
Directions:
Put the coffee beans, rosemary, thyme, garlic, and black pepper in a food processor. Pulse until well ground and combined.
Pour the mixture in a large bowl, then pour the vinegar and olive oil in the bowl. Stir to mix well.
Dunk the steak in the mixture, then wrap the bowl in plastic and refrigerate to marinate for 2 hours.
Preheat the broiler to MEDIUM.
Remove the bowl from the refrigerator, and discard the marinade.
Place the marinated steak on a baking sheet lined with aluminum foil.
Broil in the preheated broiler for 10 minutes or until the steak reaches your desired doneness. Flip the steak halfway through the cooking time.
Remove the steak from the broiler. Allow to cool for a few minutes and slice to serve.
Nutritional Information: Calories 316; Total Carbs 0g; Net Carbs 0g; Protein 31g; Fat 19g; Sugar 0g; Fiber 0g

Mushroom, Beef, and Cauliflower Rice in Lettuce

Prep Time: 5 minutes| Cook Time: 20 minutes| Servings: 4
Ingredients:
1 tablespoon avocado oil
1 cup portobello mushrooms, chopped
½ cup white onion, chopped
1 pound (454 g) 93% lean ground beef
½ teaspoon garlic powder
Salt, to taste
1 (10-ounce / 284-g) bag frozen cauliflower rice
¾ cup Cheddar cheese, shredded
12 iceberg lettuce leaves
Directions:
Heath the avocado oil in a nonstick skillet over medium heat.
Add the mushrooms and onion to the skillet and sauté for 5 minutes until the mushrooms are soft and the onion starts to become translucent.
Add the beef, garlic powder, and salt to the skillet and sauté for another 5 minutes to brown the beef.
Increase the heat to medium-high, then add the cauliflower rice and sauté for an additional 5 minutes.
Divide the mixture and cheese on all lettuce leaves with a spoon, then roll up the lettuce to seal the wrap and serve warm.
Nutritional Information: Calories 289; Total Carbs 6.9g; Net Carbs 3g; Protein 31g; Fat 14g; Sugar 3.8g; Fiber 3.1g

Cauliflower and Beef Fajita

Prep Time: 10 minutes| Cook Time: 15 minutes| Servings: 4
Ingredients:
4 tablespoons extra-virgin olive oil, divided
1 head cauliflower, riced
1 pound (454 g) sirloin steak, cut into ¼-inch-thick strips
1 red bell pepper, seeded and sliced
1 onion, thinly sliced
2 garlic cloves, minced
Juice of 2 limes
1 teaspoon chili powder
Directions:
In a large skillet over medium-high heat, heat 2 tablespoons olive oil until it shimmers. Add the cauliflower. Cook, stirring occasionally, until it softens, about 3 minutes. Set aside.
Wipe out the skillet with a paper towel. Add the remaining 2 tablespoons oil to the skillet, and heat it on medium-high until it shimmers. Add the steak and cook, stirring occasionally, until it browns, about 3 minutes. Use a slotted spoon to remove the steak from the oil in the pan and set aside.
Add the bell pepper and onion to the pan. Cook, stirring occasionally, until they start to brown, about 5 minutes.
Add the garlic and cook, stirring constantly, for 30 seconds.
Return the beef along with any juices that have collected and the cauliflower to the pan. Add the lime juice and chili powder. Cook, stirring, until everything is warmed through, 2 to 3 minutes.

Nutritional Information: Calories 311; Total Carbs 13.1g; Net Carbs 8g; Protein 27g; Fat 18g; Sugar 10g; Fiber 2.9g

Pork Diane

Prep Time: 10 minutes| Cook Time: 20 minutes| Servings: 4
Ingredients:
2 teaspoons Worcestershire sauce
1 tablespoon freshly squeezed lemon juice
¼ cup low-sodium chicken broth
2 teaspoons Dijon mustard
4 (5-ounce / 142-g) boneless pork top loin chops, about 1 inch thick
Sea salt and freshly ground black pepper, to taste
1 teaspoon extra-virgin olive oil
2 teaspoons chopped fresh chives
1 teaspoon lemon zest
Directions:
Combine the Worcestershire sauce, lemon juice, broth, and Dijon mustard in a bowl. Stir to mix well.
On a clean work surface, rub the pork chops with salt and ground black pepper.
Heat the olive oil in a nonstick skillet over medium-high heat until shimmering.
Add the pork chops and sear for 16 minutes or until well browned. Flip the pork halfway through the cooking time. Transfer to a plate and set aside.
Pour the sauce mixture in the skillet and cook for 2 minutes or until warmed through and lightly thickened. Mix in the chives and lemon zest.
Baste the pork with the sauce mixture and serve immediately.
Nutritional Information: Calories 200; Total Carbs 1g; Net Carbs 0.5g; Protein 30g; Fat 8g; Sugar 1g; Fiber 0g

Beef Tortillas

Prep Time: 15 minutes| Cook Time: 0 minutes| Servings: 6
Ingredients:
6 whole wheat flour tortillas (10-inch)
6 large romaine lettuce leaves
12 ounces (340 g) cooked deli roast beef, thinly sliced
1 cup diced red bell peppers
1 cup diced tomatoes
1 tablespoon vinegar
1 teaspoon cumin
¼ teaspoon freshly ground black pepper
1 tablespoon olive oil
Directions:
Unfold the tortillas on a clean work surface, then top each tortilla with a lettuce leaf. Divide the roast beef over the leaf.
Combine the remaining Ingredients in a bowl. Stir to mix well. Pour the mixture over the beef. Fold the tortillas over the fillings, then roll them up. Serve immediately.
Nutritional Information: Calories 295; Total Carbs 43g; Net Carbs 25g; Protein 19g; Fat 6g; Sugar 3g; Fiber 6g

Sumptuous Lamb and Pomegranate Salad

Prep Time: 8 hours 35 minutes| Cook Time: 30 minutes| Servings: 8

Ingredients:

1½ cups pomegranate juice
4 tablespoons olive oil, divided
1 tablespoon ground cinnamon
1 teaspoon cumin
1 tablespoon ground ginger
3 cloves garlic, chopped
Salt and freshly ground black pepper, to taste
1 (4-pound / 1.8-kg) lamb leg, deboned, butterflied, and fat trimmed
2 tablespoons pomegranate balsamic vinegar
2 teaspoons Dijon mustard
½ cup pomegranate seeds
5 cups baby kale
4 cups fresh green beans, blanched
¼ cup toasted walnut halves
2 fennel bulbs, thinly sliced
2 tablespoons Gorgonzola cheese

Directions:

Mix the pomegranate juice, 1 tablespoon olive oil, cinnamon, cumin, ginger, garlic, salt, and black pepper in a large bowl. Stir to mix well.
Dunk the lamb leg in the mixture, press to coat well. Wrap the bowl in plastic and refrigerate to marinate for at least 8 hours.
Remove the bowl from the refrigerate and let sit for 20 minutes. Pat the lamb dry with paper towels.
Preheat the grill to high heat.
Brush the grill grates with 1 tablespoon olive oil, then arrange the lamb on the grill grates. Grill for 30 minutes or until the internal temperature of the lamb reaches at least 145°F (63°C). Flip the lamb halfway through the cooking time.
Remove the lamb from the grill and wrap with aluminum foil. Let stand for 15 minutes.
Meanwhile, combine the vinegar, mustard, salt, black pepper, and remaining olive oil in a separate large bowl. Stir to mix well.
Add the remaining Ingredients and lamb leg to the bowl and toss to combine well. Serve immediately.

Nutritional Information: Calories 380; Total Carbs 16g; Net Carbs 8g; Protein 32g; Fat 21g; Sugar 6g; Fiber 5g

Beef and Sweet Potato Stew

Prep Time: 20 minutes| Cook Time: 1 hour 40 minutes| Servings: 8

Ingredients:

2 tablespoons olive oil
1½ pounds (680 g) lean beef stew meat
2 carrots, cut ½ inch thick slices
2 celery stalks, diced
1 onion, diced
2½ cup low-sodium beef broth
½ cup prunes, diced
1 cup hot water
2 (6-ounce / 170-g) sweet potatoes, peeled and diced into 1-inch chunks
1½ teaspoon ground cinnamon
1 teaspoon salt
1 teaspoon black pepper
¼ teaspoon parsley, chopped

Directions:

Heat the olive oil in a stockpot over high heat. Arrange the beef in a single layer in the pot and cook for 12 minutes or until browned on all sides. You may need to work in batches to avoid overcrowding. Transfer the beef to a plate and set aside.
Add carrots, celery, and onions to the pot and sauté for 5 minutes or until the onions are translucent.
Pour the beef broth over, then put the beef back to the pot. Simmer for 1 hour.
Meanwhile, soak the prunes in hot water for 20 minutes, then pat dry with paper towels. Reserve ½ cup the prune water.
Add the prunes, prune water, sweet potatoes, cinnamon, salt, and black pepper to the pot. Cover and simmer for 20 minutes until potatoes are soft.
Spoon the stew in a large bowl, then serve with chopped parsley on top.

Nutritional Information: Calories 196; Total Carbs 17g; Net Carbs 12g; Protein 19g; Fat 4g; Sugar 7g; Fiber 3g

Pork Souvlakia with Tzatziki Sauce

Prep Time: 20 minutes| Cook Time: 12 minutes| Servings: 4

Ingredients:

¼ cup lemon juice
1 tablespoon dried oregano
¼ teaspoon salt
¼ teaspoon ground black pepper
1 pound (454 g) pork tenderloin, cut into 1-inch cubes
1 tablespoon olive oil
Tzatziki Sauce:
½ cup plain Greek yogurt
1 large cucumber, peeled, deseeded and grated
1 tablespoon fresh lemon juice
4 cloves garlic, minced or grated
¼ teaspoon ground black pepper
8 bamboo skewers, soaked in water for at least 30 minutes

Directions:

Combine the lemon juice, oregano, salt, and ground black pepper in a large bowl. Stir to mix well.
Dunk the pork cubes in the bowl of mixture, then toss to coat well. Wrap the bowl in plastic and refrigerate to marinate for 10 minutes or overnight.
Preheat the oven to 450°F (235°C) or broil. Grease a baking sheet with the olive oil.
Remove the bowl from the refrigerator. Run the bamboo skewers through the pork cubes. Set the skewers on the baking sheet, then brush with marinade.
Broil the skewers in the preheated oven for 12 minutes or until well browned. Flip skewers at least 3 times during the broiling.
Meanwhile, combine the Ingredients for the tzatziki sauce in a small bowl.
Remove the skewers from the oven and baste with the tzatziki sauce and serve immediately.

Nutritional Information: Calories 260; Total Carbs 21g; Net Carbs 15g; Protein 28g; Fat 7g; Sugar 3g; Fiber 3g

Slow Cooked Roast

Prep Time: 15 minutes| Cook Time: 4 hours| Servings: 4

Ingredients:
1 tablespoon olive oil
2 medium celery stalks, halved lengthwise and cut into 3-inch pieces
4 medium carrots, scrubbed, halved lengthwise, and cut into 3-inch pieces
1 medium onion, cut in 8hs
1¼ pounds (567 g) lean chuck roast, boneless, trimmed of fat
2 teaspoons Worcestershire sauce
1 tablespoon balsamic vinegar
2 tablespoons water
1 tablespoon onion soup mix
½ teaspoon ground black pepper

Directions:
Grease a slow cooker with olive oil.
Put the celery, carrots, and onion in the slow cooker, then add the beef.
Top them with Worcestershire sauce, balsamic vinegar, and water, then sprinkle with onion soup mix and black pepper.
Cover and cook on high for 4 hours.
Allow to cool for 20 minutes, then serve them on a large plate.
Nutritional Information: Calories 250; Total Carbs 15g; Net Carbs 10g; Protein 33g; Fat 6g; Sugar 6g; Fiber 3g

Lime Lamb Cutlets

Prep Time: 4 hours 20 minutes| Cook Time: 8 minutes| Servings: 4

Ingredients:
¼ cup freshly squeezed lime juice
2 tablespoons lime zest
2 tablespoons chopped fresh parsley
Sea salt and freshly ground black pepper, to taste
1 tablespoon extra-virgin olive oil
12 lamb cutlets (about 1½ pounds / 680 g in total)

Directions:
Combine the lime juice and zest, parsley, salt, black pepper, and olive oil in a large bowl. Stir to mix well.
Dunk the lamb cutlets in the bowl of the lime mixture, then toss to coat well. Wrap the bowl in plastic and refrigerate to marinate for at least 4 hours.
Preheat the oven to 450ºF (235ºC) or broil. Line a baking sheet with aluminum foil.
Remove the bowl from the refrigerator and let sit for 10 minutes, then discard the marinade.
Arrange the lamb cutlets on the baking sheet.
Broil the lamb in the preheated oven for 8 minutes or until it reaches your desired doneness. Flip the cutlets with tongs to make sure they are cooked evenly.
Serve immediately.
Nutritional Information: Calories 297; Total Carbs 1g; Net Carbs 0.2g; Protein31; Fat 18g; Sugar 0g; Fiber 0g

Grilled Lamb Racks

Prep Time: 15 minutes| Cook Time: 20 minutes| Servings: 4

Ingredients:
1 tablespoon olive oil, plus more for brushing the grill grates
1 tablespoon garlic, minced
½ teaspoon salt
Freshly ground black pepper, to taste
2 (1-inch) sprig fresh rosemary
2 (1½-pounds / 680-g) French lamb racks, trimmed of fat, cut into 4 pieces with 2 bones, and leave one bone with an equal amount of meat

Directions:
Combine all the Ingredients in a large bowl. Toss to coat the lamb racks well.
Wrap the bowl in plastic and refrigerate to marinate for at least 2 hours.
Preheat the grill over medium heat. Brush the grill grates with olive oil.
Remove the bowl from the refrigerator, and arrange the lamb racks on the grill grates, bone side down.
Grill for 3 minutes until lightly browned, then flip the lamb racks, and cover and grill for 15 minutes or until it reaches your desired doneness.
Remove the lamb racks from the grill grates and serve hot.
Nutritional Information: Calories 192; Total Carbs 1g; Net Carbs 0.2g; Protein 22g; Fat 9g; Sugar 0g; Fiber 0g

Garlic Parmesan Topping on Baked Salmon

Prep time: 04 minutes, Cook time: 18 minutes, Serves: 4
Ingredients:
1 lb. wild caught salmon filets
2 tbsp. plant-based butter
What you'll need from store cupboard:
¼ cup reduced fat parmesan cheese, grated
¼ cup light mayonnaise
2-3 cloves garlic, diced
2 tbsp. parsley
Salt and pepper
Directions:
Preheat the oven to 350 degrees Fahrenheit, and use a piece of parchment paper, line the baking tray.
Season the salmon with salt and pepper and place it on the pan.
In a medium skillet, warm the butter over medium heat for 1 minute, stirring constantly. Reduce to a low heat setting and add the other Ingredients. Stir until all of the Ingredients are melted and mixed.
Spread equally over the salmon and bake for 15 minutes if the fish is thawed or 20 minutes if it is frozen. When a fork easily flakes the salmon, it's done.
Serve.
Nutritional Information: Calories 408; Total Carbs 4g; Net Carbs 3g; Protein 41.0g; Fat 24.0g; Sugar 1g; Fiber 0 g

Green Beans and Crispy Baked Flounder

Prep time: 10 minutes, Cook time: 20 minutes, serves 4
Ingredients:
1 lb. flounder
2 cups green beans
4 tbsp. plant-based butter
8 basil leaves
What you'll need from store cupboard:
1 ¾ oz. pork rinds
½ cup reduced fat parmesan cheese
3 cloves garlic
Salt and pepper to taste
Nonstick cooking spray
Directions:
Preheat the oven to 350 degrees Fahrenheit. Using cooking spray, coat a baking dish.
Green beans should be steamed until almost soft, around 15 minutes (less if using frozen or canned beans). Place the green beans in the dish that has been prepared.
Season the fish fillets with salt and pepper and serve over the green beans.
In a food processor, pulse the garlic, basil, pork rinds, and parmesan cheese until the mixture resembles crumbs. Sprinkle on top of the fish. Place the butter on top, cut into small pieces.
Bake for 15-20 minutes, or until the fish readily flakes with a fork.
Serve.
Nutritional Information: Calories 358; Total Carbs 5g; Net Carbs 2g; Protein 39.0g; Fat 8.0g; Sugar 1g; Fiber 2 g

Cakes of Crab

Prep time: 10 minutes, Cook time: 10 minutes, Serves: 8 (2 crab cakes per serving)
Ingredients:
1 lb. lump blue crabmeat
1 tbsp. red bell pepper, diced fine
1 tbsp. green bell pepper, diced fine
1 tbsp. fresh parsley, chopped fine
2 eggs
¼ tsp. fresh lemon juice
What you'll need from store cupboard:
¼ cup + 1 tbsp. lite mayonnaise
¼ cup Dijon mustard
2 tbsp. sunflower oil
1 tbsp. baking powder
1 tbsp. Worcestershire sauce
1 ½ tsp. Old Bay
Directions:
¼ cup mayonnaise, Dijon mustard, Worcestershire sauce, and lemon juice, whisked together in a small bowl Refrigerate until ready to serve.
Mix crab, bell peppers, parsley, eggs, 1 tablespoon mayonnaise, baking powder, and Old Bay flavour in a large mixing basin until everything is well blended.
In a large skillet, heat the oil over medium-high heat. Drop 2 teaspoons crab mixture into heated skillet once oil is hot. They'll be a little loose at first, but they'll stick together as the egg cooks.
Cook for 2 minutes, or until firm, then flip and cook for an additional minute. Place on a serving dish. With a mustard dipping sauce on the side.
Nutritional Information: Calories 96; Total Carbs 3g; Net Carbs 2g; Protein 12.0g; Fat 4.0g; Sugar 1g; Fiber 0 g

Catfish in the Cajun style

Prep time: 5 minutes, Cook time: 15 minutes, Serves: 4
Ingredients:
4 (8 oz.) catfish fillets
What you'll need from store cupboard:
2 tbsp. olive oil
2 tsp. garlic salt
2 tsp. thyme
2 tsp. paprika
½ tsp. cayenne pepper
½ tsp. red hot sauce
¼ tsp. black pepper
Nonstick cooking spray
Directions:
Preheat the oven to 450 degrees Fahrenheit. Using cooking spray, coat a 9x13-inch baking dish.
Everything except the catfish goes into a small bowl and is whisked together. Brush both sides of the fillets with the spice mixture.
Bake for 10-13 minutes, or until the fish easily flakes with a fork.
Serve.
Nutritional Information: Calories 366; Total Carbs 0g; Net Carbs 0g; Protein 35.0g; Fat 24.0g; Sugar 0g; Fiber 0g

Tomatoes & Cajun Flounder

Prep time: 10 minutes, Cook time: 15 minutes, Serves: 4
Ingredients:
4 flounder fillets
2 ½ cups tomatoes, diced
¾ cup onion, diced
¾ cup green bell pepper, diced
What you'll need from store cupboard:
2 cloves garlic, diced fine
1 tbsp. Cajun seasoning
1 tsp. olive oil
Directions:
In a large skillet, heat the oil over medium-high heat. Cook for 2 minutes, or until onion and garlic are tender. Cook for 2-3 minutes, or until tomatoes soften, before adding tomatoes, peppers, and seasonings.
Place the fish on top. Cook for 5-8 minutes, covered, on medium heat, or until fish flakes easily with a fork.
Place the fish on serving dishes and drizzle with the sauce.
Nutritional Information: Calories 194; Total Carbs 6g; Net Carbs 0g; Protein 32.0g; Fat 3.0g; Sugar 5g; Fiber 2 g

Cajun Shrimp & Roasted Vegetables

Prep time: 04 minutes, Cook time: 14 minutes, Serves: 4
Ingredients:
1 lb. large shrimp, peeled and deveined
2 zucchinis, sliced
2 yellow squash, sliced
½ bunch asparagus, cut into thirds
2 red bell pepper, cut into chunks
What you'll need from store cupboard:
2 tbsp. olive oil
2 tbsp. Cajun Seasoning
Salt & pepper, to taste
Directions:
Preheat the oven to 400 degrees Fahrenheit.
In a large mixing basin, combine the shrimp and vegetables. To coat, toss in the oil and spices.Bake for 15-20 minutes, or until vegetables are soft, on a large baking sheet.
Serve.
Nutritional Information: Calories 251; Total Carbs 13g; Net Carbs 9g; Protein 30.0g; Fat 9.0g; Sugar 6g; Fiber 4 g

Grilled Shrimp with Cilantro and Lime

Prep time: 5 minutes, Cook time: 5 minutes, Serves: 6
Ingredients:
12-pound uncooked, peeled, deveined big shrimp with tails
Juice and zest of 1 lime
2 tbsp. fresh cilantro chopped
What you'll need from store cupboard:
¼ cup olive oil
2 cloves garlic, diced fine
1 tsp. smoked paprika
¼ tsp. cumin
½ teaspoon salt
¼ tsp. cayenne pepper
Directions:
In a big Ziploc bag, place the shrimp.

In a small bowl, combine the other **Ingredients** and pour over the shrimp. Allow 20-30 minutes for marinating.
Preheat the grill. Cook the shrimp on skewers for 2-3 minutes per side, or until they turn pink. Make sure you don't overcook them.
Serve with cilantro on top.
Nutritional Information: Calories 317; Total Carbs 4g; Net Carbs 4g; Protein 39.0g; Fat 15.0g; Sugar 0g; Fiber 0 g

Frittata with Crab

Prep time: 10 minutes, Cook time: 50 minutes, Serves: 4
Ingredients:
4 eggs
2 cups lump crabmeat
1 cup half-n-half
1 cup green onions, diced
What you'll need from store cupboard:
1 cup reduced fat parmesan cheese, grated
1 tsp. salt
1 tsp. pepper
1 tsp. smoked paprika
1 tsp. Italian seasoning
Nonstick cooking spray
Directions:
Preheat the oven to 350 degrees Fahrenheit. Using cooking spray, coat the suitable springform pan or pie dish.
Whisk together the eggs and half-n-half in a large mixing bowl. Stir in the Ingredients and parmesan cheese.
Combine the onions and crab meat in a mixing bowl. Bake 35-40 minutes, or until eggs are set and top is gently browned, in prepared pan. Allow 10 minutes to cool before slicing and serving warm or at room temperature.
Nutritional Information: Calories 276; Total Carbs 5g; Net Carbs 4g; Protein 25.0g; Fat 17.0g; Sugar 1g; Fiber 1 g

Fish & Tomatoes in the Crock Pot

Prep time: 10 mins, Cook time: 2 hours 30 mins, Serves: 4
Ingredients:
1 lb. cod
1 bell pepper, diced
1 small onion, diced
What you'll need from store cupboard:
15 oz. can tomatoes, diced
1/3 cup low-sodium vegetable broth
1 clove garlic, diced fine
½ tsp. basil
½ tsp. oregano
½ tsp. salt
¼ tsp. pepper
Directions:
In the crock pot, combine the onion, bell pepper, tomatoes, and garlic. To blend, stir everything together.
Arrange the fish on top. Season with herbs and seasonings before serving. Pour the broth on top.
Cook on high for 1-2 hours or low for 2-4 hours, covered.
Nutritional Information: Calories 165; Total Carbs 11g; Net Carbs 8g; Protein 28.0g; Fat 1.0g; Sugar 6g; Fiber 3 g

Lemon Shrimp with a Crunch

Prep time: 5 minutes, Cook time: 10 minutes, Serves: 4

Ingredients:
1 lb. raw shrimp, peeled and deveined
2 tbsp. Italian parsley, roughly chopped
2 tbsp. lemon juice, divided
What you'll need from store cupboard:
⅔ cup panko bread crumbs
2½ tbsp. olive oil, divided
Salt and pepper, to taste

Directions:
Preheat the oven to 400 degrees Fahrenheit.
Sprinkle salt and pepper equally over the shrimp in a baking dish. 1 tablespoon lemon juice and 1 tablespoon olive oil, drizzled on top. Remove from the equation.
Combine parsley, remaining lemon juice, bread crumbs, remaining olive oil, and ¼ teaspoons salt and pepper in a medium mixing bowl. On top of the shrimp, equally distribute the panko mixture.
Bake for 8-10 minutes, or until the shrimp are done and the panko is golden brown.

Nutritional Information: Calories 283; Total Carbs 15g; Net Carbs 14g; Protein 28.0g; Fat 12.0g; Sugar 1g; Fiber 1 g

Tuna Steaks on the Grill

Prep time: 04 minutes, Cook time: 08 minutes, Serves: 6

Ingredients:
6 6 oz. tuna steaks
3 tbsp. fresh basil, diced
What you'll need from store cupboard:
4 ½ tsp. olive oil
¾ tsp. salt
¼ tsp. pepper
Nonstick cooking spray

Directions:
Preheat the grill to medium. Using cooking spray, coat the rack.
Drizzle oil on all sides of the tuna. Mix in the basil and season to taste with salt and pepper.Cook for 5 minutes per side on the grill; the tuna should be slightly pink in the centre. Serve.

Nutritional Information: Calories 343; Total Carbs 0g; Net Carbs 0g; Protein 51.0g; Fat 14.0g; Sugar 0g; Fiber 0 g

Noodles with Dill Smoked Salmon

Prep time: 08 minutes, Cook time: 08 minutes, Serves: 4

Ingredients:
6 oz. smoked salmon, chopped
Juice from ½ a lemon
¼ cup half-n-half
3 tbsp. plant-based butter
2 tbsp. fresh dill, diced
What you'll need from store cupboard:
Homemade noodles
½ cup low sodium chicken broth
½ cup dry white wine
1 tbsp. olive oil
2 cloves garlic, diced fine
Salt & pepper, to taste

Directions:

In a large frying pan, heat the oil and butter over moderate flame. Cook for another 30 seconds after adding the garlic.
Combine the broth, wine, and lemon juice in a mixing bowl. Cook for about 4 minutes, or until the sauce has been reduced by half.
Cook for 2 minutes, or until the noodles are done, stirring in the half-n-half.
Season the salmon to taste with salt and pepper.
Garnish with a sprig of fresh dill.

Nutritional Information: Calories 273; Total Carbs 4g; Net Carbs 4g; Protein 14.0g; Fat 21.0g; Sugar 0g; Fiber 0 g

Pea Paella

Prep time: 22 minutes, Cook time: 34 minutes, Serves: 6

Ingredients:
1 lb. chicken thighs, skinless & boneless
1 lb. medium shrimp, raw, peel & devein
1 dozen mussels, cleaned
2 chorizo sausages, cut into pieces
1 medium head cauliflower, grated
1 yellow onion, diced fine
1 green bell pepper, sliced into strips
1 cup frozen peas
What you'll need from store cupboard:
15 oz. can tomatoes, diced, drain well
2 tbsp. extra-virgin olive oil
2 tsp. garlic, diced fine
2 tsp. salt
1 tsp. saffron
½ tsp. pepper
¼ tsp. paprika
Nonstick cooking spray

Directions:
Preheat oven to broil. Applying cooking spray, coat a baking dish..
Season the chicken on both sides with salt and pepper before placing it in a baking tray. Bake for about 4 minutes per side, or until the middle is no longer pink. Allow to cool completely before serving.
Heat 1 tablespoon of oil in a medium skillet over medium heat.
Combine the onion, pepper, and garlic in a mixing bowl. Cook, turning regularly, for about 4-5 minutes, or until peppers begin to soften. Place in a mixing basin.
Cook, stirring often, for 2 minutes with the chorizo in the skillet. Drain the fat and toss it in with the vegetables.
Cut the chicken into small pieces and toss it with the vegetables once it has cooled. Add the remaining oil to a large saucepot and heat over medium heat. Add the cauliflower and seasonings once it's hot. Cook, stirring regularly, for 8-10 minutes, or until cauliflower is almost soft.
Cook the mussels and shrimp until the mussels open and the shrimp turn pink.
Stir the mixture into the tomatoes and peas in the mixing bowl to incorporate everything. Cook for another 5 minutes, or until the mussels have all opened and everything is hot. Serve.

Nutritional Information: Calories 423 Total Carbs 21g Net Carbs 15g Protein 46g Fat 18g Sugar 9g Fiber 6g

Sun-Dried Tomatoes with Garlic Shrimp

Prep time: 08 minutes, Cook time: 28 minutes, Serves: 4

Ingredients:

½ lb. shrimp, peeled and deveined
4 oz. sun-dried tomatoes
1 cup half-n-half
What you'll need from store cupboard:
1 cup reduced fat parmesan cheese
4 cloves garlic, diced fine
2 tbsp. olive oil
1 teaspoon dried basil
¼ tsp. salt
¼ tsp. paprika
¼ teaspoon crushed red pepper
½ recipe homemade pasta, cook and drain, (chapter 14)

Directions:

Heat the oil in a large pan over medium heat.
Cook for 1 minute after adding the garlic and tomatoes.
Cook for 2 minutes after adding the shrimp, seasoning with salt and paprika.
Bring to a boil with the half-n-half, basil, and crushed red pepper. Reduce the heat to a low simmer. On low heat, whisk the parmesan cheese into the hot cream and stir to melt the cheese.
Remove the pan from the heat. Toss in the spaghetti and coat with the sauce. Serve.

Nutritional Information: Calories 353; Total Carbs 23g; Net Carbs 20g; Protein 22.0g; Fat 22.0g; Sugar 3g; Fiber 3 g

Steamed Mussels in Italy

Prep time: 08 minutes, Cook time: 08 minutes, Serves: 4

Ingredients:

2 lbs. mussels, cleaned
2 plum tomatoes, peeled, seeded and diced
1 cup onion, diced
2 tbsp. fresh parsley, diced
What you'll need from store cupboard:
¼ cup dry white wine
3 cloves garlic, diced fine
3 tbsp. olive oil
2 tbsp. fresh breadcrumbs
¼ teaspoon crushed red pepper flakes

Directions:

In a large sauce saucepan over medium heat, heat the oil. Cook, stirring occasionally, until the onions are tender, about 2-3 minutes. After adding the garlic, cook for another minute.
Combine the wine, tomatoes, and pepper flakes in a mixing bowl. Bring to a boil, stir to combine. Cook for 3 to 4 minutes, or until all of the mussels have opened. Mussels that do not open should be thrown away.
Transfer the mussels to a serving basin once they have opened. Cook, stirring regularly, until the mixture thickens, then add the bread crumbs to the sauce. Stir in the parsley and pour over the mussels evenly.
Serve and enjoy.

Nutritional Information: Calories 340; Total Carbs 18g; Net Carbs 16g; Protein 29.0g; Fat 8.0g; Sugar 4g; Fiber 2 g

Salmon with Maple and Orange Glaze

Prep time: 03 minutes, Cook time: 18 minutes, Serves: 4

Ingredients:

1 ½ lb. salmon fillet
1 tbsp. orange juice
What you'll need from store cupboard:
2 tbsp. sugar-free maple syrup
2 tbsp. grainy Dijon mustard
2 tsp. garlic, diced fine
Nonstick cooking spray

Directions:

Preheat the oven to 375 degrees Fahrenheit.
Coat a baking dish with cooking spray and place the salmon skin side down in it.
Combine orange juice, syrup, mustard, and garlic in a small mixing basin. Cover the fish with foil and pour the sauce over it.
Bake for 15 minutes in the oven; uncover and bake for another 5 minutes, or until the top of the fish is caramelised and the fish readily flakes with a fork.
When done, serve and enjoy.

Nutritional Information: Calories 247 Total Carbs 6g Protein 33g Fat 11g Sugar 1g Fiber 0g

Pasta with Mediterranean Shrimp

Prep time: 14 minutes, Cook time: 18 minutes, Serves: 4

Ingredients:

1 lb. med. shrimp, peel & devein
1 lb. Trimmed asparagus, cut into 1-inch segments
½ cup sun dried tomatoes
½ cup green onions, sliced thin
What you'll need from store cupboard:
½ recipe Homemade Pasta, (chapter 15) cook & drain
8 oz. tomato sauce
1 cup boiling water
2 cloves garlic, diced
2 tbsp. clam juice
2 tbsp. apple juice, unsweetened
1 tbsp. olive oil
1 tsp. curry powder
¼ tsp. pepper

Directions:

Fill a small bowl halfway with boiling water and add the tomatoes. Drain after 5 minutes of standing.
Combine tomato sauce, clam juice, apple juice, and seasonings in a small bowl.
Heat the oil in a large skillet over medium-high heat.
Cook for 2 minutes after adding the asparagus.
Cook for another minute after adding the green onions and garlic.
Add the shrimp and mix well. Cook for 3 minutes, stirring occasionally, or until shrimp turn pink.
Heat through the tomato mixture and the sun dried tomatoes. Cook, stirring constantly, until the pasta is hot.
Serve.

Nutritional Information: Calories 296 Total Carbs 20g Net Carbs 15g Protein 37g Fat 9g Sugar 9g Fiber 5g

Lemon Trout Fillets

Prep time: 04 minutes, Cook time: 08 minutes, Serves: 6

Ingredients:
6 6 oz. trout fillets
6 lemon slices
What you'll need from store cupboard:
4 tbsp. olive oil
¾ tsp. salt
½ tsp. pepper
Italian-Style Salsa, (chapter 16)

Directions:
Season the fillets with salt and pepper before serving.
Heat the oil in a large nonstick skillet over medium-high heat.
Cook 3 fillets at a time for 2-3 minutes per side, or until fish easily flakes with a fork. Continue with the remaining fillets.
Serve with salsa and a lemon slice on top.

Nutritional Information: Calories 320 Total Carbs 2g Protein 30g Fat 21g Sugar 1g Fiber 0g

Milanese salmon

Prep time: 08 minutes, Cook time: 18minutes, Serves: 6

Ingredients:
2 ½ lb. salmon filet
2 tomatoes, sliced
½ cup olive oil
What you'll need from store cupboard:
½ cup basil pesto

Directions:
Preheat the oven to 400 degrees Fahrenheit.
Cover the edges and bottom of a 9x15-inch baking sheet with foil. Place a second large piece of foil on top of the salmon fillet on the baking sheet.
Pulse the pesto and oil until smooth in a blender or food processor. Distribute equally over the salmon. Top with tomato slices.
Wrap the foil around the salmon, tenting it at the top to keep the foil from touching the salmon. Bake for 15-25 minutes, or until salmon easily flakes with a fork.
Serve.

Nutritional Information: Calories 444; Total Carbs 2g; Net Carbs 1g; Protein 55.0g; Fat 8.0g; Sugar 1g; Fiber 0 g

Seafood & Broccoli Pasta

Prep time: 10 minutes, Cook time: 15 minutes, Serves: 6

Ingredients:
1 lb. shrimp, peel & devein
1 lb. sea scallops, pat dry
1 lb. broccoli florets, steamed
2 6.5 oz. cans clams, chopped
1 cup half-n-half
½ tablespoon olive oil
What you'll need from store cupboard:
1 cup clam juice
6 cloves garlic, diced fine
4 tbsp. reduced fat parmesan
3 tbsp. flour
1 recipe Homemade Pasta, cook & drain

Directions:

In a large pot over medium heat, heat the oil. Cook, stirring constantly, for 2 minutes after adding the garlic.
Cook for 5 minutes, or until shrimp turn pink, before adding the shrimp and scallops. Bring to a gentle boil with the clams, clam juice, and half-n-half.
Cook, stirring constantly, until the sauce has thickened. Heat the broccoli until it is fully cooked.
Serve with parmesan cheese on top of cooked spaghetti.

Nutritional Information: Calories 519 Total Carbs 28g Net Carbs 23g Protein 50g Fat 23g Sugar 7g Fiber 5g

Skillet with Shrimp and Artichokes

Prep time: 04 minutes, Cook time: 08 minutes, Serves: 4

Ingredients:
1 ½ cups shrimp, peel & devein
2 shallots, diced
1 tbsp. plant-based butter
What you'll need from store cupboard
2 12 oz. jars artichoke hearts, drain & rinse
2 cups white wine
2 cloves garlic, diced fine

Directions:
Melt butter in a large saucepan over moderate heat. Cook, stirring often, until the shallot and garlic begin to brown.
Cook for 5 minutes after adding the artichokes. Remove the pan from the heat and add the wine.
Cook, stirring occasionally, for 3 minutes.
Cook for a few minutes, just until the shrimp turn pink.
Serve.

Nutritional Information: Calories 487 Total Carbs 26g Net Carbs 17g Protein 64g Fat 5g Sugar 3g Fiber 9g

Fish Fillet Crusted with Cumin

Prep Time: 10 minutes| Cook Time: 4 minutes| Servings: 4

Ingredients:
1 tablespoon Cumin (ground)
¼ teaspoon Thyme
1 teaspoon Paprika
½ teaspoon Lemon pepper
1 pound Halibut fish fillets
½ tablespoon Canola oil
2 tablespoons Parsley (chopped)
4 Lime wedges

Directions:
Prepare a shallow bowl and add the cumin, paprika, lemon pepper, and thyme.
Mix well to combine.
Rub both sides of the fillet evenly with the prepared spice blend.
Prepare a suitable cooking skillet and place it over a medium flame. Pour in the canola oil and heat.
Place the fish fillet in the pan and cook 4 minutes per side or until the fish is opaque.
Transfer to a plate and sprinkle with parsley.
Serve with lemon wedges.

Nutritional Information: Calories 130; Total Carbs 1g; Net Carbs 0.4g; Protein 22g; Fat 4g; Sugar 0g; Fiber 0g

Pasta with a Seafood Medley

Prep time: 5 minutes, Cook time: 3 hours 10 minutes, Serves: 10
Ingredients:
24 oz. seafood mix, thaw
1 lemon, cut in wedges
¼ cup fresh parsley, diced
1 onion, diced
What you'll need from store cupboard:
28 oz. can petite tomatoes, diced
2½ cup low-sodium chicken broth
⅔ cup dry white wine
4 cloves garlic, diced fine
2 tbsp. olive oil
1 tsp. paprika
¼ tsp. salt and
¼ tsp. black pepper
1 recipe Homemade Pasta, (chapter 15)
Directions:
In a big, deep skillet, heat the oil over medium-high heat. Cook for 1 minute, or until garlic begins to smell fragrant.
Cook until the liquid has mostly evaporated, then add the wine. Increase the heat to high and toss in the tomatoes, broth, and seasonings to bring to a boil.
Reduce the heat to medium-low and cook, stirring periodically, for 7-9 minutes, or until the pasta is done.
Cook for 3-4 minutes, or until the seafood is cooked through. Serve garnished with a lemon wedge and parsley.
Nutritional Information: Calories 358 Total Carbs 24g Net Carbs 19g Protein 35g Fat 11g Sugar 11g Fiber 5g

Curry with Shrimp and Coconut

Prep time: 08 minutes, Cook time: 24 minutes, Serves: 4
Ingredients:
1 lb. extra-large shrimp, peel & devein
1 onion, diced fine
1 ¾ cup coconut milk, unsweetened
2 tbsp. fresh lemon juice
1 tbsp. fresh ginger, grated
What you'll need from store cupboard:
14.5 oz. can tomatoes, diced
3 cloves garlic, diced fine
1 tbsp. coconut oil
2 tsp. coriander
1 tsp. curry powder
1 tsp. salt, or to taste
½ tsp. turmeric
¾ tsp. black pepper
¼ tsp. cayenne
Directions:
Combine the lemon juice, ¼ teaspoon salt, ¼ teaspoon pepper, and the cayenne pepper in a medium mixing basin. Toss in the shrimp to coat. After covering, refrigerate for at least 10 minutes.
Heat the oil in a large, deep skillet over medium-high heat. Cook, stirring periodically, for about 2-3 minutes, or until the onion begins to soften.Cook for another minute after adding the remaining Ingredients.
Bring the tomatoes, juices, and coconut milk to a boil, stirring constantly. Cook for 5 minutes, stirring periodically.

Cook, stirring occasionally, until the shrimp turn pink, about 2-3 minutes. Serve.:
Nutritional Information: Calories 448 total Carbs 12g Net carbs 9g Protein 29g fat 30g Sugar 5g fiber 3g

Pasta with Shrimp in a Hot Pepper Sauce

Prep time; 08 minutes, Cook time: 22 minutes, Serves: 4
Ingredients:
¾ lb. shrimp, cooked
3 red bell peppers, chopped
1 onion, diced
8 oz. snow peas, steamed
2 tbsp. plant-based butter
What you'll need from store cupboard:
1 cup low sodium chicken broth
½ tsp. salt
½ tsp. chicken bouillon
¼ tsp. pepper
1 recipe Homemade Pasta, cook & drain
Directions:
Melt butter in a large skillet over medium-high heat. Cook, stirring occasionally, until the onions are completely translucent.
Bring to a simmer the peppers, broth, bouillon, salt, and pepper. Cover and cook for 5-10 minutes over low heat, or until peppers are tender.
Blend the mixture until it is completely smooth. Return the liquid to the pan.
Cook until the shrimp are fully cooked. Mix in the spaghetti and snow peas thoroughly. Serve.
Nutritional Information: Calories 387 Total Carbs 27g Net Carbs 21g Protein 40g Fat 14g Sugar 14g Fiber 6g

Risotto with Shrimp and Pumpkin

Prep time: 5 minutes, Cook time: 15 minutes, Serves: 3
Ingredients:
½ lb. raw shrimp, peel & devein
2 cups cauliflower, grated
¼ cup half-n-half
2 tbsp. plant-based butter
What you'll need from store cupboard:
½ cup low sodium vegetable broth
¼ cup pumpkin puree
¼ cup reduced fat parmesan cheese
2 cloves garlic, diced fine
¼ tsp. sage
¼ tsp. salt
¼ tsp. pepper
Directions:
Melt butter in a large skillet over medium-high heat. Cook for 1-2 minutes after adding the garlic.
Whisk together the broth, pumpkin, and half-and-half until smooth.
Cook for 5 minutes, or until cauliflower is soft, with the cauliflower and parmesan. Cook until the Shrimp turn pink, stirring regularly.
Season with a touch of salt and pepper before serving.
Nutritional Information: Calories 236 Total Carbs 9g Net Carbs 7g Protein 21g Fat 13g Sugar 3g Fiber 2g

Halibut from Spain

Prep time: 10 minutes, Cook time: 40 minutes, Serves: 6

Ingredients:
6 6 oz. halibut filets, pat dry
6 thick slices tomato
1 onion, sliced thin
1 cup mushrooms, sliced thin
4 ½ tsp. plant-based butter
What you'll need from store cupboard:
½ cup bread crumbs
¼ cup white wine
2 tbsp. pimientos, diced
1 tbsp. olive oil
1 ¼ tsp. salt
¼ tsp. mace
¼ tsp. cayenne pepper
¼ tsp. black pepper

Directions:
Preheat the oven to 350 degrees Fahrenheit.
Brush the oil into the bottom of a 13x9-inch baking dish.
On the bottom of the prepared dish, place the onion and pimiento.
Combine seasonings in a small bowl and sprinkle on both sides of the halibut.
In a baking dish, place the halibut. Place a piece of tomato on top of each fillet, then top with mushrooms and green onions. Pour the wine over everything.
In a skillet over medium heat, melt butter.
Cook, stirring constantly, until the bread crumbs are light brown. Sprinkle on top of the fish.
Bake for 20 minutes, covered in foil. Remove the lid and bake for another 20-25 minutes, or until the fish flakes easily with a fork.
Serve.
Nutritional Information: Calories 205 Total Carbs 13g Net Carbs 11g Protein 22g Fat 6g Sugar 4g Fiber 2g

Pasta with Sweet and Spicy Seafood

Prep time: 10 minutes, Cook time: 10 minutes, Serves: 4

Ingredients:
¼ lb. shrimp, peel & devein
¼ lb. scallops
6 oz. Chilean sea bass, cut in ½ -inch pieces
½ white onion, cut in strips
Juice of 1 lemon
½ cup fresh pineapple, diced
½ cup flat-leaf parsley, diced
What you'll need from store cupboard:
1½ cup white wine
¼ cup extra virgin olive oil
3 cloves garlic, diced fine
1½ tbsp. salt
¾ tsp. red pepper flakes
½ recipe Homemade Pasta,

Directions:
In a big pot, heat the oil over high heat. Cook, stirring regularly, until the onion is tender, about 1 minute.
Combine the garlic, shrimp, scallops, sea bass, and salt in a large mixing bowl. Cook for another minute, stirring occasionally.
Toss the spaghetti in the pot, making sure that each strand is well-coated in oil. Reduce the

heat to medium-low and stir in the wine, lemon juice, and pineapple until the pasta and fish are fully cooked, about 8 minutes.
Take the pan off the heat and add the parsley and red pepper flakes.
Serve right away.
Nutritional Information: Calories 334 Total Carbs 13g Net Carbs 11g Protein 25g Fat 21g Sugar 6g Fiber 2g

Carbonara with tuna

Prep time: 5 minutes, Cook time: 25 minutes, Serves: 4

Ingredients:
½ lb. tuna fillet, cut in pieces
2 eggs
4 tbsp. fresh parsley, diced
What you'll need from store cupboard:
½ recipe Homemade Pasta, cook & drain, (chapter 15)
½ cup reduced fat parmesan cheese
2 cloves garlic, peeled
2 tbsp. extra virgin olive oil
Salt & pepper, to taste

Directions:
In a small mixing bowl, whisk together the eggs, parmesan, and a pinch of pepper.
Heat the oil in a large skillet over medium-high heat.
Cook until the garlic is browned. Cook for another 2-3 minutes, or until the tuna is almost done. Garlic should be discarded.
Reduce the heat to a low setting and toss in the pasta. Cook, stirring constantly, for 2 minutes after adding the egg mixture. If the sauce is too thick, add a little water at a time until it reaches a creamy consistency.
Season with salt and pepper to taste, then top with parsley.
Nutritional Information: Calories 409 Total Carbs 7g Net Carbs 6g Protein 25g Fat 30g Sugar 3g Fiber 1g

Tilapia Fillet with Fruity Salsa

Prep Time: 30 minutes| Cook Time: 0 minutes| Servings: 4

Ingredients:
½ lb. (quartered) raspberries
½ (peeled, cored and chopped) fresh pineapple
1 (peeled, seeded and diced) large mango
3 (peeled and diced) kiwifruit
2 tablespoons fresh parsley, finely chopped
½ cup grape tomatoes 1 ½ lbs. tilapia fillets 1 tablespoon balsamic vinegar
½ teaspoon seasoned pepper blend

Directions:
Add the vinegar, parsley, tomatoes, mango, kiwi, strawberry, and pineapple to a bowl and wait until combined.
Add avocado oil to a saucepan on medium-high heat.
Coat the tilapia fillets with the pepper mixture.
Put the caoted fish in a hot pan and fry for 2-3 minutes until the fish is opaque and white.
Serve the salsa with the cooked tilapia.
Nutritional Information: Calories 305; Total Carbs 35g; Net Carbs 25g; Protein 36g; Fat 3g; Sugar 5g; Fiber 6g

Halibut with Vegetables

Prep Time: 25 minutes| Cook Time: 20 minutes| Servings: 4
Ingredients:
1 pound green beans, trimmed
2 red bell peppers, seeded and cut into strips
1 onion, sliced
Zest and juice of 2 lemons
3 garlic cloves, minced
2 tablespoons extra-virgin olive oil
1 teaspoon dried dill
1 teaspoon dried oregano
4 halibut fillets
½ teaspoon salt
¼ teaspoon freshly ground black pepper
Directions:
Preheat the oven to 400ºF (205ºC).
Line a baking sheet with parchment paper.
Toss the green beans, bell peppers, onion, lemon zest and juice, garlic, olive oil, dill, and oregano in a large bowl.
Transfer the vegetables to the prepared baking sheet in a single layer, leaving the juice behind in the bowl.
Gently place the halibut fillets in the bowl, and coat in the vegetable juice.
Transfer the fillets to the baking sheet, nestled between the vegetables, and drizzle them with any juice left in
the bowl.
Sprinkle the vegetables and halibut with the salt and pepper.
Bake the fish for 15 to 20 minutes until the vegetables are just tender and the fish flakes apart easily.
When done, serve and enjoy.
Nutritional Information: Calories 235; Total Carbs 16g; Net Carbs 11g; Protein 23g; Fat 9g; Sugar 2g; Fiber 3g

Sesame Tuna Steak

Prep Time: 21 minutes| Cook Time: 21 minutes| Servings: 2
Ingredients:
2 (6-ounce) Tuna steaks
2 tablespoons reduced-sodium Soy sauce
1 tablespoon Sesame oil
1 teaspoon Sesame seeds
Salt as per taste
Pepper as per taste
Directions:
Start by placing the tuna steak on a shallow plate and lightly season with pepper and salt.
Place sesame oil and soy sauce in a small bowl. Mix well and pour over the tuna steak, coat well.
Place the nonstick skillet over medium heat.
When the pan is hot, add the seasoned tuna and cook for about 3 minutes.
Flip and cook for another 3 minutes.
When finished, transfer it to a cutting board and cut it into thin slices about ½-inch thick.
Transfer to a platter and garnish with black and white sesame seeds.
Serve hot!
Nutritional Information: Calories 255; Total Carbs 1g; Net Carbs 0.2g; Protein 40g; Fat 9g; Sugar 0.1g; Fiber 0g

Cod Gratin

Prep Time: 30 minutes| Cook Time: 22 minutes| Servings: 4
Ingredients:
½ cup olive oil, divided
1-pound fresh cod
1 cup black kalamata olives, pitted and chopped
4 leeks, trimmed and sliced
1 cup whole-wheat bread crumbs
¾ cup low-sodium chicken stock
Fine-grained kosher salt and freshly ground black pepper, to taste
Directions:
Preheat the oven to 350 degrees F. Grease 4 gratin plates and the larger ovenproof dish with olive oil.
Place the cod in a large bowl and bake for 5-7 minutes. Let cool and cut into 1-inch pieces.
Add and heat the olive oil to a large saucepan. Add the olives and leeks and cook over medium-low heat until tender.
Add breadcrumbs and chicken broth and mix. Gently fold the pieces of cod.
Divide the mixture among 4 gratin plates and drizzle with olive oil. Season with salt and pepper.
Bake for 15 minutes or until heated through. When done, serve and enjoy.
Nutritional Information: Calories 578; Total Carbs 32g; Net Carbs 20g; Protein 25g; Fat 36g; Sugar 3g; Fiber 4g

Herby Parmesan Crusted Fish

Prep Time: 15 minutes| Cook Time: 12 minutes| Servings: 4
Ingredients:
⅓ cup Almonds (chopped)
¼ cup Dry bread crumbs (plain)
3 tablespoons low-fat Parmesan cheese (grated)
½ teaspoon Garlic powder
½ teaspoon Paprika
½ teaspoon Parsley flakes
¼ teaspoon Black pepper (freshly ground)
I pound Tilapia fillets
Olive oil
Directions:
Start by preheating the oven to a temperature of 450 degrees F.
Make a baking sheet and line it with foil.
Prepare a shallow bowl and add the chopped almonds, parsley, breadcrumbs, garlic powder, paprika, black pepper, and parsley flakes in it. Mix well to combine.
Place the fish on a plate and use a brush to lightly grease on both sides with olive oil.
Coat the fish with the almond and the seasoning mix, make sure both sides of the fish are even coated.
Place the coated fish on a baking sheet and bake for 12 minutes.
When done, the fish should be flaked with a fork.
Nutritional Information: Calories 225; Total Carbs 7g; Net Carbs 4g; Protein 29g; Fat 9g; Sugar 0.2g; Fiber 0.5g

Asparagus with Scallops

Prep Time: 25 minutes| Cook Time: 15 minutes| Servings: 4
Ingredients:
3 teaspoons extra-virgin olive oil, divided
1 pound asparagus, trimmed and cut into 2-inch segments
1 tablespoon plant-based butter
1 pound sea scallops
¼ cup dry white wine Juice of
1 lemon
2 garlic cloves, minced
¼ teaspoon freshly ground black pepper
Directions:
In a large skillet, heat half of the oil over medium heat.
Add the asparagus in it and sauté for 5 to 6 minutes until tender.
Remove from the skillet and cover with aluminum foil to keep warm.
Add the remaining oil and the butter to the skillet. When the butter is melted and sizzling, place the scallops in a single layer in the skillet.
Cook for about 3 minutes on one side until nicely browned. Gently flip the scallops with the tongs, and cook on the other side for another 3 minutes until browned and cooked through.
Remove and cover with foil to keep warm.
In the same skillet, combine the wine, lemon juice, garlic, and pepper.
Bring to a simmer for 1 to 2 minutes, stirring to mix in any browned pieces left in the pan.
Return the asparagus and the cooked scallops to the skillet to coat with the sauce. Serve warm.
Nutritional Information: Calories 253; Total Carbs 14g; Net Carbs 9g; Protein 26g; Fat 7g; Sugar 4g; Fiber 3g

Mediterranean Tuna Cups

Prep Time: 15 minutes| Cook Time: 20 minutes| Servings: 5
Ingredients:
White albacore tuna in water, flaked and drained 10 ounces
0.25 teaspoons Garlic salt
2 tablespoons fresh Lemon juice
0.33 cups Red onion, chopped
0.33 cups Pitted and chopped Kalamata olives
0.66 cups Non-fat, plain Greek yogurt
3 medium Cucumbers
Directions:
Cut the cucumber into 10 pieces and discard the ends. Keep the cucumber shell and use a 0.5 teaspoon to scoop out the insides.
Make sure there is a thin layer on the bottom of the slice to accommodate the tuna mixture.
Combine the olives, garlic, yogurt, onion, and lemon juice.
Mix until the mixture is smooth. Add the tuna and stir again until combined.
Take about 1 tablespoon of the tuna mixture and put it in cucumber cup.
Repeat this until all 10 cups of cucumber are filled with tuna.
Refrigerate and serve.
Nutritional Information: Calories 150; Total Carbs 2g; Net Carbs 1g; Protein 6g; Fat 1g; Sugar 0.9g; Fiber 1g

Basil-Lime Shrimp

Prep Time: 10 minutes| Cook Time: 10 minutes| Servings: 2
Ingredients:
½ cup (120 ml) lime juice
½ cup (120 ml) olive oil
¼ cup (10 g) fresh basil—Just compact sprigs into your measuring cup.
4 teaspoons (16 g) brown mustard
¼ teaspoon Splenda
4 scallions—thinly sliced, including the crisp part of the green
½ pound (225 g) shrimp
Directions:
Add all the lemon juice to Splenda in a blender and mix for just 1 to 2 seconds.
Pour the mixture into a saucepan and place at medium heat.
Reduce the heat until it boils and when it begins to boil, simmer until reduced by half.
Slice the scallions.
When the lemon juice is reduced, place the shrimp in.
Blanch for 2 minutes, then flip again and leave for a few more minutes until firm and pink.
Serve drizzled with sauce and sprinkle with sliced scallion on top.
Nutritional Information: Calories 438; Total Carbs 6g; Net Carbs 5g; Protein 35g; Fat 30g; Sugar 1g; Fiber g

Shrimp Creole

Prep Time: 110 minutes| Cook Time: 1 hour 25 minutes| Servings: 8
Ingredients:
1¾ lbs. raw shrimp, peeled
pepper, to taste
2 tablespoons canola oil
1 cup chopped onion
1 cup chopped celery
½ cup chopped bell pepper
8-oz. can no-salt-added tomato paste
8-oz. can no-salt-added tomato sauce
1 tablespoons Louisiana hot sauce
2½ cups water
3 cloves garlic, minced
1 cup chopped green onions
parsley
Directions:
Peel the shrimp.
Season with pepper to taste and set aside.
In a suitable saucepan, heat oil. Sauté onion, celery, and pepper until cooked through.
Add tomato paste and cook 5 minutes over low heat, stirring constantly.
Add tomato sauce, hot sauce, and water. Cook for 1 hour, stirring occasionally.
Stir in shrimp and garlic.
Cook another 15 minutes.
Sprinkle with green onions and parsley. Cook 2–3 more minutes.
Serve with the allowd staples.
Nutritional Information: Calories 150; Total Carbs 13g; Net Carbs 10g; Protein 15g; Fat 4g; Sugar 2g; Fiber 3g

Chipotle Spicy Fish Tacos

Prep Time: 20 minutes| Cook Time: 17 minutes| Servings: 4
Ingredients:
2 tablespoons Olive oil
½ small Yellow onion (diced)
1 Jalapeño (chopped)
2 cloves Garlic (pressed)
4 ounces Chipotle peppers soaked in adobo sauce
2 tablespoons plant-based butter
2 tablespoons lite Mayonnaise
1 pound Haddock fillets
4 Tortillas (low carb)
Directions:
Place a nonstick skillet over medium-high heat. Pour in the olive oil and let it hot.
Add the chopped onion and stir constantly for 5 minutes to prevent the onions from turning brown.
Reduce the heat and add the chopped garlic and jalapeno. Cook, stirring, about 2 minutes.
Remove the chipotle pepper from the adobo sauce and finely chop it. Transfer the chopped chipotle and adobo sauce to a hot skillet. Add the mayonnaise, butter and the fish fillet to the pepper sauce and mix well.
Cook the fish for 8 minutes or until completely cooked through. Divide into 4 equal parts.
To prepare the taco shells, make tortillas and fry them over high flame for 2 minutes on both sides.
Place the tacos on a plate and let the tacos cool if needed.
Fill the shells with ¼ of the fish mixture.
Serve hot with freshly chopped chives!
Nutritional Information: Calories 300; Total Carbs 7g; Net Carbs 4g; Protein 24g; Fat 20g; Sugar 0.4g; Fiber 2g

Tuna Bake with Cheese Swirls

Prep Time: 55 minutes| Cook Time: 25 minutes| Servings: 8
Ingredients:
½ cup diced green bell pepper
½ cup chopped onion
2 Tablespooncanola oil
6 Tablespoonflour
2 cups fat-free milk
6½- or 7-oz. can or pouch tuna
Cheese Swirls:
1½ cups reduced-fat buttermilk biscuit mix
¾ cup grated 50%-less fat cheddar cheese
½ cup fat-free milk 2 chopped pimentos (from jar)
Directions:
In the saucepan, sauté the peppers and onions in the oil until tender but not brown.
Incorporate the flour and cook for a few minutes over low heat to remove the raw flour taste.
Gently stir in the milk. Sauté over low heat, stirring constantly, until smooth.
Add Tuna. Pour into a 9 x 13 inch pan and then set aside for later use.
For cheese swirls, prepare the biscuit with milk according to the instructions on the package.
Sprinkle with cheese and chopped pimento.

Roll up Jelly roll fashion. Cut the roll into 8 pieces.
Spread gently and place on top of the tuna mixture.
Bake at 450°F for 25 minutes or until tuna mixture is foamy and cookies are golden brown. When done, serve and enjoy.
Nutritional Information: Calories 215; Total Carbs 25g; Net Carbs 20g; Protein 13g; Fat 7g; Sugar 10g; Fiber 12g

Shrimp Stewed in Curry Butter

Prep Time: 5 minutes| Cook Time: 5 minutes| Servings: 2
Ingredients:
6 tablespoons (85 g) plant-based butter
2 teaspoons curry powder
1 teaspoon minced garlic or 2 cloves garlic, crushed
24 large, raw, "easy peel" shrimp
Directions:
Melt the butter in a larger pan over the lowest heat. Mix with the curry powder and the garlic, then put the shrimp in a single layer.
Cook for 3 to 5 minutes per side or until the shrimp are tender.
Serve on a plate and scrape the extra curry butter.
Nutritional Information: Calories 218; Total Carbs 2g; Net Carbs 1g; Protein 15g; Fat 8g; Sugar 0.2g; Fiber 1g

Saigon Shrimp

Prep Time: 10 minutes| Cook Time: 5 minutes| Servings: 3
Ingredients:
½ teaspoon salt
½ teaspoon pepper
1 ½ teaspoons Splenda
3 scallions
4 tablespoons (60 ml) canola oil
1 pound (455 g) large shrimp, shelled and deveined
1 ½ teaspoons chili garlic paste
2 teaspoons minced garlic
Directions:
Combine salt, pepper, and Splenda in a small bowl or mug. Thinly slice the scallions and set them aside.
Collect all the Ingredients except for the scallions.
On the highest heat, hot oil in a wok or large saucepan.
Add the shrimp and fry for 2-3 minutes or until about ⅔ are pink.
Add the chili, garlic paste, and garlic and contine to sauté.
When the shrimp are fully cooked, sprinkle with salt, pepper, and Splendid and stir for only 10 seconds.
Turn off the heat and divide the shrimp into 3 plates.
Top each serving with a scattering of sliced scallion, serve and enjoy.
Nutritional Information: Calories 288; Total Carbs 2g; Net Carbs 0.8g; Protein 25g; Fat 7g; Sugar 1g; Fiber 1g

Shrimp in Curried Coconut Milk

Prep Time: 10 minutes| Cook Time: 15 minutes| Servings: 3

Ingredients:
½ onion
½ green pepper
2 tablespoons (28 ml) coconut oil
2 teaspoons cumin
2 teaspoons curry powder
1 ½ teaspoons ground coriander
1 ½ teaspoons chopped garlic
1 cup (235 ml) unsweetened coconut milk
½ teaspoon salt or Vege-Sal
¼ teaspoon chili garlic paste
3 cups (384) frozen cooked salad shrimp, thawed

Directions:
Place the onions and green pepper in a food processor and pulse until finely chopped. Start sautéing them in coconut oil in a deep-bottomed pan.
When the onions and peppers begin to soften, add the seasoning.
Cook for a few more minutes, add the garlic and put one more minute.
Add the coconut milk and stir. Also, stir in the salt and the garlic, and chili paste.
Now add the thawed and drained shrimp, stir and turn up the burner slightly.
Simmer for 1 to 2 minutes, thickening with a little guar, xanthan, or sugar if you feel it need it.
When done, serve and enjoy with all of the sauce.

Nutritional Information: Calories 235; Total Carbs 6g; Net Carbs 5g; Protein 28g; Fat 11g; Sugar 1g; Fiber 1g

Feta-Spinach Salmon Roast

Prep Time: 15 minutes| Cook Time: 20 minutes| Servings: 4

Ingredients:
3 ounces low-fat cheese, softened
¾ cup crumbled low-fat feta
2 scallions, thinly sliced, including the crisp part of the green
½ cup fresh spinach, chopped
2 skinless salmon fillets of roughly equal size and shape, totaling ¾ pound
Olive oil

Directions:
Preheat the oven to 350°F.
Combine the cheese and feta, mashing and stirring with a fork until well blended.
Add the scallions and spinach, and combine well.
Spread the mixture evenly over one salmon fillet. (The filling will be about ¾ inch thick.)
Top with the second salmon fillet. Brush both sides with olive oil, turning the whole thing over carefully with a spatula.
Place the loaf on a shallow baking pan, and bake for 20 minutes. Slice carefully with a sharp, serrated knife.

Nutritional Information: Calories 236; Total Carbs 24g; Net Carbs 18g; Protein 57g; Fat 9g; Sugar 6g; Fiber 4g

Barbecued Sea-Bass

Prep Time: 10 minutes| Cook Time: 10 minutes| Servings: 2

Ingredients:
1 pound (455 g) sea bass fillets
Barbecue Rub (sugar free)
4 slices nitrate-free & sugar-free bacon
2 tablespoons (30 ml) lemon juice

Directions:
Cut your sea bass fillets into serving portions.
Sprinkle both sides liberally with the barbecue rub.
Spray your big, heavy skillet with nonstick cooking spray, and place over medium-low heat.
Using a sharp kitchen shears, snip your bacon into small pieces, straight into the skillet.
Stir it about for a moment.
As soon as a little grease starts to cook out of the bacon, clear a couple of spaces for the fish, and put the fish in the pan.
Cover and set your oven timer for 4 minutes. When time is up, flip the fish, and stir the bacon around a bit, so it will cook evenly.
Re-cover the pan, and set the timer for another 3 to 4 minutes.
Peek at your fish at least once; you don't want to overcook it!
When the fish is flaky, remove to serving plates, and top with the browned bacon bits. Pour the lemon juice in the skillet, stir it around, and pour over the fish.

Nutritional Information: Calories 357; Total Carbs 13g; Net Carbs 10g; Protein 58g; Fat 18g; Sugar 4g; Fiber 6g

Tasty Fish Cakes

Prep Time: 10 minutes| Cook Time: 15 minutes| Servings: 3

Ingredients:
1-pound catfish fillet
2 green onions, minced
1 banana pepper, cored, seeded, and chopped
2 cloves garlic, minced
1 tablespoon grated or minced fresh ginger
1 tablespoon Bragg Liquid Aminos
1 tablespoon lemon juice
1 teaspoon grated lemon zest
Nonstick cooking spray

Directions:
Preheat the oven to 375°F.
Combine the fish with green onions, banana pepper, garlic, ginger, Bragg Liquid Aminos, lemon juice, and lemon zest in your food processor. Chop until combined.
Add Old Bay Seasoning to it and stir to mix.
Make patties of about 2 tablespoons of the fish mixture. Must have a total of 6 patties.
Place the patties on a baking sheet a. Bake the patties for 12-15 minutes or until crispy.
serve hot and enjoy.

Nutritional Information: Calories 66; Total Carbs 1g; Net Carbs 0g; Protein 11g; Fat 2g; Sugar 0g; Fiber 0g

Buttered Salmon with Creole Seasonings

Prep Time: 10 minutes| Cook Time: 10 minutes| Servings: 3
Ingredients:
12 ounces (340 g) salmon fillet, in 2 or three pieces
1 teaspoon purchased Creole seasoning
¼ teaspoon dried thyme
4 tablespoons (55 g) plant-based butter
1 teaspoon minced garlic or 2 cloves garlic, minced
Directions:
Sprinkle Creole seasoning and thyme evenly over the salmon.
Melt the butter in a pan over medium-low heat and add the salmon skin side down.
Cook 4 to 5 minutes per side, turning gently.
Transfer to a saucepan, skin side down, and toss the garlic with the additional butter in the saucepan.
Cook for just a minute, then rub all the garlic butter over the salmon and serve.
Nutritional Information: Calories 241; Total Carbs 2g; Net Carbs 0.1g; Protein 35g; Fat 14g; Sugar 0.2g; Fiber 0.4g

Glazed & Grilled Salmon

Prep Time: 10 minutes| Cook Time:12 minutes| Servings: 2
Ingredients:
2 tablespoons (3 g) Splenda
1 ½ teaspoons dry mustard
1 tablespoon (15 ml) reduced-sodium soy sauce
1 ½ teaspoons vinegar
¼ teaspoon blackstrap molasses
12 ounces (340 g) salmon fillet, cut into 2 or 3 serving-size pieces
Directions:
In a small bowl, combine the Splenda, mustard, soy sauce, vinegar, and molasses.
Pour 1 tablespoon of this mixture and place it on a separate plate.
Place the salmon on a plate, pour in the sauce mixture, and turn the fillets over so that both sides are coated with the sauce. rest the fish, skinless side down, for 2-3 minutes.
Heat oil in the pan and cook the salmon for 5 minutes on both sides.
When the salmon is cooked, transfer to a bowl and drizzle with the reserved seasoning mixture before serving.
Nutritional Information: Calories 189; Total Carbs 3g; Net Carbs 1g; Protein 35g; Fat 8g; Sugar 0g; Fiber 0.2g

Salmon in Citrus Vinaigrette

Prep Time: 10 minutes| Cook Time: 10 minutes| Servings: 4
Ingredients:
1 tablespoon (15 ml) coconut oil
24 ounces (680 g) salmon fillet in 4 servings
½ cup (120 ml) vinaigrette
½ cup (120 ml) lemon juice
2 ½ tablespoons (4 g) Splenda
¼ teaspoon orange extract
1 teaspoon brown mustard
1 teaspoon chili powder
2 tablespoons (28 ml) lime juice
Directions:
Grease a nonstick pan with cooking spray and set it on medium heat.
Add the coconut oil and when it melts, add the salmon in it.
Put other Ingredients in a blender and blend well.
Flip the salmon until tender.
Now add the vinaigrette mixture to the salmon and turn the burner to medium. Cook for 5 minutes or until the salmon is cooked through.
Place the salmon on a plate. Boil the vinaigrette dressing until harden into foamy syrup.
Pour the sauce over the salmon and serve.
Nutritional Information: Calories 384; Total Carbs 5g; Net Carbs 3g; Protein 34g; Fat 25g; Sugar 1g; Fiber 1.5g

Fish Cakes

Prep Time: 10 minutes| Cook Time: 6 minutes| Servings: 8
Ingredients:
1 ½ lb (680 g) boneless, skinless salmon filet
2 tablespoon (30 ml) lite mayonnaise
1 tablespoon (15 ml) finely chopped green onion tops
1 tablespoon (15 ml) finely chopped fresh dill
1 tablespoon (15 ml) freshly squeezed lemon juice
¾ (3.7 ml) sea salt
freshly ground black pepper
2 tablespoon (30 ml) vegetable oil
Directions:
Cut the fillet into ¼ inch pieces with a knife and place them in a bowl.
Add mayonnaise, green onions, dill, lemon juice, salt, and pepper to taste.
Stir quickly in the same direction for 1 minute.
Make 8 patties with the mix. It can be refrigerated for up to 6 hours or until cooked through.
Heat oil in a skillet over medium-high heat.
Add the cake and cook 2-3 minutes until lightly browned.
Flip and cook for another 2-3 minutes or until golden brown.
Serve and enjoy.
Nutritional Information: Calories 209; Total Carbs 0.3g; Net Carbs 0g; Protein 17g; Fat 15g; Sugar 0g; Fiber 0.1g

Tuna Salad

Prep Time: 5 minutes| Cook Time: 0 minutes| Servings: 2
Ingredients:
1 cup (284 g) light tuna, in water, drained
¼ cup (25 g) celery, chopped
2 tablespoons (28 g) low-fat mayonnaise
3 tablespoons (12 g) fresh dill, chopped
2 tablespoons (20 g) white onions, diced
Pepper to taste
Directions:
Mix all Ingredients in a large bowl.
Serve and enjoy.
Nutritional Information: Calories 66; Total Carbs 5g; Net Carbs 4g; Protein 5g; Fat 5g; Sugar 1g; Fiber 1g

Fish with Lemon-Dill Dip

Prep Time: 5 minutes| Cook Time: 14 minutes| Servings: 4
Ingredients:
2 (1-ounce) bags low-carb soy chips. finely ground
4 (8-ounce) fish fillets, about ¼ inch thick
2 tablespoons canola oil, divided
½ cup lite mayonnaise
3 tablespoons chopped fresh dill
2 teaspoons grated lemon zest
¼ teaspoon pepper
Directions:
Sprinkle the ground chips on a plate.
Dredge the fillet with fries to coat on both sides.
Heat 1 tablespoon of oil in a non-stick pan.
Add half of the fish and cook until opaque on the inside and golden on the outside for 3-4 minutes per side.
Carefully transfer to the plate and cover with foil to keep them warm. Repeat with additional oil and fish.
Mix mayonnaise, dill and zest in a small bowl.
Serve with pepper and alongside sauce.
Nutritional Information: Calories 520; Total Carbs 3g; Net Carbs 1g; Protein 51g; Fat 32g; Sugar 1g; Fiber 2g

Grilled Haddock with Peach-Mango Salsa

Prep Time: 10 minutes| Cook Time: 10 minutes| Servings: 4
Ingredients:
2 tablespoons olive oil
2 tablespoons lime juice
½ teaspoon salt
½ teaspoon ground pepper
1 pound haddock, cut into 4 fillets
Nonstick cooking spray
2 cups Fresh Peach-Mango Salsa
Directions:
Combine olive oil, lemon juice, salt, and pepper in a shallow bowl.
Add the haddock. Turn the fish over and cover with the marinade.
Prepare grill on high heat. Grease foil paper with cooking spray.
Place the fillet on the foil. Cook, 7 to 8 minutes per side, or until fish is tender when pricked with a fork.
Top each fish piece with ½ cup fresh peach-mango salsa and serve.
Nutritional Information: Calories 204; Total Carbs 11g; Net Carbs 7g; Protein 22g; Fat 8g; Sugar 1.4g; Fiber 2g

Crusted Catfish

Prep Time: 10 minutes| Cook Time: 25 minutes| Servings: 8
Ingredients:
8 catfish fillets
1 cup (115 g) bread crumbs
¾ cup (75 g) low-fat parmesan cheese, grated
¼ cup (15 g) fresh parsley, chopped
1 teaspoon paprika
½ teaspoon oregano
¼ teaspoon basil
½ teaspoon pepper
½ cup (112 g) melted butter
Directions:
Pat dry fish
Add the breadcrumbs, cheese, seasonings to a bowl. Mix well.
Dip the catfish in the butter and roll it in the breadcrumb mixture.
Arrange the fish in a well-greased 13 x 9 x 2-inch baking sheet.
Bake at 375°F for about 25 minutes or until the fish is crisp and tender.
Nutritional Information: Calories 412; Total Carbs 10g; Net Carbs 8g; Protein 30g; Fat 12g; Sugar 1g; Fiber 1g

Smoked Shrimp and Cheese Quesadillas

Prep Time: 10minutes| Cook Time: 5 minutes| Servings: 4
Ingredients:
4 (8") flour tortillas
4 teaspoons olive oil
2 ounces part-skim mozzarella or other mild cheese (such as fontina or baby Swiss)
1 jalapeño or banana pepper, finely chopped
2 cloves garlic, crushed
4 ounces smoked shrimp
1 cup thinly sliced red onion
½ cup roughly chopped fresh cilantro
Directions:
Preheat the oven to 375 ° F.
Gentlygrease one side of the tortilla with olive oil.
Combine the cheese, pepper, and garlic with additional olive oil. Sprinkle ½ of the cheese mixture in the middle of the oiled tortilla.
Garnish with shrimp, red onion, and cilantro.
Fold the tortilla in half to cover the
Ingredients.
Place the tortillas in a roasting pan greased with nonstick spray. Bake for 3-5 minutes or until golden brown and melted.
Serve with the tomato sauce of your choice.
Nutritional Information: Calories 272; Total Carbs 32g; Net Carbs 15g; Protein 11g; Fat 11g; Sugar 15g; Fiber 3g

Slow-Roasted Salmon

Prep Time:10 minutes| Cook Time: 25 minutes| Servings: 4
Ingredients:
2 teaspoons extra-virgin olive oil
4 (5-ounce) salmon fillets with skin, at room temperature
1 cup finely minced fresh chives
Sea or kosher salt and freshly ground white pepper to taste (optional)
Nonstick cooking spray
Sage sprigs for garnish
Directions:
Preheat the oven to 250°F. Rub ½ teaspoon of olive oil into the salmon fillet.
Completely cover the fillet with chives. Gently press in chives. Season with salt and pepper if needed.
Place fillets skin side down on a non-stick baking dish.
Bake for 25 minutestender. Decorate with sage sprigs.
Nutritional Information: Calories 257; Total Carbs 1g; Net Carbs 1g; Protein 25g; Fat 16g; Sugar 0g; Fiber 0g

Spicy Fish Fillet

Prep Time: 5 minutes| Cook Time: 10 minutes| Servings:2
Ingredients:
½ cup cornmeal
½ teaspoon salt
1 teaspoon chipotle seasoning
1 egg
2 tablespoons 1% milk
16 ounces flounder, cut into 4 pieces
2 tablespoons olive oil
Directions:
In a shallow bowl, toast the corn, salt, and chipotle together.
Place the eggs and milk in a shallow bowl.
Dip the fish in the egg mixture. Place the fillet with the corn mixture.
Heat the olive oil in a non-stick pan. cook fillets until golden and crispy, about 6-7 minutes per side.
Nutritional Information: Calories 230; Total Carbs 9g; Net Carbs 6g; Protein 24g; Fat 10g; Sugar 1.4g; Fiber 1g

Simple Salmon Patties

Prep Time: 15 minutes| Cook Time: 10 minutes| Servings: 4
Ingredients:
2 cups flaked cooked salmon
6 soda crackers, crushed
1 egg
½ cup skim milk
1 small onion, chopped
1 tablespoon chopped fresh parsley
1 tablespoon unbleached all-purpose flour
1 tablespoon olive oil
Pure Rice Flour (optional)
Directions:
Place the salmon in a bowl.
Add the mashed crackers, eggs, milk, onion, parsley, and flour. Mix well. Make 5 patties.
Heat oil in a medium-high nonstick skillet. Fry on both sides until golden, about 10 minutes.
Serve hot with salad and enjoy.
Nutritional Information: Calories 168; Total Carbs 3g; Net Carbs 1g; Protein 17g; Fat 9g; Sugar 1g; Fiber 0.5g

Tuna-Noodle Casserole

Prep Time: 15 minutes| Cook Time: 15minutes| Servings: 4
Ingredients:
1 ½ cups egg noodles
1 recipe Condensed Cream of Mushroom Soup
1 teaspoon steamed chopped onion
1 tablespoon steamed chopped celery
½ cup skim milk
1 ounce shredded low-fat American, Cheddar, or Colby cheese
1 cup frozen mixed peas and carrots
1 cup steamed sliced fresh mushrooms
1 can water-packed tuna, drained
Directions:
Cook egg noodles according to package instructions. Drain and return to the pan
Add all the Ingredients to the pan. Stir to mix.
Cook over medium heat, stirring occasionally until the cheese melts.
Serve hot and enjoy.

Nutritional Information: Calories 245; Total Carbs 33g; Net Carbs 20g; Protein 20g; Fat 4g; Sugar 12g; Fiber 15g

Honey-Soy Broiled Salmon

Prep Time: 35 minutes| Cook Time: 20 minutes| Servings: 4
Ingredients:
1 scallion, minced
2 tablespoons reduced-sodium soy sauce
1 tablespoon vinegar
1 tablespoon honey
1 teaspoon minced fresh ginger
1 pound center-cut salmon fillet, skinned and cut into 4 portions
1 teaspoon toasted sesame seeds
Directions:
Whisk scallion, soy sauce, vinegar, honey and ginger in a medium bowl until the honey is dissolved.
Place salmon in a sealable plastic bag, add 3 tablespoons of the sauce and refrigerate; let marinate for 15 minutes.
Reserve the remaining sauce.
Preheat broiler. Line a small baking pan with foil and coat with cooking spray.
Transfer the salmon to the pan, skinned-side down. (Discard the marinade.)
Broil the salmon 4 to 6 inches from the heat source until cooked through, 6 to 10 minutes.
Nutritional Information: Calories 257; Total Carbs 23g; Net Carbs 18g; Protein 28g; Fat 18g; Sugar 6g; Fiber 4g

Shrimp Pie with Rice Crust

Prep Time: 10 minutes| Cook Time: 35 minutes| Servings: 4
Ingredients:
1 ½ cups cooked white rice
2 teaspoons dried parsley
2 tablespoons grated onion
1 teaspoon olive oil
1 tablespoon plant-based butter
1 clove garlic, crushed
1 pound shrimp, peeled and deveined
1 recipe Condensed Cream of Mushroom Soup (see recipe in Chapter 4)
1 teaspoon lemon juice
1 cup sliced steamed mushrooms
Directions:
Preheat the oven to 350°F. Add the rice, parsley, and onion. Mix well. Use olive oil to coat 10" pie plate; Combine the rice and press down the sides and bottom evenly. It works best if the rice is wet. Add 1 teaspoon of water if needed.
Melt the butter in a non-stick pan at medium heat. saute garlic and shrimps, stir frequently, for 5 minutes, until pink.
Add the soup and lemon juice to the pan. Stir until smooth and firm, about 5 minutes.
Stir Mushrooms in a soup mixture; Pour over the rice "crust". Bake for 30 minutes or until the top is lightly browned.
Serve hot.
Nutritional Information: Calories 273; Total Carbs 27g; Net Carbs 18g; Protein 27g; Fat 6g; Sugar 2g; Fiber 12g

Tuna Casserole

Prep Time: 10 minutes| Cook Time: 25 minutes| Servings: 8

Ingredients:
Sauce **Ingredients:**
1 cup sour cream
2 eggs
½ tablespoon minced onion, dried
1 teaspoon dill weed
½ teaspoon orange zest
½ teaspoon seasoning salt
Other Ingredients
1 pound cauliflower, cut into bite-sized pieces (may be fresh or frozen)
1 6-ounce can of tuna, drained
Cooking oil spray
1 ½ cups low-fat cheese, shredded (Monterey jack, Co-Jack, Cheddar, or a blend)

Directions:
Combine the sauce Ingredients in a mixing bowl.
Add the cauliflower into the sauce, then the tuna and coat well in sauce.
Spray a 9" x 13" baking dish with cooking oil spray and pour the cauliflower tuna mixture into the baking dish.
Top it with the cheese.
Bake it at 350°F for about 25 minutes or until the cheese is thoroughly melted and starting to become golden brown.
Serve hot and enjoy.
Nutritional Information: Calories 390; Total Carbs 10g; Net Carbs 6g; Protein 27g; Fat 28g; Sugar 1.4g; Fiber 3g

Chicken Chili with Black Beans

Prep Time: 10 minutes| Cook Time: 25 minutes| Servings: 2
Ingredients:
1 and ¾ pounds of cubed chicken breasts, skinless boneless
2 medium-sized chopped red peppers
1 big chopped onion
3 tablespoons olive oil
1 can green chilies, chopped
4 minced garlic cloves
2 tablespoons chili powder
2 teaspoons ground cumin
1 teaspoon ground coriander
2 cans of drained and rinsed black beans
1 can Italian tomatoes, stewed
1 cup low-sodium chicken broth
½-1 cup water
Directions:
Cook red peppers, onions, and chicken in a greased Dutch oven, until the chicken is longer pink, about 5 minutes.
Add the garlic, red pepper, cumin, red pepper powder and cilantro and boil for another 1 minute.
Bring to a boil with tomatoes, beans, ½ cup water, and broth. Reduce heat to low and cook for 15 minutes, stirring frequently, adding water as needed.
Serve hot and enjoy.
Nutritional Information: Calories 163; Total Carbs 21g; Net Carbs 18g; Protein 22g; Fat 6g; Sugar 0g; Fiber 4g

Cabbage Roll Mexican Soup

Prep Time: 5 minutes| Cook Time: 25 minutes| Servings: 6
Ingredients:
1 pound lean beef
½ teaspoon salt
¾ teaspoon garlic powder
¼ teaspoon pepper
1 tablespoon olive oil
1 medium chopped onion
6 cups chopped cabbage
3 cans of green chilies, chopped
2 cups water
1 can less sodium-containing beef broth
2 tablespoons fresh cilantro, minced
Directions:
Place the beef with the Ingredients in a large saucepan and cook over medium-high heat until no pink, about 5-7 minutes, then crumble.
Remove the pan from the heat.
In the same skillet, heat oil over medium to high heat and sauté cabbage and onions until tender and crisp, about 4 to 6 minutes.
Boil with beef, water, chili, and broth.
Lower the heat, cover, and let stand 10 minutes to blend the flavors.
Add the cilantro and mix well. If desired, use sour cream and Pico de Gallo.
Nutritional Information: Calories 282; Total Carbs 10g; Net Carbs 8g; Protein 9g; Fat 1g; Sugar 0.4g; Fiber 4g

Red Pepper Hummus

Prep Time: 10 minutes| Cook Time: 10 minutes| Servings: 8
Ingredients:
1 tablespoon olive oil
1 can garbanzo beans
1 medium-sized bell pepper (red)
1 fresh lime
¼ teaspoon garlic powder
1 tablespoon tahini
1 ½ tablespoons water
¼ teaspoon ground black pepper
½ teaspoon salt
Directions:
Add all Ingredients in a blender or food processor.
Blend until completely smooth.
Plate it top with olive oil and serve.
Nutritional Information: Calories 216; Total Carbs 15.1g; Net Carbs 12g; Protein 3.4g; Fat 3.4g; Sugar 0.5g; Fiber 4.2g

Moroccan Lentil Soup

Prep Time: 5 minutes| Cook Time: 1 hour 25 minutes| Servings: 3
Ingredients:
2 cups chopped onions
2 teaspoon olive oil
2 cups chopped carrots
1 teaspoon of ground cumin
4 cloves of garlic, minced
1 teaspoon of ground coriander
¼ teaspoon of ground cinnamon
1 teaspoon of ground turmeric
¼ teaspoon of ground pepper
4 cups fresh chopped spinach
2 cups water
6 cups low-sodium vegetable broth
2 tablespoons lemon juice
3 cups chopped cauliflower
1 chopped tomato (28-ounce of the can)
2 tablespoons tomato paste
1 ¾ cups lentils
½ cup fresh chopped cilantro
Directions:
Heat a little oil in a saucepan over medium heat, then add the onions and carrots, stirring occasionally, until tender, about 10 minutes.
Mix in a little garlic and cook for ½ minute.
Add the cumin, cilantro, turmeric, cinnamon, and black pepper. Stir until fragrant, about 60 seconds.
Add the broth, cauliflower, water, tomatoes, lentils, and tomato paste and bring to a boil.
Reduce heat and cook until lentils are tender, but not half liquid, about 45-55 minutes, half volume and stir occasionally.
Stir in spinach and cook for 5 minutes until soft.
Add the lemon and cilantro juice before serving.
Nutritional Information: Calories 27.5; Total Carbs 10g; Net Carbs 8g; Protein 9.3g; Fat 1.5g; Sugar 1g; Fiber 3g

Slow Cooker Chicken-Tortilla Soup

Prep Time: 20 minutes| Cook Time: 8 hour 20 minutes| Servings: 2

Ingredients:
1 ¼-pounds skinless chicken thighs
½ of chopped bell pepper (red)
1 small chopped onion
1 chopped clove of garlic
1 can diced tomatoes
2 cups low-sodium chicken stock
1 can tomato sauce
1 teaspoon chili powder
1 can green chilies (chopped)
1 teaspoon dried oregano
Salt as per taste
¾ teaspoon ground cumin
2 ½ tablespoons fresh cilantro, chopped
Fresh black pepper, grounded
Tortilla chips and sliced jalapenos for serving
3 ounces halved green beans
2 sliced and halved yellow squash
1 tablespoon lime juice, fresh

Directions:
Place onion, bell pepper, chicken, broth, garlic, tomato sauce, chopped tomatoes, chili powder, chili, cumin, and oregano in the slow cooker. Season with pepper and salt.
Cover chicken until ready to simmer for 7 to 8 hours. Or heat for 3 hours and 4 hours at high.
Add the green beans and zucchini, cover, and simmer for 30 minutes.
Then remove the chicken, discard the bones and shred the meat. Return to slow cooker.
Combine the cilantro and lemon juice.
Top with jalapeño and cilantro, and tortilla chips on the side.

Nutritional Information: Calories 158; Total Carbs 18g; Net Carbs 12g; Protein 26g; Fat 8g; Sugar 2g; Fiber 4g

White Bean and Chicken Soup

Prep Time: 5 minutes| Cook Time: 20 minutes| Servings: 2

Ingredients:
2 leeks, light green and white parts only, which are cut into quarter-inch rounds
2 teaspoons olive oil
1 roasted 2-pound chicken, discarded skin, removed meat from the bones, shredded
1 tablespoonfresh sage, chopped
2 cups water
2 cans of less sodium in chicken broth
1 can 15-ounce rinsed cannellini bean

Directions:
Heat the oil in a Dutch oven over medium-high heat.
Add a leek, then cook and stir until tender, about 3 minutes.
Add sage and cook until fragrant, about ½ minute.
Add the broth and a little water, increase the temperature to high, cover and bring to a boil.
Add the chicken and beans and simmer, uncovered, stirring occasionally, until heated through, about 3 minutes. Serve hot.

Nutritional Information: Calories 146; Total Carbs 14.8g; Net Carbs 10g; Protein 35.1g; Fat 5.8g; Sugar 1.2g; Fiber 2.9g

Beef and Mushroom Soup

Prep Time: 30 minutes| Cook Time: 55 minutes| Servings: 4

Ingredients:
12 ounces trimmed sirloin beef steak
1 tablespoon canola oil
4 cups sliced mushrooms
¼ cup chopped shallot
2 minced cloves of garlic
4 cups less sodium in beef broth
¼ teaspoon black pepper
1 cup chopped carrot
½ teaspoon salt
1 can undrained diced tomatoes with no salt
½ teaspoon of dried and crushed leaf thyme
½ cup chopped celery
1 bay leaf
2 cups fresh chopped kale

Directions:
Cut the beef into ¾-inch cubes and cook the beef over medium to high heat with oil in a 44 to 55-quart oven.
Remove the beef and set it aside.
Put the shallot, mushrooms, and garlic in a saucepan and boil for 4 to 5 minutes, stirring occasionally.
Return the beef to the pan and add the broth, carrots, tomatoes, bay leaves, celery, salt, thyme, and pepper.
Stir to separate the brown from the bottom of the pot. Then bring to the boil and reduce the heat. Cover and simmer for 20-25 minutes.
Stir in the kale. Boil lightly for 5 -10 minutes.
Remove the bay leaves before putting them in a bowl.

Nutritional Information: Calories 210; Total Carbs 10.5g; Net Carbs 8g; Protein 14.9g; Fat 5.1g; Sugar 0.7g; Fiber 3g

Green Herbed Hummus

Prep Time: 10 minutes| Cook Time: 0 minutes| Servings: 5

Ingredients:
½ cup basil leaves
1 garbanzo beans rinsed and drained chickpeas
Salt and black pepper
1 clove of garlic
½ teaspoon balsamic vinegar
1 tablespoon olive oil
½ teaspoon soy sauce

Directions:
In a hand blender, combine the basil, chickpeas, garbanozo beans, and garlic. Pulse several times. Use a spatula to push the mixture out of the edge of the processor container.
When you mix the Ingredients again, drizzle with a little olive oil. Blend until the soy sauce and vinegar combine well. Salt and pepper to taste.
Serve with toasted bread.

Nutritional Information: Calories 298; Total Carbs 21g; Net Carbs 14g; Protein 4.7g; Fat 3.8g; Sugar 0.9g; Fiber 4.1g

Potato Pot Soup

Prep Time: 20 minutes| Cook Time: 40 minutes| Servings: 5

Ingredients:
½ cup light sour cream
2 slices of halved non-nitrate bacon
1 tablespoon ubsalted butter
½ teaspoon salt
½ cup chopped onion
¼ cup chives
2 cups less sodium-containing chicken broth
1 ½ pound russet potatoes which are diced and peeled
¼ teaspoon pepper

Directions:
Add a little butter to the multicooker and heat until the butter is melted.
Add the bacon and cook for 4 to 5 minutes, turning occasionally until golden brown.
Transfer it to a paper towel to drain off and let the bacon and butter drip into the pan.
Put the onions in the multicooker and simmer for 2-3 minutes, stirring until tender, then add the potatoes and broth and cook.
Close the lid and cook for 10 minutes over high heat. Reduce the pressure and puree the soup until soft and slightly crumbly.
Add a little sour cream and stir until smooth.
Mix ¼ cup of cheese with salt and pepper. Mix until the cheese is melted.
Now serve it and top with mashed bacon, scallion greens, and the remaining quarter cup of cheese.

Nutritional Information: Calories 156; Total Carbs 10g; Net Carbs 8g; Protein 3.2g; Fat 4.1g; Sugar 0.2g; Fiber 3g

Coconut and Chicken Soup

Prep Time: 20 minutes| Cook Time: 30 minutes| Servings: 2

Ingredients:
1 pound thinly sliced chicken breast
Salt & pepper
1 tablespoon coconut oil
1 small sized onion which is thinly sliced
2 minced garlic cloves
1-inch minced and peeled ginger piece
1 medium-sized zucchini, which is cut into ¼, diced
0.75 pounds of pumpkin
1 red-colored bell pepper
1 jalapeño pepper
14 ounces part-skim coconut milk (lite)
2 cups low-sodium chicken broth
1 lime juice

Directions:
Season the chicken breasts finely with salt and pepper. Heat the coconut oil over medium heat in a large saucepan and add the chicken breast.
Sauté chicken over high heat for 4 to 5 minutes until red on the outside. Add the onion, garlic, and ginger and sauté for 2-3 minutes.
Add the zucchini and pumpkin and mix. Add the bell peppers, jalapeño peppers, chicken broth, coconut milk, and lemon juice, and stir.
When it comes to a boil, reduce the heat, cover and simmer for about 20 minutes.
Remove from the heat and season with salt and pepper at the end.

Nutritional Information: Calories 186; Total Carbs 12g; Net Carbs 9g; Protein 17g; Fat 13g; Sugar 1.4g; Fiber 5g

Vegetables Soup

Prep Time: 25 minutes| Cook Time: 1 hour 20 minutes| Servings: 16

Ingredients:
8 sliced of medium carrots
1 tablespoon olive oil
2 large chopped onions
1 big chopped and seeded green pepper
4 chopped celery ribs
1 minced garlic clove
2 cups frozen green beans
2 cups chopped cabbage
2 cups frozen peas
1 can garbanzo beans
1 cup frozen corn
One bay leaf
1-½ teaspoon parsley flakes, dried
2 teaspoon chicken bouillon cubes
2 cups V8 juice
1 teaspoon salt
1 teaspoon dried thyme
1 teaspoon dried marjoram
½ teaspoon dried basil
4 cups water
¼ teaspoon pepper
1 can undrained diced tomatoes

Directions:
Place the onion, carrot, bell pepper, and celery in a saucepan and cook over medium to high heat until tender and crisp.
Cook for 1 minute, stirring constantly.
Bring the rest of the Ingredients to a boil and continue.
Reduce heat to low, cover, and cook for 1 to 1 hour 30 minutes or until vegetables are tender.
Remove the bay leaves before serving.

Nutritional Information: Calories 218; Total Carbs 20g; Net Carbs 18g; Protein 4g; Fat 2g; Sugar 0.14g; Fiber 3.2g

Apple Ladybug

Prep Time: 10 minutes| Cook Time: 0 minutes| Servings: 4

Ingredients:
8 thin sticks of pretzel
¼ cup raisins
2 red apples
1 tablespoon peanut butter

Directions:
Using a knife, cut the apples into 2 equal pieces and remove the insides.
Place all the ½ apples on a small, flat plate.
Brush the backs of the apple ladybugs with peanut butter and add the raisins to the sink in place.
To make the antenna, slip one end of each pretzel stick into something like a raisin and slip the second end of the liquid into it.
Serve and enjoy fresh apple ladybugs.

Nutritional Information: Calories 187; Total Carbs 23.2g; Net Carbs 18g; Protein 2.1g; Fat 2.3g; Sugar 1.4g; Fiber 2.3g

Kabocha Squash with Cauliflower Soup

Prep Time: 10 minutes| Cook Time: 20 minutes| Servings: 4
Ingredients:
½ yellow-colored diced onion
2 tablespoons olive oil
3 cloves of minced garlic
2 and a ½ cups cauliflower florets
1 tablespoon minced ginger
¼ teaspoon pepper
2 and a ½ cups kabocha squash, cubed
¼ teaspoon cayenne
½ teaspoon ground cardamom
2 leaves of bay
½ cup almond vanilla milk, unsweetened
4 cups low-sodium vegetable broth
½ teaspoon salt
Directions:
Heat olive oil in a saucepan over medium heat.
Put the garlic, onion, and ginger in a mixing bowl and mix. Sauté for 3 minutes or until the onions are translucent and starting to flavor.
In a large mixing bowl, place the squash, cauliflower, cayenne pepper, cardamom, and bay leaves. Mix everything then pour into the broth.
Bring the mixture to a boil then lower the heat to low.
Cook for 10 minutes or until the fork is easily absorbed by the zucchini.
Puree the Ingredients with a spoon or under high pressure.
When the soup mixes slowly, return it to the pot over low heat.
Add the almond milk and season with pepper and salt.
Nutritional Information: Calories 248; Total Carbs 12g; Net Carbs 9g; Protein 3g; Fat 8g; Sugar 0.1g; Fiber 2.8g

Vegan Mushroom Soup

Prep Time: 10 minutes| Cook Time: 30 minutes| Servings: 4
Ingredients:
1 teaspoon olive oil
1 large diced onion
1 clove of garlic
16 ounces mushrooms
8 sprigs of thyme (leaves set aside and removed)
2 cups vegetable broth with low sodium
14 ounces coconut milk, canned and unsweetened
1 tablespoon coconut Aminos
Pepper and salt
Directions:
Cut all the garlic, onion, and mushrooms into small pieces.
In a large saucepan, add the garlic, onion, oil, and mushrooms heated to medium heat and mix.
Cook for another 8 to 10 minutes, until the mushrooms, start to lose liquid.
Mix the other Ingredients until they are well combined. Bring the soup to a boil or simmer, then reduce the heat to low and cook for another 15 minutes.

Fill the blender halfway with the soup. Mix until smooth, then add to the soup. This adds extra creaminess to the soup.
Garnish with a little thyme and coconut milk and serve.
Nutritional Information: Calories 176; Total Carbs 13g; Net Carbs 10g; Protein 3g; Fat 16g; Sugar 0.8g; Fiber 4g

Beans and Greens Turkey Soup

Prep Time: 15 minutes| Cook Time: 2 hours| Servings: 2
Ingredients:
9 cups water
1 remaining turkey skeleton
2 ribs of celery, cut into half-inch pieces
1 can drained and rinsed northern beans,
1 medium-sized onion
1 package frozen spinach, chopped
¼ teaspoon pepper
2 teaspoons granules of chicken bouillon
3 tablespoons chopped onion
1 teaspoon salt
Directions:
In a saucepan, combine the celery, turkey, water, and onion.
Boil slowly. Lower the heat, cover, and cook for 2 hours.
Remove the turkey and let it cool. Remove the vegetables and strain the liquid with a cotton-lined colander.
Remove excess fat. Remove the bones, remove the meat and cut it into small pieces. Discard the bones.
Return the meat and broth to the pan. Beans, chopped onion, spinach, broth, pepper, and salt are added to the pan. Boil soup. Lower the heat, cover, and simmer for 10 minutes.
Serve hot and enjoy.
Nutritional Information: Calories 321; Total Carbs 10g; Net Carbs 9g; Protein 10g; Fat 2g; Sugar 1g; Fiber 3g

Fruit Leather

Prep Time: 20 minutes| Cook Time: 5 hours| Servings: 2
Ingredients:
4 cups pears
¼ cup lemon juice
1 cup sugar
4 cups apple
Directions:
Preheat oven at 150 ℉.
Line the baking sheet with wrap.
In a blender, put the sugar, apples, lemon juice, and pears. Close and mix until the mixture is completely smooth.
Using a spatula, distribute the mixture evenly in the prepared baking dish.
Bake for 5 to 6 hours with the oven door half open.
Whenever the edges of the fruit are not sticky and can be torn like leather.
Remove it and place it to cool down.
Serve and enjoy.
Nutritional Information: Calories 243; Total Carbs 23.5g; Net Carbs 15g; Protein 0.3g; Fat 0.1g; Sugar 1.4g; Fiber 9.2g

Autumn Bisque

Prep Time: 25 minutes| Cook Time: 50 minutes| Servings: 2

Ingredients:
2 teaspoons fresh chives, minced
¼ cup dairy-free margarine
2 teaspoons fresh parsley, minced
2 tablespoons olive oil
½ teaspoon lemon zest, grated
2 big cubed and peeled rutabagas
3 medium-sized chopped leeks only white portion
1 big cubed and peeled celery root
1 big cubed carrot
2 cups unsweetened almond milk
7 cups vegetable stock
3 cloves of minced garlic
2 teaspoons fresh thyme, minced
1 teaspoon salt
1-½ teaspoons fresh rosemary, minced
½ teaspoon ground pepper, coarsely
2 tablespoons fresh chives, minced

Directions:
Put the first 4 Ingredients in a bowl. Use a measuring spoon to shape the mix in 12 packets.
Cool on a baking sheet greased with foil until frozen.
Heat the oil in a 6-quart soup pot and sauté the celeriac, rutabagas, carrots, and leeks over medium heat for 8 minutes. Add the garlic and simmer for 2 minutes. Add the herbs, broth, pepper, and salt and bring to a boil.
Lower the heat and cover. Cook for 30 to 35 minutes or until the vegetables are cooked through.
Mix the soup using a blender. Alternatively, place it in part of the blender and allow it to cool slightly before returning it to the pot. Add milk and heat until hot.
Take the herbed margarine out of the freezer 15 minutes before eating it. Garnish with margarine and chives.
Nutritional Information: Calories 218; Total Carbs 20g; Net Carbs 18g; Protein 3g; Fat 6g; Sugar 0.6g; Fiber 4g

English Pub Pea Soup

Prep Time: 15 minutes| Cook Time: 5 hours| Servings: 2

Ingredients:
2 chopped celery ribs
1 and a ½ cups green peas, dried and split
1 big chopped carrot
4 cups water
1 sweet chopped onion
1 bottle of light beer
½ cup 2% milk
1 tablespoon English mustard, prepared
¼ cup fresh parsley, minced
1 ham bone, meaty
¼ teaspoon pepper
½ teaspoon salt
¼ teaspoon ground nutmeg

Directions:
Place ham in a 4-quart slow cooker. In it, you need to add peas, carrots, celery, and onions. In a salad bowl, put the beer, water, and mustard. Pour it over the vegetables.

Cook for 5 hours and 6 hours. Cover over high heat or until the peas are cooked. Remove the ham bones from the soup.
Cut the fat and let it cool slightly before removing the meat from the bones. Remove the bones and fat.
Put the meat in a slow cooker and cut it into small pieces.
Place the rest of the Ingredients in a mixing bowl.
Add chopped parsley on top.
Nutritional Information: Calories 211; Total Carbs 25g; Net Carbs 20g; Protein 9g; Fat 1g; Sugar 0g; Fiber 6g

Red Pepper & Roasted Cauliflower Soup

Prep Time: 50 minutes| Cook Time: 25 minutes| Servings: 6

Ingredients:
1 big head of cauliflower
2 medium-sized red peppers (sweet), seeded and halved
4 tablespoons olive oil
2 minced garlic cloves
1 cup sweet onion, chopped
2 and a ½ teaspoons fresh rosemary, minced
¼ cup flour (all-purpose)
⅛ to ¼ teaspoon cayenne pepper
½ teaspoon paprika
4 cups low-sodium chicken stock
½ teaspoon salt
1 cup 2% milk
¼ teaspoon pepper

Directions:
Preheat the broiler. Place the peppers , skin side up, on the bright paper lined with the foil.
Cook for five minutes or until the fire dropped or skin moves to brown. Remove the middle of the pepper out and set aside it for 20 minutes. Your oven can be preheated at 400 degrees F and set the oven on bake mode.
Spread cauliflower in a pan with two tablespoons of oil. Roast, regularly stir for 25-30 minutes.
Remove seeds and skin from the pepper before cutting them. Heat the extra oil in 6 quarts soup pot on high heat. Cook, soft, pepper, and cauliflower and stir regularly.
Approximately 6-8 minutes. Add rosemary, garlic, and paprika and continue cooking and mix for 1 minute. After adding flour, cook and fry for a minute.
Boil the stock until thickened. Put peppers and crashes and mix well. Puree the soup until creamy with a hand blender.
Add hot milk and seasoning in it and cook for a while.
Add cheese if desire and serve hot.
Nutritional Information: Calories 263; Total Carbs 19g; Net Carbs 15g; Protein 8g; Fat 10g; Sugar 1.1g; Fiber 2.9g

White Turkey Chili

Prep Time: 15 minutes| Cook Time: 70 minutes| Servings: 6

Ingredients:
½ cup chopped onion
2 tablespoons canola oil
3 minced garlic cloves
1 lb. of skinless, boneless breast of turkey
2 and a ½ teaspoons ground cumin
½ pound ground turkey
1 teaspoon of water
1 can chickpeas or garbanzo beans
3 cups chicken broth
1 teaspoon minced jalapeno pepper
¼ teaspoon dried savory
½ teaspoon of dried marjoram
2 teaspoons cornstarch

Directions:
Heat the oil in a large saucepan over medium heat.
Add the onion and simmer until tender, about 5 minutes. Boil another 1 minute after adding the garlic, add the cumin and boil another 5 minutes.
Divide the turkey chunks until no pink.
Add the broth, jalapenos, beans, marjoram, pepper, and salt to taste. Boil soup.
Lower the heat to low, cover, and cook for 45 minutes, stirring occasionally. Cook for another 15 minutes before serving.
The cornstarch should be dissolved in water and then mixed with the chilies. Cook for 2 minutes, stirring occasionally.
Serve with cheese and chopped red onions, if desired.

Nutritional Information: Calories 274; Total Carbs 15g; Net Carbs 13g; Protein 29g; Fat 12g; Sugar 0g; Fiber 6g

Baked Tortilla Chips

Prep Time: 10 minutes| Cook Time: 15 minutes| Servings: 6

Ingredients:
1 tablespoon vegetable oil
1 package corn tortillas
1 teaspoon salt
3 tablespoon lime juice
1 teaspoon chili powder
1 teaspoon ground cumin

Directions:
Preheat your oven to 350 ° F.
Cut all the tortillas into large 8 pieces and arrange them together in a thin layer on a baking sheet.
Combine oil and lemon juice.
Sprinkle all tortilla pieces with the mixture until slightly moist.
In a small bowl, combine the pepper, cumin, and salt. Sprinkle the spice mix over the chips and bake for 7 minutes.
Turn the pan halfway through and bake another 8 minutes until the chips are crispy but not completely golden.
Serve with salsa, guacamole.

Nutritional Information: Calories 298; Total Carbs 26g; Net Carbs 20g; Protein 3.3g; Fat 4.1g; Sugar 2g; Fiber 4g

Popcorn

Prep Time: 2 minutes| Cook Time: 3 minutes| Servings: 3

Ingredients:
1 teaspoon vegetable oil
½ cup un-popped popcorn
½ teaspoon salt

Directions:
In a mug, combine the popcorn with oil. Spread the salt over and the covered corn in a wrapping paper.
Microwave on high for 2-3 minutes, or till pauses of approximately 2 seconds after pops are heard.
To prevent steam, cautiously open your bag and put it into the serving dish.

Nutritional Information: Calories 195; Total Carbs 24.6g; Net Carbs 20g; Protein 4.1g; Fat 3.1g; Sugar 0.4g; Fiber 6g

Salsa

Prep Time: 10 minutes| Cook Time: 0 minutes| Servings: 4

Ingredients:
1 minced jalapeno pepper
1 chopped onion
4 large chopped tomatoes
½ cup fresh cilantro, chopped
Salt as per taste
1 tablespoon lime juice
3 minced cloves of garlic
1 diced tomatillo

Directions:
In a bowl, combine onion, tomatoes, garlic, cilantro, tomatillo, lime juice, and salt until well incorporated.
Taste after adding ½ of the jalapeño pepper.
Mix the remaining ½ jalapeño if you want your salsa to be spicier.
Cover and refrigerate the salsa until it is ready for serving.

Nutritional Information: Calories 283; Total Carbs 11.7g; Net Carbs 7g; Protein 2.3g; Fat 0.5g; Sugar 1g; Fiber 5g

Fried Carrot Slices

Prep Time: 10 minutes | Cook Time: 20 minutes | Serve: 1

Ingredients:
3 ounces carrots, peeled and cut into thin slices diagonally
½ tablespoon extra-virgin olive oil
¼ teaspoon arrowroot starch
⅛ teaspoons red chili powder
⅛ teaspoon ground cinnamon
Salt and ground black pepper, as required

Directions:
Preheat the oven to 425 degrees Fahrenheit. To use parchment paper, line a rimmed baking sheet.
Combine all of the Ingredients in a mixing bowl.
Arrange the carrot sticks to the baking sheet lined with a piece of parchment paper and bake for 20 minutes, tossing halfway through.
When done, serve and enjoy.

Nutritional Information: Calories 99 Total Carbs 8g Net Carbs 5.6g Protein 0.8g Fat 7.1 g Sugar 4g Fiber 2.4g

Baked Banana Chips

Prep Time: 10 minutes| Cook Time: 2 hours| Servings: 2
Ingredients:
1 teaspoon lemon juice
2 bananas, just-ripe
Directions:
Preheat the oven at 225 ℉.
Line the baking sheet with baking paper.
Distribute banana slices evenly over the baking sheet in an even layer. Brush lemon juice on the slices.
Bake the chips for 90 minutes in a preheated oven. Allow bananas chips to cool for at least five minutes before eating.
Nutritional Information: Calories 264; Total Carbs 27.2g; Net Carbs 20g; Protein 1.3g; Fat 0.4g; Sugar 11g; Fiber 12g

Jicama Appetizer

Prep Time: 10 minutes| Cook Time: 0 minutes| Servings: 4
Ingredients:
2 tablespoons chili powder
2 tablespoons lime juice
1 cut and peeled jicama
Directions:
In a bowl, place jicama and toss it with the fresh lemon juice and some chili powder.
Plate and serve right away.
Nutritional Information: Calories 203; Total Carbs 17.3g; Net Carbs 15g; Protein 1.7g; Fat 0.8g; Sugar 0.9g; Fiber 4.2g

Guacamole

Prep Time: 10 minutes| Cook Time: 0 minutes| Servings: 2
Ingredients:
⅛ to a quarter of teaspoon salt
1 tablespoon lemon juice
2 medium-sized ripe avocados
¼ cup chunky salsa
Directions:
Peel avocados and chopped.
Placed the avocado in a small bowl. Add lemon juice in it.
Toss in the salsa and season with salt, then mash roughly with the fork.
Chill until ready to serve.
Nutritional Information: Calories 162; Total Carbs 3g; Net Carbs 2g; Protein g; Fat 5g; Sugar 0g; Fiber 2g

Garlic Hummus

Prep Time: 10 minutes| Cook Time: 0 minutes| Servings: 2
Ingredients:
½ teaspoon salt
¼ cup tahini
1 can chickpeas with no salt
¼ cup olive oil
½ teaspoon chili powder
1 clove of garlic
¼ cup lemon juice
1 teaspoon ground cumin
Directions:
Add all Ingredients along chickpea liquid in a hand blender and blend until smooth.

Scrape of the container edges and blend until all the Ingredients well combined.
Serve top with olive oil and enjoy with bread.
Nutritional Information: Calories 152; Total Carbs 9.7g; Net Carbs 6.2g; Protein 3.7g; Fat 11.9g; Sugar 0.2g; Fiber 4.6g

Creamy Tomato Soup

Prep Time: 0 minutes| Cook Time: 5 minutes| Servings: 1
Ingredients:
1 tablespoon cream cheese, with less fat
¼ cup less sodium-containing chicken broth
¾ cup tomato puree, canned with no salt
Directions:
In a large heat-resistant bowl, put the broth, tomatoes, and cream cheese.
Microwave for 2 minutes over high heat, stirring occasionally until cooked through and creamy.
Nutritional Information: Calories 111; Total Carbs 18.3g; Net Carbs 11g; Protein 5.1g; Fat 2.7g; Sugar 0.2g; Fiber 5g

Gazpacho with Strawberries

Prep time: 10 minutes, Cook time: 00 minutes, Serves: 1
Ingredients:
1½ ounces fresh strawberries, hulled and sliced
2 tablespoons red bell pepper, seeded and chopped
¼ tablespoon onion, chopped
¼ tablespoon fresh basil leaves
¼ of small garlic clove, chopped
¼ teaspoon olive oil
¼ teaspoon balsamic vinegar
Directions:
Add all Ingredients to a small blender and pulse until smooth.
Place the gazpacho in a serving basin.
Before serving, cover and refrigerate to chill.
Nutritional Information: Calories 30 Total Carbs 5g Net Carbs 3.7g Protein 1g Fat 1.5g Sugar 2.3g Fiber 1.3g

Roasted Cinnamon Almonds

Prep Time: 5 minutes | Cook Time: 10 minutes | Serve: 1
Ingredients:
2 tablespoons whole almonds
Pinch of ground cinnamon
Pinch of ground cumin
Pinch of ground coriander
Salt and ground black pepper, as required
¼ tablespoon olive oil
Directions:
Preheat the oven to 350 degrees Fahrenheit.
In a mixing bowl, thoroughly mix up all of the Ingredients.
Arrange the almonds to the baking dish lined with a piece of parchment. Roast for about 10 minutes, flipping twice during the process.
Remove the almonds from the oven and cool thoroughly before serving.
Nutritional Information: Calories 100 Total Carbs 2.9g Net Carbs 1.2g Protein 2.6g Fat 8.5g Sugar 0.5g Fiber 1.7g

Mini Meatball with Apricot Dip

Prep Time: 15 minutes| Cook Time: 25 minutes| Servings: 1

Ingredients:
¼ cup bread crumbs, seasoned and dry
1 lb. of ground beef
2 egg whites
¼ teaspoon salt
2 tablespoons mustard of Dijon-style
2 tablespoons water
⅛ teaspoon pepper
¾ cup barbecue sauce
¾ cup apricot preserves

Directions:
Preheat the oven at 400 ℉.
In a large bowl, combine the breadcrumbs, ground beef, water, egg whites, salt, and pepper and mix gently.
Make 36 balls, ½ inches in diameter. Place on a steamed grill pan for cooking.
Preheat the oven to 400 ° F and bake for 15-17 minutes.
Meanwhile, heat a small skillet over medium heat to warm the jams, mustard, and barbecue sauce. Bring to a boil, then transfer to low heat and cook, uncovered, 3 to 5 minutes or until the sauce thickens slightly.
place meatballs in the slow cooker until heated through and cook for another 2-3 minutes.
Place the pork in a slow cooker set to the low heat option. Cover securely.
Meatballs can be kept in it for up to 2-3 hours by mixing them regularly.
Nutritional Information: Calories 128; Total Carbs 7g; Net Carbs 4g; Protein 3g; Fat 1g; Sugar 0g; Fiber 2.4g

Gazpacho with Avocados

Prep time: 10 minutes, Cook time: 00 minutes, Serves: 1

Ingredients:
½ of avocado, peeled, pitted and chopped
1 tablespoon fresh cilantro leaves
½ cup low-sodium vegetable broth
¼ tablespoon fresh lemon juice
⅛ teaspoon ground cumin
⅛ teaspoon cayenne pepper
Salt, as required

Directions:
Combine all of the Ingredients in a high-powered blender and pulse until smooth.
Place the soup in a large mixing bowl.
Refrigerate with lid on for at least 2-3 hours.
Enjoy.
Nutritional Information: Calories 155 Total Carbs 7g Net Carbs 2.4g Protein 2.5g Fat 11g Sugar 0.5g Fiber 4.6g

Guacamole with Avocados

Prep time: 10 minutes, Cook time: 00 minutes, Serves: 1

Ingredients:
¼ of ripe avocados, peeled, pitted and chopped
1 tablespoon red onion, chopped
½ of small garlic clove, minced
¼ of Serrano pepper, seeded and chopped
¼ of tomato, seeded and chopped
½ tablespoon fresh cilantro leaves, chopped
¼ tablespoon fresh lime juice

Salt, as required
Directions:
Add avocado to a bowl and mash it completely with a fork. Stir in the remaining Ingredients carefully to mix.
Serve right away.
Nutritional Information: Calories 68 Total Carbs 4.6g Net Carbs 2.2g Protein 0.9g Fat 5.6g Sugar 1.1g Fiber 2.4g

Salsa de Strawberry

Prep time: 10 minutes, Cook time: 00 minutes, Serves: 1

Ingredients:
¼ cup fresh strawberries, hulled and chopped
½ of small tomato, seeded and chopped
1 tablespoon red onion, finely chopped
½ of small garlic clove, minced
¼ tablespoon fresh lime juice
⅛ teaspoon olive oil

Directions:
Combine all of the Ingredients in a mixing bowl and gently toss to combine.
Serve right away.
Nutritional Information: Calories 31 Total Carbs 6g Net Carbs 4.5g Protein 0.9g Fat 0.8g Sugar 3.3g Fiber 1.5g

Salsa de Tomas

Prep time: 10 minutes, Cook time: 00 minutes, Serves: 1

Ingredients:
½ of tomato, chopped
¼ of small red onion, chopped
1 tablespoon fresh cilantro leaves, chopped
¼ of jalapeño pepper, seeded and chopped finely
¼ of small garlic clove, minced finely
½ teaspoon fresh lime juice
1 teaspoon extra-virgin olive oil
Salt and ground black pepper, as required
Directions:
Combine all of the Ingredients in a mixing bowl and gently toss to combine.
Serve right away.
Nutritional Information: Calories 55 Total Carbs 3.4g Net Carbs 2.5g Protein 0.9g Fat 4.8g Sugar 1.7g Fiber 0.9g

Roasted Peanuts

Prep Time: 5 minutes | Cook Time: 20 minutes | Serve: 1

Ingredients:
3 tablespoons raw peanuts
Pinch of salt
Directions:
Preheat the oven to 350 degrees Fahrenheit.
Spread the peanuts on a small baking sheet and roast for 15-20 minutes.
Remove the peanuts from the oven and place them in a mixing dish, add the salt and toss well.
Before serving, set aside to cool fully.
Nutritional Information: Calories 155 Total Carbs 4.4g Net Carbs 2.1g Protein 0.5g Fat 10.5 g Sugar 1.1g Fiber 2.3g

Salsa with Tomatoes and Olives

Prep time: 10 minutes, Cook time: 00 minutes, Serves: 1
Ingredients:
2 ounces cherry tomatoes, quartered
¼ of shallot, chopped finely
2-3 Kalamata olives, pitted and chopped
¼ of garlic clove, minced
½ tablespoon fresh mint leaves, chopped
½ tablespoon fresh parsley, chopped
¼ teaspoon olive oil
¼ teaspoon fresh lemon juice
Salt and ground black pepper, as required
Directions:
Combine all of the Ingredients in a mixing bowl and gently toss to combine.
Before serving, set aside for about 10-15 minutes.
Nutritional Information: Calories 37 Total Carbs 4.2g Net Carbs 3g Protein 0.9g Fat 4.8g Sugar 1.6g Fiber 1.2g

Fat-Free Yogurt with Egg

Prep time: 10 minutes, Cook time: 00 minutes, Serves: 1
Ingredients:
1 hard-boiled egg
¾ tablespoon fat-free plain Greek yogurt
Pinch of salt
¼ tablespoon Dijon mustard
Pinch of cayenne pepper
Directions:
Peel the egg and cut it in half vertically with a sharp knife. Remove the yolk using a spoon.
Pulse the egg yolk, yoghurt, and salt in a small blender until smooth.
Fill a bowl halfway with the yogurt mixture. Stir in the mustard and combine well.
Use a spoon to place the yoghurt mixture evenly on each egg half.
With a pinch of cayenne pepper on top, serve.
Nutritional Information: Calories 71 Total Carbs 1g Net Carbs 3g Protein 0.9g Fat 4.8g Sugar 0.7g Fiber 0.2g

Egg with Avocado

Prep time: 10 minutes, Cook time: 00 minutes, Serves: 1
Ingredients:
1 hard-boiled egg
¼ of small avocado, peeled, pitted and chopped
¼ teaspoon freshly squeezed lime juice
Pinch of salt
Pinch of cayenne pepper
Directions:
Peel the egg and cut it in half vertically with a sharp knife. Remove the yolk using a spoon.
Add half of the egg yolk, avocado, lime juice, and salt to a bowl and mash with a fork until well blended.
Evenly spoon the avocado mixture into each egg half.
Serve with a dash of cayenne pepper on top.
Nutritional Information: Calories 122 Total Carbs 2.9g Net Carbs 3g Protein 0.9g Fat 4.8g Sugar 0.7g Fiber 0.2g

Paprika Chickpeas

Prep Time: 5 minutes | Cook Time: 45 minutes | Serve: 1
Ingredients:
2 tablespoons cooked chickpeas
½ of small garlic clove, minced
⅛ teaspoon dried oregano, crushed
Pinch of ground cumin
Pinch of smoked paprika
Pinch of cayenne pepper
Salt, as required
½ teaspoon olive oil
Directions:
Preheat the oven to 400 degrees Fahrenheit.
Roast the chickpeas on the sprayed baking sheet for about 30 minutes, tossing them every 10 minutes.
While cooking, add and mix up garlic, thyme, and spices in a small mixing bowl.
When the time is up, take the baking sheet out of the oven, drizzle the oil over the chickpeas and sprinkle with the garlic mixture.
Toss well and cook for another 10-15 minutes.
Turn off the oven but leave the baking sheet in for another 10 minutes.
Remove the chickpeas from the oven and set aside to cool completely before serving.
Nutritional Information: Calories 59 Total Carbs 7.3g Net Carbs 5.7g Protein 1.6g Fat 2.8g Sugar 0.1g Fiber 1.6g

Garlic Veggie Balls

Prep Time: 08 minutes | Cook Time: 24 minutes | Serve: 2
Ingredients:
½ of medium sweet potato, peeled and cubed into ½-inch size
½ tablespoon unsweetened coconut milk
¼ cup fresh spinach, chopped
¼ of medium shallot, chopped finely
¼ teaspoon ground cumin
⅛ teaspoon granulated garlic
Pinch of ground turmeric
Salt and ground black pepper, as required
1-2 tablespoons ground flax seeds
Directions:
Preheat the oven to 400 degrees Fahrenheit.
Utilizing parchment paper, line a large baking sheet. Place a steamer basket in a pan of boiling water. Steam the sweet potato for around 10-15 minutes in a steamer basket.
Remove the sweet potato from the steamer basket and place it in a bowl. Mash in the coconut milk thoroughly. Mix in the remaining Ingredients, except the flax seeds, until thoroughly incorporated.
From the mixture, make 1½-2-inch balls.
Place the balls in a single layer on the prepared baking sheet and top with flax seeds. Pre - heat to 200 degrees Fahrenheit and bake for 20 to 25 minutes.
Warm the dish before serving.
Nutritional Information: Calories 63 Total Carbs 9g Net Carbs 12.8g Protein 1.6g Fat 7.5 g Sugar 2.5g Fiber 2.4g

Roasted Cashews with Lemon Juice

Prep Time: 5 minutes | Cook Time: 10 minutes | Serve: 1
Ingredients:
2 tablespoons raw cashews
⅛ teaspoon ground cumin
Pinch of cayenne pepper
Pinch of salt
¼ teaspoon fresh lemon juice
Directions:
Preheat the oven to 400 degrees Fahrenheit.
Toss the cashews and spices together in a dish to evenly coat them.
Spread the cashews in the roasting pan lined with a piece of foil, then Roast for 8-10 minutes.
Remove the cashews from the oven and cool thoroughly before serving.
Serve with the lemon juice.
Nutritional Information: Calories 101 Total Carbs 5.9g Net Carbs 5.3g Protein 2.7g Fat 8.1g Sugar 0.9g Fiber 0.6g

Paprika Roasted Pecans

Prep Time: 5 minutes | Cook Time: 12 minutes | Serve: 1
Ingredients:
2 tablespoons pecan halves
½ teaspoon extra-virgin olive oil
⅛ teaspoon fresh rosemary, chopped
Pinch of smoked paprika
Pinch of cayenne pepper
Pinch of salt
Directions:
Preheat the oven to 350 degrees F.
Thoroughly mix up all of the Ingredients in a mixing basin in a small bowl.
Place the pecans on the baking sheet lined with a piece of parchment paper.
Cook for 10 to 12 minutes, flipping twice during the cooking time.
Remove the baking sheet from the oven and set it aside to cool.
Serve and enjoy.
Nutritional Information: Calories 126 Total Carbs 2.5g Net Carbs 0.6g Protein 1.6g Fat 8.1g Sugar 0.6g Fiber 1.8g

Simple Roasted Walnuts

Prep Time: 5 minutes | Cook Time: 12 minutes | Serve: 1
Ingredients:
2 tablespoons walnuts pieces
½ teaspoon olive oil
Directions:
Preheat the oven to 375 degrees Fahrenheit.
With parchment paper, arrange a baking sheet.Toss the walnuts with the oil in a mixing dish to evenly coat them.
On the baking sheet lined with a piece of parchment papper, spread the walnut.
Bake for 12 minutes, stirring halfway through.
Before serving, remove the pan from the oven and set it aside to cool fully.
Nutritional Information: Calories 43 Total Carbs 0.5g Net Carbs 0.3g Protein 0.5g Fat 4.6g Sugar 0.1g Fiber 0.2g

Easy-to-Make Banana Chips

Prep Time: 5 minutes | Cook Time1 hour | Serve: 1
Ingredients:
½ of small banana, peeled and cut into ¼-inch thick slices
Directions:
Preheat the oven to 350 degrees Fahrenheit.
Place the banana slices on the baking sheet lined with a piece of baking paper and then bake for 1 hour.
When done, serve and enjoy.
Nutritional Information: Calories 45 Total Carbs 11g Net Carbs 9.7g Protein 0.6g Fat 0.2 g Sugar 5g Fiber 1.3g

Nutmeg Apple Chips

Prep Time: 5 minutes | Cook Time: 2 hours | Serve: 1
Ingredients:
¼ teaspoon ground cinnamon
Pinch of ground ginger
Pinch of ground cloves
Pinch of ground nutmeg
½ Fuji apple rounds, thinly sliced and cored
Directions:
Preheat the oven to 200 degrees Fahrenheit.
Prepare a baking sheet with parchment paper.
Combine all spices in a mixing dish.
Arrange the apple slices on the baking sheet lined with a piece of parchment paper and generously season with the spice mixture, then bake for 1 hour.
Sprinkle the spice mixture on the other side and bake for another 1 hour.
When done, serve and enjoy.
Nutritional Information: Calories 44 Total Carbs 11g Net Carbs 8.1g Protein 0.1g Fat 0.2 g Sugar 5g Fiber 2.9g

Oregano Chicken Nuggets

Prep Time: 10 minutes | Cook Time: 30 minutes | Serve: 1
Ingredients:
2-3 ounces skinless, boneless chicken breasts, cut into 2x1-inch chunks
1 small egg
2-3 tablespoons almond flour
Pinch of dried oregano, crushed
Salt and ground black pepper, as required
Directions:
Preheat the oven to 350 degrees Fahrenheit.
In a shallow basin, crack the egg and whisk it vigorously.
In a separate shallow bowl, whisk together the flour, oregano, onion powder, garlic powder, salt, and black pepper.
After dipping the chicken nuggets in the beaten egg, uniformly coat them in the flour mixture.
Lay the chicken nuggets on the sprayed baking sheet and bake for 30 minutes, or until golden brown.
When done, serve and enjoy.
Nutritional Information: Calories 215 Total Carbs 9g Net Carbs 13.1g Protein 16.6g Fat 13.2 g Sugar 0.8g Fiber 1.6g

Salty Kale Chips

Prep Time: 5 minutes | Cook Time: 15 minutes | Serve: 1
Ingredients:
2 ounces fresh kale leaves, stemmed and torn
Salt, as required
¼ tablespoon olive oil
Directions:
Preheat the oven to 350 degrees Fahrenheit.
Arrange the kale pieces on the baking sheet lined with a piece of parchment paper and bake for 10-15 minutes.
Remove the kale chips from the oven and set aside to cool before serving.
Nutritional Information: Calories 58 Total Carbs 5.7g Net Carbs 4.8g Protein 0.8g Fat 3.5 g Sugar 0g Fiber 0.9g

Simple Homemade Spinach Chips

Prep Time: 5 minutes | Cook Time: 8 minutes | Serve: 1
Ingredients:
1 cup fresh spinach leaves
½ teaspoon extra-virgin olive oil
Salt, as required
Directions:
Preheat the oven to 325 degrees Fahrenheit.
Add spinach leaves to a bowl and sprinkle with the olive oil, use your hands to rub the spinach leaves until they are coated well with the oil.
Arrange the leaves in a single layer on the baking sheet lined with a piece of parchment paper and bake for 8 minutes.
When done, remove the spinach chips from the oven and set aside to cool before serving.
Nutritional Information: Calories 27 Total Carbs 1.1g Net Carbs 4.8g Protein 0.9g Fat 2.5 g Sugar 0.1g Fiber 0.7g

Paprika Zucchini Chips

Prep Time: 10 minutes | Cook Time: 2 hours | Serve: 1
Ingredients:
½ of zucchini, cut into ⅛-inch thick rounds
1 teaspoon olive oil
⅛ teaspoon smoked paprika
⅛ teaspoon ground cumin,
Pinch of salt
Directions:
Preheat the oven to 235 degrees Fahrenheit.
With parchment paper, line a baking sheet.
Use the paper towels to squeeze the zucchini slices to remove the extra moisture.
Combine all Ingredients in a mixing basin.
Distribute zucchini slices on the baking sheet lined with a piece of parchment paper and bake for about 1½-2 hours, or until golden and crisp.
When done, remove the zucchini chips from the oven and set aside to cool before serving.
Nutritional Information: Calories 51 Total Carbs 2,2g Net Carbs 1.4g Protein 0.8g Fat 4.9 g Sugar 1.1g Fiber 0.8g

Dehydrated Orange Slice

Prep Time: 5 minutes | Cook Time: 10 hours | Serve: 1
Ingredients:
½ of seedless navel orange, sliced thinly
Salt, as required
Directions:
Preheat the oven at 135 degrees Fahrenheit on Dehydrate mode.
Place slices of orange on the suitable sheet and then dehydrate the orange slices for a 10 hours.
Nutritional Information: Calories 23 Total Carbs 5.6g Net Carbs 4.4g Protein 0.5g Fat 0.1 g Sugar 4g Fiber 1.2g

Fried Sweet Potato Wedges

Prep Time: 10 minutes | Cook Time: 25 minutes | Serve: 1
Ingredients:
½ of sweet potato, peeled and cut into wedges
¼ teaspoon ground turmeric
¼ teaspoon ground cinnamon
Salt and ground black pepper, as required
½ tablespoon extra-virgin olive oil
Directions:
Preheat the oven to 425 degrees Fahrenheit.
Wrap a piece of foil around a baking sheet.
Combine all Ingredients in a mixing basin.
Spread the sweet potato wedges out evenly on the baking sheet lined with a piece of foil and bake for 25 minutes, flipping once after 15 minutes.
Serve right away.
Nutritional Information: Calories 148 Total Carbs 13g Net Carbs 10.6g Protein 15.6g Fat 0.1 g Sugar 3.9g Fiber 2.4g

Tasty Parsnip Fries

Prep Time: 5 minutes | Cook Time: 10 minutes | Serve: 1
Ingredients:
2 ounces parsnip, peeled and sliced
1 teaspoon olive oil
Directions:
Preheat the oven to 390 degrees Fahrenheit (180 degrees Celsius).
In a mixing bowl, toss the parsnip slices and oil well.
Arrange the parsnip slices to the prepared baking sheet and bake for 30 minutes, turning halfway through.
Serve immediately.
Nutritional Information: Calories 83 Total Carbs 10.2g Net Carbs 7.4g Protein 0.7g Fat 4.8 g Sugar 2.7g Fiber 2.8g

Roasted Cauliflower Floerts

Prep Time: 10 minutes | Cook Time: 30 minutes | Serve: 1
Ingredients:
¼ cup cauliflower florets
½ teaspoon olive oil
Pinch of red chili powder
Salt and ground black pepper, as required
Directions:
Preheat the oven to 450 degrees Fahrenheit. A small roasting pan should be greased.
Combine all Ingredients in a mixing basin.
Spread the cauliflower mixture on the sprayed roasting pan and roast for 25-30 minutes.
Serve warm.
Nutritional Information: Calories 27 Total Carbs 1.5g Net Carbs 0.8g Protein 0.5g Fat 11.3 g Sugar 0.6g Fiber 0.7g

Almond Chicken Fingers

Prep Time: 10 minutes | Cook Time: 18 minutes | Serve: 1

Ingredients:
1 small egg
2-3 tablespoons almond meal
Pinch of ground turmeric
Salt and ground black pepper, as required
¼ pound skinless, boneless chicken breast, cut into strips

Directions:
Preheat the oven to 375 degrees Fahrenheit.
Utilizing parchment paper, line a large baking sheet.
Crack the egg in a small dish.
Combine almond meal and spices in a separate shallow dish.
Each chicken strip should be dipped in beaten egg and then evenly coated in almond meal mixture.
Lay the chicken strips in a single layer on the baking sheet lined with a piece of parchment paper and bake for 16-18 minutes.
Serve warm.

Nutritional Information: Calories 264 Total Carbs 3g Net Carbs 1.4g Protein 32.5g Fat 13.7 g Sugar 0.8g Fiber 1.6g

Paprika Buffalo Chicken Wings

Prep Time: 10 minutes | Cook Time: 20 minutes | Serve: 1

Ingredients:
⅓ pound chicken wings
1 tablespoon red hot sauce
¾ tablespoon olive oil
¼ teaspoon paprika
Pinch of cayenne pepper
Salt and ground black pepper, as required

Directions:
Cut the wing tips and then each wing at the joint.
In a mixing bowl, combine the spicy sauce, oil, paprika, cayenne pepper, salt, and black pepper with a wooden spoon.
In a small bowl, add 2 tablespoons of the marinade.
Gently coat the chicken wings with the remaining marinade in the bowl and marinate for 30-40 minutes at room temperature.
Preheat your oven to 425 degrees F and then arrange the suitable cooking pan in it.
Remove the wings from the bowl and toss away any leftover marinade.
Lay the wings on the cooking pan.
Broil for about 20 minutes, flipping halfway through.
Remove the chicken wings from the oven and coat evenly with the remaining marinade.
Serve immediately.

Nutritional Information: Calories 380 Total Carbs 0.7g Net Carbs 0.4g Protein 43.9g Fat 18.5 g Sugar 0.3g Fiber 0.3g

Cayenne Broccoli Tots

Prep Time: 10 minutes | Cook Time: 35 minutes | Serves: 3

Ingredients:
4 ounces frozen chopped broccoli
1 small egg
⅛ teaspoon dried oregano
⅛ teaspoon cayenne pepper
Pinch of red pepper flakes, crushed
Salt , as required
Freshly ground white pepper, as required
¼ cup low-fat cheddar cheese, grated
¼ cup almond flour
Olive oil cooking spray

Directions:
Preheat the oven to 400 degrees Fahrenheit.
Line a baking sheet with parchment paper that has been gently oiled.
Place the broccoli florets in a microwave-safe basin and microwave for about 5 minutes, stirring halfway through. Remove the water from the broccoli completely.
In a mixing bowl, whisk together the eggs, oregano, cayenne pepper, red pepper flakes, salt, and white pepper. Combine the cooked broccoli, cheddar cheese, and almond flour in a mixing bowl.
Make small, equal-sized patties from the Ingredients using slightly wet palms.
Arrange the patties in a single layer on the prepared baking pans, about 2-inch apart.
Spray each patty lightly with the cooking spray.
Cook for 15 minutes on each side, or until golden brown on both sides.
Warm the dish before serving.

Nutritional Information: Calories 161 Total Carbs 6.8g Net Carbs 3.8g Protein 7.4g Fat 10.6 g Sugar 1.7g Fiber 3g

Garlic Chicken Wings

Prep Time: 10 minutes | Cook Time: 1 hour | Serve: 1

Ingredients:
⅓ pound chicken wings
¼ tablespoon fresh lemon juice
1 (¼-inch) piece fresh ginger, minced
½ of small garlic clove, minced
¼ tablespoon baking powder
Salt and ground black pepper, as required

Directions:
Cut the wingtips off first, then each wing at the joint.
Mix up the lemon juice, ginger, and garlic in a mixing bowl. Toss in the chicken wings to thoroughly coat them. Refrigerate for 15-20 minutes to marinate.
Preheat the oven to 250 degrees Fahrenheit.
Place a rack in the oven's bottom third. On a baking pan, place a sprayed rack.
Remove the wings from the basin and blot them dry with paper towels.
Combine the wings, baking powder, salt, and black pepper in a zip-lock bag. To coat each well, close the bag and shake it.
Arrange the wings on the baking sheet. Bake for about 30 minutes, tossing out the pan drippings halfway through.
When the time is up, increase the cooking temperature to 425 degrees Fahrenheit. Place the baking sheet with the wings on the top oven rack and bake for 25-30 minutes, or until golden and crisp.
Serve immediately.

Nutritional Information: Calories 292 Total Carbs 1.8 g Net Carbs 1.7g Protein 43.8g Fat 11.3 g Sugar 0.1g Fiber 0.1g

Pepper Zucchini Sticks

Prep Time: 10 minutes | Cook Time: 25 minutes | Serve: 1

Ingredients:
½ of zucchini, cut into thick slices
2 tablespoons almond flour
Salt and ground black pepper, as required
1 small egg

Directions:
Preheat the oven to 425 degrees Fahrenheit.
Utilising parchment paper, line a baking sheet.
In a shallow bowl, crack the egg and whisk it vigorously.
In another shallow bowl, whisk together the flour, salt, and black pepper until thoroughly blended.
After dipping the zucchini sticks in the beaten egg, uniformly coat them in the flour mixture.
Lay the zucchini sticks on the baking sheet and bake for 25 minutes, or until golden brown, flipping halfway through.
When done, serve and enjoy.
Nutritional Information: Calories 152 Total Carbs 4.8g Net Carbs 2.6g Protein 5.4g Fat 11.3 g Sugar 1.8g Fiber 2.2g

Baked Sweet Potato Balls

Prep Time: 10 minutes | Cook Time: 30 minutes | Serve: 2

Ingredients:
¾ cup cooked sweet potato, peeled and mashed
½ tablespoon coconut oil, softened
Pinch of salt
½ of egg
2-3 tablespoons almond meal

Directions:
Preheat the oven to 400 degrees Fahrenheit.
Utilizing parchment paper, line a large baking sheet.
Combine the mashed sweet potato, coconut oil, and salt in a mixing dish.
Crack the eggs into a shallow bowl and thoroughly beat them.
In another shallow bowl, add the almond meal.
Form the mixture into little balls and slightly flatten each one; coat the balls with the egg mixture and the with the almond meal.
Arrange the coated balls to the baking sheet lined with a piece of parchment paper and bake for about 25-30 minutes, or until totally done.
Serve and enjoy.
Nutritional Information: Calories 148 Total Carbs 16g Net Carbs 12.8g Protein 4.2g Fat 7.5 g Sugar 6g Fiber 3.2g

Sesame Spinach Fritters

Prep Time: 10 minutes | Cook Time: 10 minutes | Serve: 1

Ingredients:
3-4 tablespoons chickpea flour
¼ teaspoons white sesame seeds
⅛ teaspoon garam masala powder
Pinch of ground cumin
Pinch of baking soda
Salt, as required
¼ cup water
4 fresh spinach leaves
2-4 tablespoons olive oil
Directions:

Mix all of the Ingredients in a bowl, except the spinach and oil, until a smooth consistency forms.
Heat the oil in a small pot over moderate heat.
In two batches, evenly coat each spinach leaf in the chickpea flour mixture and set in the hot oil.
Cook for about 3-5 minutes with rotating occasionally, or until golden brown on both sides.
Drain the fritters on a dish lined with paper towels.
Enjoy.
Nutritional Information: Calories 189 Total Carbs 10.4g Net Carbs 8.3g Protein 4.1g Fat 15.2 g Sugar 1.9g Fiber 2.1g

Baked Chicken Thigh Pieces

Prep Time: 10 minutes | Cook Time: 25 minutes | Serve: 1

Ingredients:
¼ pound boneless chicken thigh, cut into bite-sized pieces
2 ounces unsweetened coconut milk
¼ teaspoons ground turmeric
Salt and ground black pepper, as required
1 tablespoon coconut flour
2 tablespoons unsweetened desiccated coconut
1 teaspoon olive oil

Directions:
Combine the chicken, coconut milk, turmeric, salt, and black pepper in a mixing bowl.
Refrigerate with lid on overnight.
Preheat the oven to 390 degrees Fahrenheit.
Combine coconut flour and desiccated coconut in a shallow dish. Coat the chicken pieces evenly in the coconut mixture.
Arrange the coated thigh pieces to the baking sheet and equally drizzle with the oil.
Bake for 20 to 25 minutes.
When done, serve immediately.
Nutritional Information: Calories 248 Total Carbs 6.8g Net Carbs 2.9g Protein 23.6g Fat 13.5 g Sugar 0.5g Fiber 3.9g

Parmesan Pepper Chicken Wings

Prep Time: 10 minutes | Cook Time: 30 minutes | Serve: 1

Ingredients:
⅓ pound chicken wings
Pinch of baking powder
Salt and ground black pepper, as required
1-2 tablespoons low-fat Parmesan cheese, grated

Directions:
Preheat the oven to 250 degrees Fahrenheit.
Place a rack in the lower part of the oven. On a foil-lined baking sheet, place a greased rack.
Toss the wings in a basin with the baking powder, salt, and black pepper to thoroughly coat them.
Arrange the wings in a single layer on the preheated rack in the baking sheet Preheat the oven to 350°F (180°C) and bake for 30 minutes.
Serve immediately with a cheese garnish.
Nutritional Information: Calories 348 Total Carbs 0.4g Net Carbs 0.4g Protein 29.1g Fat 17.1 g Sugar 0g Fiber 0g

Crispy Apple Slices

Prep Time: 20 minutes| Cook Time: 30 minutes| Servings: 8
Ingredients:
5 cups Granny Smith apples, peeled and sliced
3 tablespoons plant-based butter
What you'll need from the store cupboard
½ cup rolled oats
¼ cup + 2 tablespoon Splenda
3 tablespoon flour
1 teaspoon lemon juice
¾ teaspoon apple pie spice, divided
Directions:
Preheat the oven to 375°F.
Combine apples, 2 tablespoons Splenda, lemon juice, and ½ teaspoon apple pie spice in a bowl until apples are well coated. Place apples in a greased square baking pan.
Combine oats, flour, ¼ Splenda, and remaining apple pie spice in a bowl. add butter and mix until mixture resembles coarse crumbs.
Sprinkle the crumbs evenly over apples.
Bake the apple crsip for 30 to 35 minutes, or until apples are tender and topping is golden brown.
Serve warm.
Nutritional Information: Calories 153; Total Carbs 27g; Net Carbs 23g; Protein 1g; Fat 5g; Sugar 18g; Fiber 4g

Apricot Soufflé

Prep Time: 5 minutes| Cook Time: 30 minutes| Servings: 6
Ingredients:
4 egg whites
3 egg yolks, beaten
3 tablespoon plant-based butter
What you'll need from store cupboard
¾ cup sugar-free apricot fruit spread
⅓ cup dried apricots, diced fine
¼ cup warm water
2 tablespoon flour
¼ teaspoon cream of tartar
⅛ teaspoon salt
Directions:
Preheat the oven to 325 °F for 10 minutes.
In a sauce pan, melt plant-based butter over medium heat.
Stir in flour and cook until bubbly.
In a small bowl, stir together the fruit spread and water and add it to the saucepan with the apricots. Cook, stirring, 3 minutes or until mixture thickens. Whisk in egg yolks.
Let cool to room temperature, stirring occasionally.
Beat egg whites, salt, and cream of tartar in a medium bowl on high speed until stiff peaks form. Gently fold into cooled apricot mixture.
Spoon the apricot batter into a 1-½ quart soufflé dish.
Bake the soufflé for 30 minutes, or until puffed and golden brown.
Serve immediately.
Nutritional Information: Calories 116; Total Carbs 7g; Net Carbs 4g; Protein 4g; Fat 8g; Sugar 1g; Fiber 0g

Baked Maple Custard

Prep Time: 5 minutes| Cook Time: 1 hour 15 minutes| Servings: 6
Ingredients
2 ½ cup half-and-½
½ cup egg substitute
What you'll need from store cupboard
3 cup boiling water
¼ cup Splenda
2 tablespoon sugarfree maple syrup
2 teaspoon vanilla
Dash nutmeg
Nonstick cooking spray
Directions:
Heat oven to 325°F.
Lightly spray 6 custard cups or ramekins with cooking spray.
In a large bowl, combine half -n-half, egg yolks, Splenda, vanilla, and nutmeg.
Pour evenly into prepared custard cups.
Place the cups in a 13x9-inch baking dish.
Pour boiling water around the cup, being careful not to splash it. Bake the cups for 1 hour and 15 minutes.
Remove the cups from the pan and let them cool completely.
Cover and let cool overnight.
Drizzle with maple syrup before serving.
Nutritional Information: Calories 190; Total Carbs 15g; Net Carbs 10g; Protein 5g; Fat 12g; Sugar 8g; Fiber 0g

Blackberry Crostata

Prep Time: 10 minutes| Cook Time: 25 minutes| Servings: 6
Ingredients:
1 9-inch pie crust, unbaked
2 cup fresh blackberries
Juice and zest of 1 lemon
2 tablespoonbutter, soft
What you'll need from store cupboard:
3 tablespoon Splenda, divided
2 tablespoon cornstarch
Directions:
Heat oven to 425°F. Line a large baking sheet with parchment paper and unroll pie crust in pan.
In a medium bowl, combine blackberries, 2 tablespoons of Splenda, lemon juice, zest, and cornstarch.
Spoon onto the crust but leave a 2-inch edge.
Fold and crimp the edges.
Top the berries with 1 tablespoon of butter.
Brush remaining butter around edges of crust and sprinkle crust and fruit with the remaining Splenda.
Bake for 20 to 22 minutes or until golden brown.
Chop and cool before eating.
Nutritional Information: Calories 206; Total Carbs 24g; Net Carbs 21g; Protein 2g; Fat 11g; Sugar 9g; Fiber 3g

Apple Pear & Pecan Cups

Prep Time: 10 minutes| Cook Time: 25 minutes| Servings: 24

Ingredients:
1 Granny Smith apple, sliced, leave peel on
1 Red Delicious apple, sliced, leave peel on
1 ripe pear, sliced, leave peel on
3 eggs
½ cup plain fat-free yogurt
1 tablespoon lemon juice
1 tablespoon plant-based butter
What you'll need from store cupboard:
1 package spice cake mix
1 ¼ cup water, divided
½ cup pecan pieces
1 tablespoon Splenda
1 teaspoon cinnamon
½ teaspoon vanilla
¼ teaspoon nutmeg
Nonstick cooking spray

Directions:
Preheat the oven to 350°F for 10 minutes.
Grease jelly-roll pan with nonstick cooking spray.
In a large bowl, beat cake mix with 1 cup water, eggs and yogurt until smooth.
Pour the cake batter into prepared pan and bake for 20 minutes until fully cooked. Cool completely.
Toss pecans over med-high heat in a skillet until lightly browned.
In a skillet, add the remaining ¼ cup water, sliced fruit, juice and spices and boil to medium heat for 3 minutes until fruits are tender crisp.
Remove the fruits from heat and stir in Splenda, plant-based butter, vanilla, and toasted pecans. Spoon evenly over cake.
Slice and serve.
Nutritional Information: Calories 130; Total Carbs 20g; Net Carbs 18g; Protein 2g; Fat 5g; Sugar 10g; Fiber 1g

Autumn Skillet Cake

Prep Time: 10 minutes| Cook Time: 30 minutes| Servings: 10

Ingredients:
3 eggs, room temperature
1 cup fresh cranberries
4 oz. reduced-fat cream cheese, soft
3 tablespoon fat free sour cream
2 tablespoon planted-based butter, melted
What you'll need from store cupboard:
2 cup almond flour, sifted
¾ cup Splenda
¾ cup pumpkin puree
1 ½ tablespoon baking powder
2 teaspoon cinnamon
1 teaspoon pumpkin spice
1 teaspoon ginger
¼ teaspoon nutmeg
¼ teaspoon salt
Nonstick cooking spray

Directions:
Preheat the oven to 350 °F.
Grease a 9-inch cast iron skillet or cake pan with cooking spray.
In a bowl, beat Splenda, butter and cream cheese until thoroughly combined.
Add eggs, one at a time, beating after each.

Add pumpkin and spices in the butter mix and combine. Add the dry Ingredients and mix well. Stir in the sour cream. Pour into prepared pan. Sprinkle cranberries over the batter and with the back of a spoon, push them half-way into the batter.
Bake 30 minutes or the cake passes the toothpick test. Cool completely before serving.
Nutritional Information: Calories 280; Total Carbs 23g; Net Carbs 20g; Protein 7g; Fat 17g; Sugar 16g; Fiber 3g

Chocolate Orange Bread Pudding

Prep Time: 10 minutes| Cook Time: 35 minutes| Servings: 8

Ingredients:
4 cups French baguette cubes
1 ½ cups skim milk
3 eggs, lightly beaten
1-2 teaspoon orange zest, grated
What you'll need from store cupboard
¼ cup Splenda
¼ cup sugar-free chocolate ice cream topping
3 tablespoon unsweetened cocoa powder
1 teaspoon low-sugar vanilla
¾ teaspoon cinnamon

Directions:
Heat oven to 350°F.
In a medium bowl, combine the Splenda and cocoa. Whisk milk, egg, zest, vanilla, and cinnamon until well combined.
Place square bread on an 8-inch square baking sheet. Pour the milk mixture evenly over the top.
Bake for 35 minutes or until a medium knife is clean. Let cool for 5-10 minutes.
Place the cake on a plate and sprinkle lightly with an ice cream topping.
Serve and enjoy.
Nutritional Information: Calories 139; Total Carbs 23g; Net Carbs 22g; Protein 6g; Fat 2g; Sugar 9g; Fiber 1g

Broiled Stone Fruit

Prep Time: 5 minutes| Cook Time: 5 minutes| Servings: 2

Ingredients:
1 peach
1 nectarine
2 tablespoon sugar-free whipped topping
What you'll need from store cupboard:
1 tablespoon Splenda
Nonstick cooking spray

Directions:
Heat the oven for baking. Place foil on a thin baking sheet and spray with the cooking spray.
Cut the peach and nectarine in half and remove the seeds.
Place one side off the prepared plate. Broil for 3 minutes.
Turn fruit over and sprinkle with Splenda.
Cook for another 2-3 minutes.
Transfer 1 fruit each to a bowl and top with 1 tablespoon of the whipped topping.
Serve and enjoy.
Nutritional Information: Calories 101; Total Carbs 22g; Net Carbs 20g; Protein 1g; Fat 1g; Sugar 19g; Fiber 2g

Café Mocha Torte

Prep Time: 15 minutes| Cook Time: 25 minutes| Servings: 14

Ingredients:
8 eggs
1 cup plant-based butter, cut into cubes
What you'll need from store cupboard:
1 lb. bittersweet chocolate, chopped
¼ cup brewed coffee, room temperature
Nonstick cooking spray

Directions:
Preheat the oven to 325 degrees F.
Spray cooking spray on the 8-inch springform pan. Line bottom side with parchment paper and spray again.
Wrap the outside with a double layer of foil and place them in a 9 x 13-inch baking sheet.
Add water in a small pot and bring to boil. Beat eggs in a large bowl on medium speed until doubled in size, about 5 minutes.
Place chocolate, plant-based butter, and coffee in a microwave-safe bowl stirring every 30 seconds, until chocolate melts and the mixture is soft.
Fold ⅓ of the eggs in the chocolate until almost combined. Add the remaining egg, ⅓ at a time and fold until combined.
Pour into the prepared pan. Pour boiling water around the pan until it reaches halfway up the side.
Bake for 22-25 minutes or until the cake is slightly puffed and the edges are just starting to harden.
Remove from the double boiler and let cool completely.
Cover with plastic wrap and let cool for 6 hours or overnight. About 30 minutes before cooking, brush the edges and remove both sides of the pan.
Cut and serve.

Nutritional Information: Calories 260; Total Carbs 12g; Net Carbs 11g; Protein 5g; Fat 21g; Sugar 11g; Fiber 1g

Chocolate Cherry Cake Roll

Prep Time: 10 minutes| Cook Time: 15 minutes| Servings: 10

Ingredients:
10 maraschino cherries, drained and patted dry
4 eggs, room temperature
1 cup sugar-free Cool Whip, thawed
⅔ cup maraschino cherries, chop, drain and pat dry
½ cup reduced-fat cream cheese, soft
What you'll need from the store cupboard
⅓ cup flour
½ cup Splenda for baking
¼ cup unsweetened cocoa powder
1 tablespoon sugar-free hot fudge ice cream topping
¼ teaspoon baking soda
¼ teaspoon salt
Unsweetened cocoa powder
Nonstick cooking spray

Directions:
Preheat the oven to 375 degrees F. Spray a large sheet baking pan and spray with the cooking spray.

In a small bowl, combine the flour, ¼ cup cocoa powder, baking soda, and salt.
Beat the eggs in a large bowl at high speed for 5 minutes,
Slowly add the sweetener and continue beating until the mixture is thick and lemon-colored.
Stir in the dry Ingredients.
Spread evenly over the prepared pan. Bake for 15 minutes.
Place a clean paper towel on the cutting board and sprinkle with cocoa powder. Place the cake on a towel and carefully remove the parchment. Start at the short end and wrap the towel around it. Cool on a wire rack for 1 hour.
Preparing the filling: In a small bowl, beat the cream cheese until tender. Add ½ cup of the whipped topping and mix gently and slowly until combined. Stir in another ½ cup of whipped topping. Fold the chopped cherries.
Unwrap the cake and remove the towel. Spread the filling to within 1-inch of the edges.
Roll the cake again and cut off the ends.
Cover and refrigerate for at least 2 hours or overnight.
Reheat fudge toppings, drizzle over cake, garnish with whole cherries and serve in slices.

Nutritional Information: Calories 163; Total Carbs 25g; Net Carbs 18g; Protein 5g; Fat 3g; Sugar 12g; Fiber 0g

Unbaked Blueberry Cheesecake

Prep Time: 5 minutes| Cook Time: 0 minutes+3 hours| Servings: 8

Ingredients:
16 oz. fat free cream cheese, softened
1 cup sugar-free frozen whipped topping, thawed
¾ cup blueberries
1 tablespoon plant-based butter, melted
What you'll need from store cupboard
8 zwieback toasts
1 cup boiling water
⅓ cup Splenda
1 envelope unflavored gelatin
1 teaspoon sugar-free vanilla

Directions:
Place the toast and plant-based butter in the food processor. Pulse until mixture resembles coarse crumbs.
Press the mixture to the bottom of the 9 inches spring foam.
Place gelatin in a medium bowl and add boiling water. Stir until gelatin is completely dissolved.
In a large bowl, whisk the cream cheese, Splenda, and vanilla on medium speed until combined. Beat the whipping toppings.
Add the gelatin in a stream while stirring at a low speed.
Increase speed to medium and hold for 4 minutes or until smooth and creamy.
Gently fold in the berries and spread over the crust.
Cover and refrigerate for 3 hours or until frozen.

Nutritional Information: Calories 316; Total Carbs 20g; Net Carbs 18g; Protein 6g; Fat 23g; Sugar 10g; Fiber 0g

Cinnamon Bread Pudding

Prep Time: 10 minutes| Cook Time: 45 minutes| Servings: 6
Ingredients:
4 cups day-old French or Italian bread, cut into ¾-inch cubes
2 cups skim milk
2 egg whites
1 egg
4 tablespoon plant-based butter, sliced
What you'll need from the store cupboard
5 teaspoon Splenda
1 ½ teaspoon cinnamon
¼ teaspoon salt
⅛ teaspoon ground cloves
Directions:
Preheat the oven to 350 degrees F.
In a suitable saucepan, bring the milk and plant-based butter to a boil. Remove from the heat and stir until the plant-based butter is completely dissolved. Let cool for 10 minutes.
Beat eggs and whites in a large bowl until foamy. Add Splenda, spices, and salt. Whisk until smooth, then add the cold milk and bread.
Transfer the mixture to a 1½-quart baking sheet. Place on a rack in the roasting pan and add 1-inch of hot water to the roasting pan.
Bake for 40 to 45 minutes until the pudding hardens and the knife in the middle is clean.
Nutritional Information: Calories 362; Total Carbs 25g; Net Carbs 23g; Protein 14g; Fat 10g; Sugar 10g; Fiber 2g

Unsweetened Chocolate Coffee Cupcakes

Prep Time: 10 minutes| Cook Time: 20 minutes| Servings: 24
Ingredients:
2 eggs
½ cup fat free sour cream
½ cup plant-based butter, melted
What you'll need from store cupboard:
2 cup Splenda
1 cup almond flour, sifted
1 cup strong coffee, room temperature
4 oz. unsweetened chocolate
½ cup coconut flour
3 teaspoon of baking powder
½ teaspoon-salt
Directions:
Preheat the oven to 350 degrees F.
Line 12-cup muffin cups with cupcake liners.
Melt the chocolate.
Add the Splenda, almond and coconut powder, baking powder, and sea salt.
In a small bowl, combine the coffee, sour cream, and butter. Add the butter mixture to the dry Ingredients and keep beating on low speed until well combined.
Add and beat the eggs one at a time. Stir in chocolate until well combined.
Pour batter into prepared cups and bake for 20-25 minutes.
Let cool completely before serving.
Nutritional Information: Calories 173; Total Carbs 20g; Net Carbs 19g; Protein 2g; Fat 9g; Sugar 16g; Fiber 1g

German Chocolate Cake Bars

Prep Time: 10 minutes| Cook Time: 5 minutes| Servings: 20
Directions:
2 cup unsweetened coconut flakes
1 cup coconut milk, divided
¾ cup chopped pecans
¾ cup dark baking chocolate, chopped
What you'll need from the store cupboard
1 ½ cup almond flour cracker crumbs (chapter 4)
½ cup + 2 tablespoon powdered sugar substitute
½ cup coconut oil
Nonstick cooking spray
Directions:
Spray an 8 x 8-inch baking sheet with cooking spray.
In a large bowl, combine the coconut, ½ cup sugar substitute, cracker crumbs, and pecans and mix.
Add ½ cup of milk and oil to a suitable saucepan and cook over medium heat until oil and mixture are heated through. Pour in the coconut mixture and stir to combine.
Spread evenly on a baking dish and let cool for 1-2 hours.
In a clean saucepan, put the chocolate and milk over medium-low heat. Continue cooking, stirring, until the chocolate melts and the mixture is tender. Add 2 tablespoons of the sugar substitute and stir to combine.
Pour the chocolate over the coconut layer and let cool for 1 hour or until firm.
Cut into squares to serve.
Nutritional Information: Calories 245; Total Carbs 12g; Net Carbs 9g; Protein 3g; Fat 19g; Sugar 7g; Fiber 3g

Mini Bread Puddings

Prep Time: 5 minutes| Cook Time: 35 minutes| Servings: 12
Ingredients:
6 slices cinnamon bread, cut into cubes
1 ¼ cup skim milk
½ cup egg substitute
1 tablespoon plant-based butter, melted
What you'll need from store cupboard
⅓ cup Splenda
1 teaspoon vanilla
⅛ teaspoon salt
⅛ teaspoon nutmeg
Directions:
Preheat the oven to 350 ° F. line in 12 medium muffin cups.
In a large bowl, combine milk, egg yolks, Splenda, vanilla, salt, and nutmeg until blended.
Add the cubed bread and stir until moist. Take 15 minutes of rest. Pour evenly into the prepared baking dish. Sprinkle plant-based butter evenly on top.
Bake for 30 to 35 minutes or until puffed and golden.
Remove from the oven and let cool completely.
Nutritional Information: Calories 105; Total Carbs 15g; Net Carbs 15g; Protein 4g; Fat 2g; Sugar 9g; Fiber 1g

Peanut Butter Pie

Prep Time: 10minutes| Cook Time: 0 minutes+ 4 hours chilling time| Servings: 8

Ingredients:
1 ½ cup skim milk
1 ½ cup frozen fat-free whipped topping, thawed and divided
1 small pkg. sugar-free instant vanilla pudding mix
1 (1 ½ oz.) pkg. sugar-free peanut butter cups, chopped

What you'll need from the store cupboard
1 (9-inch) reduced-fat graham cracker pie crust
⅓ cup reduced-fat peanut butter
½ teaspoon sugar-free vanilla

Directions:
In a large bowl, combine milk and pudding until thickened. Add the peanuts, vanilla, and 1 cup of whipped cream and whisk. Stir in peanut butter cups.

Pour over in pie crust and spread whipped cream more on top. Cover and chill at least 4 hours before eating.

Nutritional Information: Calories 191; Total Carbs 27g; Net Carbs 20g; Protein 4g; Fat 6g; Sugar 6g; Fiber 0g

Moist Butter Cake

Prep Time: 15 minutes| Cook Time: 30 minutes| Servings: 14

Ingredients:
3 eggs
¾ cup plant-based butter, divided
½ cup fat free sour cream

What you'll need from store cupboard:
2 cup almond flour, packed
1 cup Splenda, divided
1 teaspoon baking powder
2 tablespoon water
1 tablespoon+ 1 teaspoon low-sugar vanilla, divided
Butter flavored cooking spray

Directions:
Preheat the oven to 350 degrees F.
Sprinkle cooking oil to bake on a Bundt cake pan.
In a large bowl, combine the flour, sour cream, ½ cup of plant-based butter, 3 eggs, ⅔ cup of Splenda, baking powder, and 1 teaspoon of vanilla and whisk until well combined.
Pour into prepared pan and bake for 30 to 35 minutes.
Melt ¼ cup of plant-based butter in a small saucepan over medium heat.
Add ⅓ cup of Splenda, a tablespoon of vanilla, and water and stir. Keep stirring until Splenda is completely dissolved.
Use a skewer to poke holes across the cake.
Pour the syrup mixture evenly over the cake so that all the holes are filled. Turn the pan for a few minutes until the syrup is absorbed into the cake.
Leave to cool for 1 hour. Turn onto the plate, cut, and serve.

Nutritional Information: Calories 259; Total Carbs 18g; Net Carbs 16g; Protein 4g; Fat 17g; Sugar 15g; Fiber 2g

Coffee Tiramisu

Prep Time: 15 minutes| Cook Time: 0 minutes + 4 hours chilling time | Servings: 15

Ingredients:
2 (8 oz.) pkgs. reduced-fat cream cheese, soft
2 cup fat-free sour cream
2 (3 oz.) pkgs ladyfingers, split
¼ cup skim milk
2 tablespoon coffee liqueur

What you'll need from store cupboard:
⅔ cup Splenda
½ cup strong brewed coffee
2 tablespoons unsweetened cocoa powder, sifted
½ teaspoon vanilla

Directions:
Combine sour cream, cream cheese, sugar substitute, milk, and vanilla in a large mixing bowl. Beat on high until smooth in texture.
Stir coffee and liqueur in a small bowl.
Place lady fingers, cut side up, in a 2-quart baking dish.
Brush the lady fingers with ½ the coffee mixture. Spread ½ the blended cheese mixture over top. Repeat layers.
Sprinkle cocoa powder over top.
Cover the cake with foil and chill 4 hours or overnight. Cut into squares to serve.

Nutritional Information: Calories 208; Total Carbs 24g; Net Carbs 15g; Protein 6g; Fat 8g; Sugar 14g; Fiber 0g

Toffee Apple Pies

Prep Time: 20 minutes| Cook Time: 25 minutes| Servings: 12

Ingredients:
2 9-inch pie crusts, soft
2 cup Gala apples, diced fine
1 egg, beaten
1 tablespoon plant-based butter, cut in 12 cubes
1 ½ teaspoon fresh lemon juice

What you'll need from store cupboard:
2 tablespoontoffee bits
1 tablespoon Splenda
½ teaspoon cinnamon
Nonstick cooking spray

Directions:
Preheat the oven to 375 °F.
Grease a cookie sheet with cooking spray.
Stie apples, toffee, Splenda, lemon juice, and cinnamon in a mixing bowl.
Roll pie crusts separately and cut into a 3-inch crust with cookie cutter. Place 12 crusts on greased pan.
Brush the dough with ½ egg.
Spoon a tablespoon of apple mixture on each crust, leaving ½- inch edge. Top with pat of butter.
Place second dough round on top and seal edges closed with a fork.
Brush with remaining egg.
Bake the mini tarts for 25 minutes, or until golden brown.
Serve warm.

Nutritional Information: Calories 154; Total Carbs 17g; Net Carbs 16g; Protein 1g; Fat 9g; Sugar 6g; Fiber 1g

Caramel Pecan Pie

Prep Time: 5 minutes| Cook Time: 35 minutes| Servings: 8
Ingredients:
1 cup pecans, chopped
¾ cup almond milk, unsweetened
⅓ cup plant-based butter, melted
1 tablespoon plant-based butter, cold
What you'll need from the store cupboard
2 cup almond flour
½ cup + 2 tablespoons Splenda for baking
1 teaspoon vanilla
1 teaspoon Arrowroot powder
¾ teaspoon sea salt
½ teaspoon vanilla
½ teaspoon maple syrup, sugar-free
Nonstick cooking spray
Directions:
Preheat the oven to 350 degrees F. Spray 9-inch pie pan with cooking spray.
In a medium bowl, combine the flour, melted plant-based butter, 2 tablespoons of Splenda, and vanilla. Mix until the Ingredients are well combined.
Press down on the bottom and sides of the prepared pan.
Bake for 12-15 minutes or until the edges are golden. Take out and set aside for later use.
In a small saucepan, combine the milk, remaining Splenda, arrowroot, salt, ½ teaspoon of vanilla, and syrup.
Cook over medium heat until it begins to boil, stirring constantly. Continue cooking, about 2-3 minutes.
Remove from heat and let cool. Mix with the ½ pecans.
Pour the filling in the crust and garnish with the remaining pecans.
Bake for about 15 minutes or until filling begins to bubble. Let cool completely before eating.
Nutritional Information: Calories 375; Total Carbs 20g; Net Carbs 15g; Protein 7g; Fat 30g; Sugar 14g; Fiber 5g

Peach Custard Tart

Prep Time: 5 minutes| Cook Time: 40 minutes| Servings: 8
Ingredients:
12 oz. frozen unsweetened peach slices, thaw and drain
2 eggs, separated
1 cup skim milk
4 tablespoon cold plant-based butter, cut into pieces
What you'll need from store cupboard:
1 cup flour
3 tablespoon Splenda
2-3 tablespoon cold water
1 teaspoon low-sugar vanilla
¼ teaspoon + ⅛ teaspoon salt, divided
¼ teaspoon nutmeg
Directions:
Preheat the oven to 400 degrees F.
In a large bowl, combine the flour and ¼ teaspoon of salt.
With a pastry blender, chop the plant-based butter until the mixture resembles coarse crumbs. Stir in cold water, one tablespoon at a time, until moist.

Roll out the dough into an 11-inch circle on a lightly floured surface. Place bottom of 9 "pie dish with removable bottom. Turn bottom edges over and pierce sides and bottom with a fork. Beat an egg white with a fork in a small bowl. Gently rub the crust with an egg. Place the pan on a baking sheet and bake for 10 minutes. cool.
In a large bowl, combine the egg whites, Splenda, vanilla, nutmeg, and ⅛ tsp. salt until blended.
Pour the milk into the measuring cup and microwave for 1 minute. Do not boil.
Cover the egg mixture until the milk is combined. Place the peaches at the bottom of the crust and pour the egg mixture over them.
Bake for 25-30 minutes or until light. Cool to room temperature. Cover and cool at least 2 hours before serving.
Nutritional Information: Calories 180; Total Carbs 22g; Net Carbs 21g; Protein 5g; Fat 7g; Sugar 9g; Fiber 1g

Raspberry Lemon Cheesecake

Prep Time: 5 minutes| Cook Time: 40 minutes| Servings: 12
Ingredients:
2 cups raspberries
1 cup fat-free sour cream
¾ cup fat-free cream cheese, softened
½ cup egg substitute
2 tablespoon lemon juice
2 teaspoon lemon zest, divided
What you'll need from store cupboard:
½ cup + 3 tablespoon Splenda
1 teaspoon vanilla
Nonstick cooking spray
Directions:
Preheat the oven to 350°F.
Grease 8-inch square baking pan with cooking spray.
Beat the cream cheese, ½ cup Splenda, and vanilla on high speed until smooth in a large mixing bowl.
Add juice, 1 teaspoon zest, and egg substitute in the cream mix and beat until thoroughly combined.
Pour the batter into prepared pan.
Bake the batter for 40 minutes or until firm to the touch.
Remove the cake from oven and cool completely.
Add the sour cream and 1 tablespoon Splenda in a small bowl and stir well until smooth.
Spoon the cream evenly over cooled cheesecake. Cover the cake and refrigerate overnight.
Before serving, toss the berries and 2 tablespoons Splenda in small bowl and place aside for 30 minutes. Stir in the remaining zest and spoon the berry mixture over the top of the cheesecake.
Cut into 12 bars and serve.
Nutritional Information: Calories 114; Total Carbs 18g; Net Carbs 17g; Protein 3g; Fat 5g; Sugar 14g; Fiber 1g

Mini Lime Pudding

Prep Time: 5 minutes| Cook Time: 10 minutes| Servings: 8
Ingredients:
4 sheets phyllo dough
¾ cup skim milk
¾ cup fat-free whipped topping, thawed
½ cup egg substitute
½ cup fat free sour cream
6 tablespoonfresh lime juice
What you'll need from store cupboard
2 tablespoon cornstarch
½ cup Splenda
Butter-flavored cooking spray
Directions:
In a medium saucepan, combine the milk, juice, and cornstarch.
Cook over medium heat for 2-3 minutes or until thickened, stirring constantly. Remove from heat.
Add the egg substitute and whisk for 30 seconds. Combine sour cream and Splenda.
Cover and stay until completely chilled.
Preheat the oven to 350 degrees F. Spray 8 cups of muffins with cooking spray.
Place 1 sheet of phyllo on cutting board and spray gently with cooking spray. Repeat this for other sheets so that they are stacked on top.
Divide the filo dough into 8 equal parts and gently place them in a muffin pan, pressing firmly on the bottom and sides.
Bake for 8 to 10 minutes or until golden brown. Remove from the pan and let cool.
Pour lemon mixture evenly into 8 cups and garnish with whipped toppings.
Garnish with fresh lemon slices, if desired.
Nutritional Information: Calories 82; Total Carbs 13g; Net Carbs 12g; Protein 3g; Fat 1g; Sugar 10g; Fiber 1g

Pumpkin Ice Cream with Candied Pecans

Prep Time: 15 minutes| Cook Time: 0 minutes+ 1 hour chilling time| Servings: 8
Ingredients:
2 eggs
2 cup almond milk, unsweetened, divided
1 cup half-n-half
What you'll need from store cupboard:
1 cup pumpkin
1 envelope unflavored gelatin
¾ cup Splenda
¾ cup Candied Pecans
2 teaspoon pumpkin pie spice
Directions:
Pour a glass of almond milk into a small bowl. Sprinkle gelatin over it. Leave it for about 5 minutes.
Whisk together the Splenda and eggs in a large saucepan.
Add the pumpkin and pumpkin spices. Add the gelatin in it and whisk.
When the mixture begins to boil, remove it from the heat.
Let cool at room temperature for 5 minutes, then refrigerate for 45 minutes uncovered, stirring occasionally. Do not refrigerate for long periods. Otherwise, the mixture will harden.

Take the pumpkin out of the refrigerator and whisk half -n- half and add the cup with the almond milk.
Pour into ICE FREEZER and freeze according to the manufacturer's instructions.
Once the ice cream has reached the desired consistency, transfer it to a container with a lid that is suitable for the freezer. Add the candied pecans, cover, and place in the freezer to make the ice cream firmer.
Nutritional Information: Calories 254; Total Carbs 26g; Net Carbs 24g; Protein 5g; Fat 13g; Sugar 22g; Fiber 2g

Raspberry Almond Clafoutis

Prep Time: 10 minutes| Cook Time: 1 hour| Servings: 8
Ingredients:
1 pint raspberries, rinse and pat dry
3 eggs
¾ cup almond milk, unsweetened
¼ cup half-n-half
4 tablespoonplant-based butter
What you'll need from store cupboard:
½ cup almond flour
⅓ cup Splenda
¼ cup almonds, sliced
1 tablespooncoconut flour
1 ½ teaspoon vanilla
½ teaspoon baking powder
¼ teaspoon allspice
¼ teaspoon almond extract
Nonstick cooking spray
Directions:
Preheat the oven to 350 °F.
Grease 9-inch pie dish with cooking spray and place on a baking sheet.
Spread the berries, in a single layer, in the pie dish.
Add the flours, baking powder, and allspice in a mixing bowl and stir well.
In a small saucepan ,add the plant-based butter and melt it over low heat. Whisk Splenda in melted plant-based butter until smooth.
In a bowl ,pour the plant-based butter and whisk in eggs, one at a time. Add extracts and dry Ingredients in it.
Stir in the almond milk and half-n-half and mix well.
Pour the batter in pie dish and spread the raspberries and almonds on top.
Bake it for 50-60 minutes, or center is set and top is lightly browned. Cool to room temperature before serving.
Nutritional Information: Calories 273; Total Carbs 19g; Net Carbs 13g; Protein 7g; Fat 19g; Sugar 11g; Fiber 6g

Chocolate Raspberry Soufflés

Prep Time: 10 minutes| Cook Time: 10 minutes| Servings: 6
Ingredients:
1 cup fresh raspberries
4 egg whites
What you'll need from store cupboard:
½ oz. dark chocolate, chopped
6 teaspoon Splenda
1 teaspoon plant-based butter, soft
Directions:
Preheat the oven to 400 °F for 10 minutes.
Grease the 6 small ramekins with plant-based butter.
Add rassberry in a blender and puree well.Stain the puree and add 1 tablespoon splenda in it and set aside.
In a mixing bowl,beat egg whites until thickened and start adding the remaining Splenda, gradually, until the mixture forms stiff glossy peaks.
Gently fold ⅓ of the egg whites into the raspberry puree.
Fold the raspberry puree mixture into the remaining egg whites and fold gently until evenly mixed.
Spoon the raspberry egg mixture into the ramekins filling them ½ full.
Divide the chopped chocolate between the ramekins and then fill to the top with soufflé mixture.
Place ramekins on a baking sheetand bake for 9 minutes until golden brown and puffed up.
Serve immediately.
Nutritional Information: Calories 60; Total Carbs 8g; Net Carbs 7g; Protein 3g; Fat 1g; Sugar 16g; Fiber 1g

Raspberry Peach Cobbler

Prep Time: 15 minutes| Cook Time: 40 minutes| Servings: 8
Ingredients:
1 ¼ lbs. peaches, peeled and sliced
2 cups fresh raspberries
½ cup low-fat buttermilk
2 tablespoon cold plant-based butter, cut into pieces
1 teaspoon lemon zest
What you'll need from store cupboard
¾ cup + 2 tablespoon flour, divided
4 tablespoon+ 2 teaspoon Splenda, divided
½ teaspoon baking powder
½ teaspoon baking soda
⅛ teaspoon salt
Nonstick cooking spray
Directions:
Preheat the oven to 425 °F.
Grease an 11×7-inch baking dish with cooking spray.
In a large bowl, stir 2 tablespoons of Splenda and 2 tablespoons of flour.
Add the fruit and zest in the flour mix and toss to coat.
Pour the flour coated fruits into prepared baking dish.
Bake the fruits for 15 minutesuntil fruit is bubbling around the edges.
Combine remaining flour, 2 tablespoons of Splenda, baking powder, baking soda, and salt

in a mixing bowl. Cut in plant-based butter until it resembles coarse crumbs.
Stir the buttermilk in the flour mix just until moistened.
Remove the fruit from the oven. Pour the buttermilk mixture top on the bubbling fruits.
Sprinkle the remaining 2 teaspoons of Splenda over the top and bake for 18-20 minutes or top is lightly browned.
Serve warm.
Nutritional Information: Calories 130; Total Carbs 22g; Net Carbs 19g; Protein 2g; Fat 3g; Sugar 10g; Fiber 3g

Sweet Potato Crème Brule

Prep Time: 10 minutes| Cook Time: 1 hour 5 minutes| Servings: 12
Ingredients:
7 egg yolks
1 ¼ cup sweet potato, bake, peel & mash
2 cup half-n-half
1 tablespoonfresh lemon juice
What you'll need from store cupboard:
¾ cup Splenda
¼ cup + ⅓ cup Splenda brown sugar
3 teaspoon vanilla
Butter flavored cooking spray
Directions:
Preheat the oven to 325 °F.
Grease a 10-inch metal quiche dish with cooking spray.
Combine sweet potato, ¼ cup Splenda brown sugar, and lemon juice in a mixing bowl and pour it in prepared baking dish.
In a suitable saucepan, whisk together half-n-half, Splenda, egg yolks, and vanilla over medium-low heat for 15 minutes until well incorporated. Cook and stirring frequently, until hot, do not boil.
Pour the sauce over sweet potato mixture.
Place dish in a shallow baking pan and put in the oven.
Pour enough boiling water to cover ½ way up the sides of the quiche dish.
Bake the quiche for 1 hour until full set and golden brown from top.
Cool on rack. Cover and refrigerate 8 hours or overnight.
Heat the oven to broil setting.
Sprinkle quiche with ⅓ cup Splenda brown sugar and place it on a baking sheet. Broil it for 3-5 minutes or until sugar has melted.
Cool 5 minutes before serving.
Nutritional Information: Calories 193; Total Carbs 24g; Net Carbs 20g; Protein 3g; Fat 7g; Sugar 21g; Fiber 0g

Tropical Fruit Tart

Prep Time: 10 minutes| Cook Time: 10 minutes| Servings: 8

Ingredients:

1 mango, peeled, pitted and sliced thin

1 banana, sliced thin

2 egg whites

What you'll need from store cupboard

15 ¼ oz. can pineapple chunks in juice, undrained

3 ½ oz. can unsweetened flaked coconut

1 cup cornflakes, crushed

3 teaspoons Splenda

2 teaspoon cornstarch

1 teaspoon coconut extract

Nonstick cooking spray

Directions:

Preheat the oven to 425 °F.

Grease a 9-inch springform pan with cooking spray.

Combine cornflakes, coconut, and egg whites in a suitable bowl and toss until blended. Press the mix firmly over the bottom and ½-inch up the sides of the prepared baking pan to make crust. Bake the crust for 8 minutes or until edges start to brown. Cool completely.

Add pineapple juice into a small saucepan along with cornstarch and stir until smooth . Stir and cook the slurry for a minutes over high heat. Remove from heat and cool completely.

Once cooled, stir in Splenda and coconut extract.

Combine pineapple, mango, and banana in a bowl, add over baked crust and drizzle with pineapple juice mixture.

Cover and chill at least 2 hours before serving.

Nutritional Information: Calories120; Total Carbs 19g; Net Carbs 17g; Protein 2g; Fat 4g; Sugar 13g; Fiber 2g

4-Week Diet Plan

Week-1

Day-1
Breakfast: Sprouted Toast with Avocado
Lunch: Mushroom and Rice Bowl with Hazelnuts
Snack: Baked Banana Chips
Dinner: Veggie Macaroni Pie
Dessert: Unsweetened Chocolate Coffee Cupcakes

Day-2
Breakfast: Quinoa Burrito
Lunch: Cajun Shrimp & Roasted Vegetables
Snack: Fried Carrot Slices
Dinner: Roasted Brussels Sprouts with Tomatoes
Dessert: Crispy Apple Slices

Day-3
Breakfast: Pancakes with Coconut
Lunch: Turkey Burgers
Snack: Salty Kale Chips
Dinner: Cauliflower Soup
Dessert: German Chocolate Cake Bars

Day-4
Breakfast: Scrambled Eggs and Onion for Lox
Lunch: Chicken with Balsamic Kale
Snack: English Pub Pea Soup
Dinner: Baked Asparagus with Cashews
Dessert: Apple Pear & Pecan Cups

Day-5
Breakfast: Breakfast Salad
Lunch: Chicken Chili with Black Beans
Snack: Cayenne Broccoli Tots
Dinner: Gingery Eggplant
Dessert: Mini Bread Puddings

Day-6
Breakfast: Tex-Mex Migas
Lunch: Black Eyed Beans and Rice Bowl
Snack: Salsa de Strawberry
Dinner: Green Beans with Onion
Dessert: Apricot Soufflé

Day-7
Breakfast: Traditional Omelet with Turmeric
Lunch: Salmon in Citrus Vinaigrette
Snack: Garlic Veggie Balls
Dinner: Classic Brussels Sprouts
Dessert: Mini Lime Pudding

Week-2

Day-1
Breakfast: Savory Egg Muffins
Lunch: Chicken Thighs with Dandelion Greens
Snack: Simple Roasted Walnuts
Dinner: Roasted Veggies
Dessert: Autumn Skillet Cake

Day-2
Breakfast: Pancakes with Blueberry and Peaches
Lunch: Chickpea Spaghetti Bolognese
Snack: Gazpacho with Strawberries
Dinner: Portobello Mushrooms with Spinach
Dessert: Peach Custard Tart

Day-3
Breakfast: Black Beans and Egg Tacos
Lunch: Ritzy Chicken Cacciatore
Snack: Apple Ladybug
Dinner: Lemony Broccoli
Dessert: Baked Maple Custard

Day-4
Breakfast: Spinach Rolls
Lunch: Tilapia Fillet with Fruity Salsa
Snack: Easy-to-Make Banana
Dinner: Black Bean Fritters
Dessert: Raspberry Almond Clafoutis

Day-5
Breakfast: Hite Sandwich
Lunch: Turkey and Cabbage Broth
Snack: Red Pepper Hummus
Dinner: Eggplant Pizzas
Dessert: Blackberry Crostata

Day-6
Breakfast: Paleo Hash
Lunch: Chicken and Veggies Roast
Snack: Egg with Avocado
Dinner: Baby Spinach Salad with Walnuts
Dessert: Raspberry Lemon Cheesecake

Day-7
Breakfast: Berry Parfaits
Lunch: Spicy Fish Fillet
Snack: Garlic Hummus
Dinner: Flavorful Peppery Mushrooms
Dessert: Unbaked Blueberry Cheesecake

Week-3	Week-4

Day-1
Breakfast: French Toast with Blueberries
Lunch: Chicken Leg Roast
Snack: Dehydrated Orange Slice
Dinner: Squash with Black Pepper
Dessert: Raspberry Peach Cobbler

Day-1
Breakfast: Veggie Wrap
Lunch: Cod Gratin
Snack: Paprika Zucchini Chips
Dinner: Kidney Beans Bowl
Dessert: Cinnamon Bread Pudding

Day-2
Breakfast: Strawberry Coconut Breakfast Cake
Lunch: Tuna-Noodle Casserole
Snack: Roasted Cinnamon Almonds
Dinner: Lemon Garlic Green Beans
Dessert: Broiled Stone Fruit

Day-2
Breakfast: Quinoa Porridge with Blueberries
Lunch: Chicken Casserole
Snack: Paprika Chickpeas
Dinner: Greek-Style Vegetable Bake
Dessert: Tropical Fruit Tart

Day-3
Breakfast: Breakfast Bark with Berries
Lunch: Sesame Chicken and Cucumber Soba
Snack: Nutmeg Apple Chips
Dinner: Curried Black-Eyed Peas
Dessert: Sweet Potato Crème Brule

Day-3
Breakfast: Egg and Avocado Toasts
Lunch: Lemon Trout Fillets
Snack: Green Herbed Hummus
Dinner: Garlic Onion and Tomato
Dessert: Blackberry Crostata

Day-4
Breakfast: Berry Avocado Smoothie
Lunch: Baked Zucchini on Whole Wheat Bread
Snack: Mini Meatball with Apricot Dip
Dinner: Pepperoni Pita
Dessert: Café Mocha Torte

Day-4
Breakfast: Simple Amaranth Porridge
Lunch: Tuna Salad
Snack: Fruit Leather
Dinner: Jicama Slices with Avocado
Dessert: Café Mocha Torte

Day-5
Breakfast: Coconut Porridge
Lunch: Chicken Zucchini Patties with Salsa
Snack: Roasted Peanuts
Dinner: Golden Onion Rings
Dessert: Coffee Tiramisu

Day-5
Breakfast: Avocado Toast
Lunch: Cashew Chicken
Snack: Gazpacho with Avocados
Dinner: Lettuce Wraps with Chestnuts
Dessert: Cinnamon Bread Pudding

Day-6
Breakfast: Hummus Toast
Lunch: Peppery Bok Choy with Almonds
Snack: Roasted Cashews with Lemon Juice
Dinner: Garlic Spinach Quiches
Dessert: Caramel Pecan Pie

Day-6
Breakfast: Huevos Rancheros
Lunch: Jerked Chicken Breasts
Snack: Simple Homemade Spinach Chips
Dinner: Eggplant and Bulgur Pilaf with Basil
Dessert: Coffee Tiramisu

Day-7
Breakfast: Summer Fruits Smoothie
Lunch: Stuffed Chicken Breasts
Snack: Paprika Roasted Pecans
Dinner: Beans Chili
Dessert: Toffee Apple Pies

Day-7
Breakfast: Bulgur Porridge
Lunch: Tomatoes & Cajun Flounder
Snack: Guacamole
Dinner: Baked Eggs with Vegetables
Dessert: Toffee Apple Pies

Conclusion

Type -2 diabetes is a chronic condition in which the body controls and uses glucose for fat. These long-term infections cause too much sugar in the arteries. Finally, high blood sugar can damage blood vessels, the nervous system, and the immune system. There is no cure for type 2 diabetes mellitus, but weight loss, eating a healthy diet, and exercising can help control the disease.

The best way to control your diabetes is healthy living with proper exercise and walking for 30 minutes to 1 hour a day. Drink water regularly and keep yourself hydrated. Eat healthy low carbs and steep out fat and sodium from your daily food intake. For your health always choose high-quality proteins, a vitamin-rich diet, and dietary fiber in your diet. This leads you to manage your healthy lifestyle, weight loss as well as manage type-2 diabetes.

This amazing cookbook will help you to regulate your healthy eating habits as it can be restricted to what to eat and what not. The amazing diet plans in the book help you manage to eat healthy as well as the yummy food for managing a healthy lifestyle and remission your type-2 diabetes.

This unique cookbook is specially designed under the supervision of nutritionists and doctors and it completely guides you to have a healthy full meal all day long from yummy breakfast to delicious snacks as well. The diet plan and the motivation encourage you to set your healthy lifestyle without worrying about this situation. Go grab the wonderful "Type-2 Diabetes cookbook" now and start living healthy.

Appendix 1 Measurement Conversion Chart

WEIGHT EQUIVALENTS

US STANDARD	METRIC (APPROXINATE)
1 ounce	28 g
2 ounces	57 g
5 ounces	142 g
10 ounces	284 g
15 ounces	425 g
16 ounces (1 pound)	455 g
1.5pounds	680 g
2pounds	907 g

VOLUME EQUIVALENTS (DRY)

US STANDARD	METRIC (APPROXIMATE)
⅛ teaspoon	0.5 mL
¼ teaspoon	1 mL
½ teaspoon	2 mL
¾ teaspoon	4 mL
1 teaspoon	5 mL
1 teaspoon	15 mL
¼ cup	59 mL
½ cup	118 mL
¾ cup	177 mL
1 cup	235 mL
2 cups	475 mL
3 cups	700 mL
4 cups	1 L

TEMPERATURES EQUIVALENTS

FAHRENHEIT(F)	CELSIUS© (APPROXIMATE
225 °F	107 °C
250 °F	120 °C
275 °F	135 °C
300 °F	150 °C
325 °F	160 °C
350 °F	180 °C
375 °F	190 °C
400 °F	205 °C
425 °F	220 °C
450 °F	235 °C
475 °F	245 °C
500 °F	260 °C

VOLUME EQUIVALENTS (LIQUID)

US STANDARD	US STANDARD (OUNCES)	METRIC
2 tablespoons	1 fl.oz	30 mL
¼ cup	2 fl.oz	60 mL
½ cup	4 fl.oz	120 mL
1 cup	8 fl.oz	240 mL
1½ cup	12 fl.oz	355 mL
2 cups or 1 pint	16 fl.oz	475 mL
4 cups or 1 quart	32 fl.oz	1 L
1 gallon	128 fl.oz	4 L

Made in United States
North Haven, CT
16 February 2023